Krista Schlueter

JEFF WEISS

WAITING FOR BRITNEY SPEARS

Jeff Weiss was born and raised in Los Angeles. His writing has appeared in the *Los Angeles Times*, *The New York Times*, *GQ*, and *Pitchfork*, and has been repeatedly anthologized in *Da Capo Best Music Writing*. He has profiled everyone from Kendrick Lamar to the Beat Generation poets, André 3000 to Paul Thomas Anderson. In 2023, *Rolling Stone* named him one of the "50 Innovators Shaping Rap's Next 50 Years." He is the founder and editor in chief of the culture website POW. *Waiting for Britney Spears* is his first book.

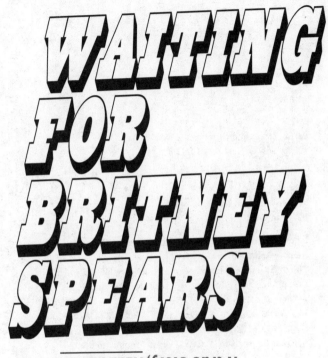

WAITING FOR BRITNEY SPEARS

A true story, ALLEGEDLY!

Jeff Weiss

MCD 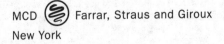 Farrar, Straus and Giroux
New York

MCD
Farrar, Straus and Giroux
120 Broadway, New York 10271

Copyright © 2025 by Jeff Weiss
All rights reserved
Printed in the United States of America
First edition, 2025

Library of Congress Cataloging-in-Publication Data
Names: Weiss, Jeff, 1981– author.
Title: Waiting for Britney Spears : a true story, allegedly / Jeff Weiss.
Description: First edition. | New York : MCD / Farrar, Straus and
    Giroux, 2025.
Identifiers: LCCN 2024056987 | ISBN 9780374606138 (paperback)
Subjects: LCSH: Spears, Britney. | Singers—United States—Biography. |
    Gonzo journalism. | LCGFT: Creative nonfiction.
Classification: LCC ML420.S714 W45 2025 | DDC 782.42164092 [B]—
    dc23/eng/20241126
LC record available at https://lccn.loc.gov/2024056987

Our books may be purchased in bulk for promotional, educational, or
business use. Please contact your local bookseller or the Macmillan
Corporate and Premium Sales Department at 1-800-221-7945, extension
5442, or by email at MacmillanSpecialMarkets@macmillan.com.

www.mcdbooks.com • www.fsgbooks.com
Follow us on social media at @mcdbooks and @fsgbooks

10 9 8 7 6 5 4 3 2 1

This is a true story, although some names and details have been
changed, some characters merged, and poetic license applied to some of
the author's interactions.

To Grandma Rita,

who introduced to me to glamour and art, and

who would've been the next Shirley Temple if

her father hadn't vowed that no daughter of his

would enter Hollywood Babylon

Let us not then speak ill of our generation, it is not any unhappier than its predecessors . . . Let us not speak well of it either.

—SAMUEL BECKETT

WAITING FOR BRITNEY SPEARS

1

An **EXCLUSIVE** look into 1998's *HOTTEST* video!!!

Summer Lovin'!
Local Teen Glimpses Louisiana Apparition!

I MUST CONFESS:
Revelations from the Neon Coast

It exploded like a cluster bomb filled with candy. Sugary bass vibrations shook the steel handle of the heavy gymnasium door. In the vacant spaces between notes, sneakers squeaked and basketballs thumped on hardwood. A piano riff turned the keys into the ignition of the next century. In this adolescent corridor scented with pheromones, fresh sweat, and mall perfume, a half moan, half growl *oh, bay-bee, bay-bee* announced itself on the loudspeakers. No one stood a chance.

In scolding red letters, the sign on the door said DO NOT ENTER. The only exceptions were credentialed cast and crew. It felt more like a loose recommendation. An hour earlier, I'd been practicing on the same court. By the time that I left the training room, production had already begun on a music video for what my high school hoops coach described as "some no-name pop star no one ever heard of."

No one gave it much thought. It was the westside of LA, two miles from the beach, and they were always filming something here. Normally, the guys on my team would've hung around to try to flirt with the girls on set, but this was the last Friday of summer school, and nothing short of Destiny's Child could've kept them on campus.

I had nowhere to be that sweltering afternoon. So I lingered in the hallway linking the locker room to the outside world, between beige cinder-block walls with chipped paint and cuneiform tags for Venice 13 and Shoreline Crip, eavesdropping on a pop song addictive enough to erode my bubble gum aversion. This was the furthest thing from the Snoop, Nate Dogg, and 'Pac that ran every half-decent sound system from Long Beach to Chatsworth that summer. But as the late great Makaveli also said, *I won't deny it.* Whoever sang behind that door had discovered how to heal every ailment except the loneliness that was killing her. *Is she asking to be hit one more time?*

I only half trust anyone who thinks that they understand the past, let alone those who claim to see the future. But once in a while, if you're suspiciously lucky or pleasantly cursed, you can glimpse the light. The question was presented to me on that August afternoon in '98: *How was I supposed to know?* The catch is that you rarely do. When I was sixteen, there was only inalterable destiny and dim instinct. A lacquered mirage of limitless peace and prosperity. All outcomes were divinely ordained. At every angle, the horizon appeared jiggy.

The gym door was propped open. No one would notice if I casually slipped through, especially in warm-up sweats that fit naturally into the video's basketball motif. I'd been raised to believe that it was better to beg for forgiveness than ask permission. If you pop shit, apologize. We grew up writing on walls and breaking into homes under construction to skate the empty pools. At worst, this was mild civil disobedience. After all, it was a public school, and they kept telling us we were here to learn.

I won't lie and tell you that the second I entered that old art deco field house, the tempo slowed, my heart raced, the temperature soared, and the color spectrum became Skittles. It wasn't anything like that. Behind the backboard, in white block script, the wall still advertised our team, the Gondoliers, named after the crumbling nearby water canals, built a century before by a scheming developer trying to construct a counterfeit duchy.

Our pep squad was absent. They'd been replaced by a dozen MTV-ready backup dancers gossiping at half-court in tracksuits and tank tops. On the same hard maple the team had just departed, a bizarro roster bricked dunks in anonymous white jerseys. In the wooden bleachers, extras snapped gum and waited for the cameras to roll. The casting director had recruited a racially diverse but spiritually homogenous cross section of "jocks," who all looked like they'd been made in test tubes in a bunker beneath the Third Street Promenade American Eagle.

Label executives, production coordinators, assistant directors, wardrobe stylists, and hair and makeup artists whirled around a girl my age with wispy butterscotch bangs and double Dutch pigtails. She looked like she'd won a Noxzema contest. A dream weaver but still the girl next door. This year's model but suspended in a hazy teenage idyll. Sexy enough for *Rolling Stone*, safe enough for the Christmas cover of *Seventeen*.

She wore burgundy warm-up pants and an electric-lemon sports bra. Depending on who was approaching, her oval Coca-Cola eyes aimed to please. To the graying men in designer blazers, she was polite and appreciative, flashing a beignet smile, batting long eyelashes, lowering her head in deference. A charming effect that left them marching off convinced that the kids might actually be all right.

Hair and makeup hung close for last-minute touch-ups. Dancers joined every few minutes, barely older than the star herself. They whispered intimate details into her ear, inducing snorts of laughter. I tried to read their lips, but it wasn't hard to figure out what they were talking about. Without subtlety, they scoped the guys on set, conspiratorially resting their hands on each other's shoulders.

She was born to win yearbook superlatives. The mean girls had to respect her abnormal talent and natural beauty. Plus, she was just so *nice*. The one dating the quarterback but still kind to the science fair nerds. She radiated nonchalance and country-girl humility. There were the mannered traces of the professional child, but her theater-kid goofiness disarmed any cynicism. To her inner circle, she comically wrinkled her face, bugged her eyes, scrunched her nose, and playfully slapped wrists. There was nothing not to like.

I watched as an elfin forty-four-year-old with a black Kangol, forty-waist jeans, and a soul patch sidled up to her. It had to be the director because he was shadowed by two assistants with clipboards, and when he gestured imperiously, a soundman cranked the song's volume way down. He wanted a final huddle with the talent. For a minute, the ingenue listened intently to his game plan—furrowing her eyebrows and biting her nails.

After the director finished his chat, the singer pointed out a few spots on the floor, then called the choreographer to the conclave. They talked in animated but respectful debate. In slow motion, the girl popped up from her chair and gracefully executed a hip thrust, hair whip, and spin—then made an air diagram to indicate that the backup dancers would follow. Both men beamed and nodded. Strutting off, the director held up ten fingers to the crew.

A flustered stylist in a powder-blue hoodie beelined from the opposite end of the gym, clutching two massive Kmart bags full of clothes. Her exasperation revealed that this wasn't her first store run today. Nervously flipping a swoosh of hair, the supplicant presented them at the star's feet. Sifting through the outfits, the girl selected a white blouse and gray skirt, mouthed *perfect*, and folded her hands to her heart with gratitude.

"You know this was originally *Mighty Morphin Power Rangers* themed?"

The comment came from a balding bystander in business casual. If not for the diamond in his left ear, you would've thought that he worked in aerospace engineering. I looked behind me to see if he was talking to someone else.

"Huh?"

"The video. It was supposed to be some half-animated kiddie superhero bullshit."

"Oh. That would've been fucking awful."

"Would've killed her career before it began." He smirks. "But she told Nigel how embarrassing the idea was. She needed to daydream in class about hot boys, and then y'know, one thing leads to another and everyone starts dancing. That's why we're filming where they shot *Grease*."

"Who is she?"

"In three months from now, everyone in your school will know her name," he says, noticing the GONDOLIERS stamped on my sweats.

"You see that wardrobe girl walking up to her?" he continues.

I nod.

"She wanted to dress her in jeans and a T-shirt, but this morning, Britney told her that it was totally wrong and they should be wearing uniforms tied up from the waist. So she schlepped to Kmart and got her that school-girl getup."

"Only rich preps wear uniforms in LA."

"LA isn't the rest of the country." He flashes a self-satisfied grin. "That's why we signed her. She's *relatable*." He stretches the syllables like Silly Putty.

"Your little sister will buy her dolls and shoes. Your girlfriend will buy her perfume. *You'll* want to date her."

"She's not really my type," I lie.

"She's *everybody's* type." He pauses and reassesses me. "Y'know, students aren't supposed to be in here."

"They said I could be an extra."

He shrugs.

"So what do you think of the song?"

"Catchy, I guess. I'm more into rap."

"I signed Tribe Called Quest. Ever hear of Jive?"

"Yeah, record industry rule number four thousand eighty."

He catches the allusion to the Q-Tip lyric about how all record company people are shady, and sputters for a few seconds about how Jive is *actually* an artist-friendly paragon of virtue. It goes nowhere, so he calibrates.

"I've A&R'd for Too Short and KRS-One. We signed UGK and E-40. R. Kelly and Aaliyah. Look, I love hip-hop and R&B, but you know how many CDs the Back-street Boys and *NSYNC sold this summer?"

"No disrespect, but that's some fake Disney Channel trash."

"Those royalties are very real. And this kid, Britney,

is going to be the biggest of them all. Like five Spice Girls in one. We've already got her an eight hundred number, and put her on a mall tour sponsored by the teen magazines. She's got Sunglass Hut and Pepsi deals and a Tommy Hilfiger modeling gig. About to start opening for *NSYNC too. Trust me, we'll make her *the star.*"

"Why her?"

How does lightning select its target? You can stick a copper rod on the roof of your house, but there are no guarantees it'll strike. Fate is agnostic: luck plus looks plus talent plus timing. About a year earlier, Britney's entertainment lawyer, a shrewd New York hustler trying to transition into management, sent out her demo to every major label. He'd procured a Toni Braxton song for Britney to sing—one that Braxton's A&Rs had discarded for being too juvenile and poppy. The plan was to imitate the R&B singer, but make the sultriness implicit. The age and aesthetic differences would make the translation seem new.

The photos refined the idea. Here was the all-American girl at the end of history. Jean shorts and a picnic basket, petting a puppy on a front lawn in front of a ramshackle wooden porch. The pride of Kentwood, Louisiana (population 2,205). A button-nosed cuteness to indulge record industry dreams about the millions to be made off a Bayou Barbie.

A few behemoths showed interest. Besides Jive, Mercury and Epic auditioned Britney in New York. She tiptoed in in a black cocktail dress and high heels, covering songs from her idols, Mariah Carey and Whitney Houston. A tremendous level of difficulty for anyone, let alone a fifteen-year-old who worked part-time shelling crawfish at her great-grandmother's seafood deli. Mercury said, "We don't get it." Epic's VP of A&R described the "shy little girl" as a "hand puppet" without presence or hunger. But the man before me knew that there was something different.

"*Why her?*" He grunts, looking at Britney. "She isn't *really* a songwriter and might not have the greatest voice in the world. She's a knockout but no runway model. But she's got 'it.' She can stare at the camera and melt you into a puddle of hair gel. She's what everyone's always looking for. You can't explain magic."

He'd been waiting for a captive audience. If—no, *when*—Britney blew up, everyone else would receive the accolades. First the star, then her producers, the songwriters, the label CEO and president, her management, her mom and dad, the marketing gurus. Until somewhere toward the bottom—in between the video director and the choreographer—was the A&R who discovered her. The historical footnote who heard that off-key Toni Braxton cover and imagined a lost city of gold in the Louisiana marshes. And as we waited for the action to begin, he retold the complete story.

◆

The Disney version of *Cinderella* was released in 1950, but variants of the folktale date back to antiquity. In this one, the girl comes from a land snubbed by time, where the scenic highways are surrounded by cicada-choked woods and billboards that read, JESUS CHRIST IS LORD. Kentwood had once been the dairy capital of the South, but by the time Britney took her first breaths in December '81, the hamlet on the Mississippi state line was crumbling into the soft-boiled earth. A Main Street once graced by festive Fourth of July parades rotted in the swollen humidity—a postindustrial ruin of shuttered brick storefronts with splintered windows. Walmart crushed the independent farms that once fringed the countryside. The Sonic drive-in was now the principal source of life.

Here was real-life Johnny Reb country. Overripe live oak and magnolia trees grazed against the loose-jowled clouds. A church on almost every corner and blood in the soil. The dirt roads were lined with decomposing shacks full of rusting pickups with shovels, shotguns, and Confederate decals. Segregation remained informal but unyielding. Britney went to the all-white Parklane Academy, where the only Black faces were the janitors'. In Kentwood, you still frequently heard laments about the speed and force with which integration occurred. The flag of Jefferson Davis flew everywhere.

The A&R described her parents as unsophisticated bumpkins. Britney's dad, Jamie, was too unreliable for steady construction work, a drunk "always disappearing." He racked up gambling debts and ran the gym he owned into bankruptcy. His manipulative and controlling streak came from his own father, a tyrannical Baton Rouge cop fired for allegedly shooting an unarmed man. When Jamie was fourteen, his mother drove out to the cemetery east of Kentwood and shot herself in the heart atop the gravestone of her infant son, who had died eight years earlier. It was said to be her fourth and final suicide attempt. No note was found. Britney's widowed grandfather eventually married his stepsister.

Britney's mother was the daughter of a dairy farmer and his British war bride. The future Lynne Spears met her husband at the town swimming pool on her college summer break. He was the all-state high school quarterback, a half decade removed from glory, already divorced and struggling to find reliable work as a welder at oil refineries. She was an education major at Southeastern Louisiana. After a month of dating, they eloped in upstate New York, where he was temporarily employed. Her family was furious. She dropped out of college. Nine months later, Britney's older brother, Bryan, was born.

The gift was obvious. Britney's solo on the Christmas carol "What Child Is This?" was so impressive that the whole Baptist church told the family that their four-year-old was Broadway bound. Lynne and Jamie weren't exactly the stage parent cliché, but their dedication was absolute enough to skip paying taxes to cover their daughter's dance, gymnastics, and singing lessons. For a few summers, Britney studied with the finest instructors in Manhattan, landing an understudy role alongside Natalie Portman in an off-Broadway musical. She played an ambitious prodigy, "born to entertain" and willing to kill for fame.

Star Search was supposed to be her first big break, but

Britney lost in the second round of the syndicated singing contest to a little lord in a bolo tie. The appearance was preceded by a midshow Q&A, where Ed McMahon asked the ten-year-old whether or not she had a boyfriend. In bangs and a ruffled dress, she sneered, "No, boys are mean!" The host, eligible for social security, replied: "Well, what about me?"

Child stardom beckoned again a year later. Attempting to graft '90s hip-hop edge onto the *aw-shucks* wholesomeness of the *New Mickey Mouse Club*, Disney introduced Britney, Christina Aguilera, Justin Timberlake, and Ryan Gosling into what was now branded *MMC*. Britney moved to Orlando with her mother and sister, performing comedy sketches and synthetic reggae duets with Timberlake. But at season's end, the show was canceled. A year after Kentwood sent her off to Disney World with an official "Britney Spears Day," she returned home to play freshman basketball, work a cash register for minimum wage, and tip the occasional cow.

There was a brief dalliance with a girl group, Innosense, managed by Timberlake's mother and Lou Pearlman, the sleazy Geppetto behind the Backstreet Boys and *NSYNC. But the solo route seemed preferable. Britney kept singing and sending out demos until one day this man before me decided that she was destined for stardom. Jive offered a $500 advance, a ninety-day probationary contract, and a penthouse on the Upper East Side, where she could live for a month while recording her debut album.

"We all liked those songs. The head of the label even gave her a deal off them," the A&R tells me. "There was only one problem: no smashes."

"Don't you pay the DJs to make that happen?"

"Very funny." He shakes me off, pursing his lips, eyes heavy underneath his glasses. "You think it's so easy, but if it was so easy, every label could make their own Britney."

"I'm sure they're trying."

"They most certainly will," he continues. "But dynamite is worthless without a detonator. So we shipped her off to Sweden."

Stockholm had become the Motown of teen pop. Even I knew it was where all the Backstreet Boys and *NSYNC hits came from.

I nod and offer a patronizing "That's crazy." He is undeterred.

"This song was written for TLC."

"And they passed."

"Well, yeah, T-Boz said that it wasn't TLC enough, but that's a $100 million fuckup! The guy who wrote it is about to be the biggest producer in pop."

You have to admire the prophecy. Maybe someone else might've eventually seen it, but when it mattered, this man was the only one who did. He glimpsed four-dimensional space where others saw only a blank cipher. And I never even got his name.

The camera operators peer through the lens to double-check the sight lines. On the floor, the basketball players attempt to distract the dancers. Minions tell Britney, "This is it." The assistant director screams: "One minute! Quiet on set!!"

"Shouldn't you be out there?" The A&R bobs his head at the bleachers, where extras pretend to be fans watching the halftime performance.

"Oh, right." I salute him. Slowly trotting out onto the freshly waxed wood, I sneak up into the stands, and pick a seat right above half-court.

When the red and yellow lights blink on, Britney becomes incandescent. She's like an old movie retouched for color. Love bludgeons me before I fully understand what it means. It requires only a caramel-blonde whip of hair, a harem dancer hip shimmy, a lashing of apricot arms, a dizzying 360-degree whirl, and a graceful floor slide. I saw the sign, an immaculate conception, a fated tarot. Only a higher power could have blessed me to bear witness to the taping of the ". . . Baby One More Time" video.

It's the way she clutches the basketball in the bleachers, belting, "Show me how you want it to be." It's the panting tigress, "oh, bay-bee, bay-bee," which conveys the desolate longing and dumbstruck lust that define adolescence. It's the plaintive agony with which she coos, "My loneliness is *killin'* me." I wanted to call the jeweler, the florist, and tell all my previous paramours to stop paging me.

The drums hit hard and bright as pink diamonds. Bass rumbles. Hugging the basketball for emotional support, Britney lip-syncs several rows beneath me, her eyes emitting voltage. Locked in the nexus between sin and salvation, her carnal purr rewires my limbic system.

> *Oh, baby, baby, how was I supposed to know*
> *Oh, pretty baby, I shouldn't have let you go*

The pianos sigh. The ticking snares add melodrama. Her vocal-fried timbre indiscriminately wanders between club and church, bedroom and homeroom. I squint and run my fingers through my spiked sickles of hair. Craning my neck, I try to project a switchblade cool. She's bound to turn around, wistfully gaze into the rafters, and lock eyes with me.

Her attention instead hovers on the cinematic idée fixe: an Abercrombie model with an abandoned-cornfield stare, damp brown hair, and a bone-saw jawline. In a black tank top, he somberly bounces a basketball, pretending to be unaware that Britney Spears is *obsessed* with him. I wonder if that's her real boyfriend. Where did I go wrong? I could take this goof one-on-one. Did I mention his real name is Chad? Later on, I learn that this interloper interrupting my fantasy is actually her cousin. Same last name and everything. But let's not get ahead of ourselves.

The bridge ends, the beat drops, the scene switches. Britney commands a synchronized dance routine at center court. Her hips writhe when she mouths that hook.

The fragile girl transforms into the leader of the ceremony: gymnast, enchantress, chanteuse.

Every celebrity crush became irrelevant. Mariah, Janet, Topanga, Kelly Kapowski? No, *she's the one*. And yes, I'll admit, it's a bit mortifying. How can I be this susceptible to something so transparently manufactured? I mean, I couldn't stand the boy bands and their soggy garlic aioli R&B. A bunch of completely interchangeable thirty-year-old cornballs, imitating street slang in ski goggles and frosted tips. On bus rides, my teammates and I rapped every word to Suga Free and DJ Quik verses. How do you go from their "I'd Rather Give You My Bitch" to falling for Swedish apple-pie pop and the Jive marketing plan? But one look in those pleading eyes and I was a sudden convert to the Britney Spears experience.

Nothing like Britney existed in my corner of precolonial Venice, where the perception of innocence made you a moving target. I was raised in the shadow of the boardwalk, where the freaks had free rein and the fake Rastas sold oregano to gullible tourists, and 40s were as easily purchased as Dr Pepper. If you wandered off campus, you needed to know which blocks had beef. Two-parent homes were alien.

My own family split up a few years earlier. I'll spare you the boring details beyond just saying that it was some typical LA shit: dad leaves for a younger woman and starts a second family in his fifties. My mom and I lived in a cramped bungalow without AC, where you constantly heard the neighbors screaming in Spanish through the walls. She painted watercolors of people looking at the ocean and horses running after trains, stuff like that. Her day job involved assisting an aging celebrity photographer whose claim to fame was that his father had been the fourth-most-famous silent film comedian.

Britney was the opposite of everything I'd known. A sequined mirage and airbrushed myth. It felt like I'd just watched a comet be born.

This would be one of the last days of her life where she could step off a set and disappear anonymously into the crowd. But fame, fortune, and adoration felt far more pressing. And I can't pretend to you that I didn't want it for myself too—just to understand what it would be like to live in a world where no one could say no. Maybe then she'd give me the time of day.

It won't be today. They perform the dance routine a couple more times. Each rendering becomes more rote. When the director finally shouts, "Okay, perfect. That's a wrap," I'm already doubting the intensity of the infatuation. Maybe my mind is playing tricks on me.

In the fall, when the video monopolizes MTV, I'm reminded that she actually was everything I wanted her to be. Of course, my uncredited extra appearance is a great story to tell at parties. By then, she belongs to the world, inhabiting the stratosphere of awards shows, sold-out tours, and multimillion-dollar homes with vistas that usually belong only to corporate criminals. I languished through another boring year of high school, getting told exactly what to do and how to do it by teachers, coaches, and parents. Alarms at 6:30 a.m., practices until it got dark, and studying until I passed out in front of *Simpsons* reruns.

That afternoon, after the cameras stop filming, the congregation offers Britney effusive congratulations. The executives are euphoric that their investment is assured. The director sees a Moonman in his future. The A&R gives me a Michael Jordan shrug.

I stand up to leave, bound down the stairs, and approach the exit. But one of the production coordinators, presumably the one in charge of casting, stops me.

"'Scuse me, are you sure you're supposed to be here?" he asks, a sprightly man with cellophane hair and a ponytail.

I nod and smile at him, never breaking stride, busting open the steel gymnasium doors and adjusting my eyes to what now feels like an insufficient sun.

THE MAGAZINE'S LAIR:
NEVER BEFORE SEEN TOUR!

EXPLOSIVE NEW HIRE!
Does He Have WHAT IT TAKES?

MILLENNIALS EXPLAINED

I did everything that you're supposed to do. I got a partial basketball scholarship to a small Southern California college that you've probably never heard of. I studied relatively hard, stuck mostly to the illegal substances that were smokable, and graduated with minor honors shortly after the start of the Iraq War. Fame and wealth were surely imminent. Even if I didn't end up walking red carpets, it seemed inevitable that I would find employment I didn't hate, which would allow me to afford rent, pay back my loans, and eat shrimp burritos.

None of that happened, at least not right away. I was ignored by museums, schools public and private, magazines, newspapers, book and record stores. Rejection letters, I could handle. It's almost soothing to get a formal

fuck off email. But no response breeds an ennui that none
of your friends want to hear about—to say nothing of the
novel that's always almost done. In retrospect, it's shocking that no one wanted to hire me. I was delusional, self-
involved, and depressive. A model employee.

The Soviets had been defeated. Unfettered belief in
democracy, technology, and the holy forces of multina-
tional capital swept the globe. Progress was infinite. Righ-
teousness merely required reading the right books, or at
least watching the right adaptations. The unsigned contract then circulating among my generation pledged to
render those twentieth-century evils obsolete. Poverty,
racism, angst, and privation could be eradicated within
this final reordering of the personal and political. A shiny
suit sparkling in every closet.

My dreams were only possible in an outdated world.
There was no *Saturday Evening Post* to cover six months
of my rent for a short story set in the chopped and screwed
age. This constant rejection somewhat relieved the pres-
sure that Earth would probably burn in an ecological ho-
locaust sometime late in the century.

The desire to write felt dumb and uncontrollable. On
Sunday mornings, I'd usually wake up hungover, my
pockets filled with ethereal and unremembered gibber-
ish scribbled on bar napkins. To afford the rent on the
two-bedroom apartment that I shared with three room-
mates, I took any random gig I could find. I ghostwrote
term papers about salsa dancing for a fortysomething
college student ($150 a pop), taught remedial English to
children at a chain tutoring center ($11 an hour), sat in

the occasional focus group ($75 in cash, plus all the cold-cut sandwiches I could pocket). I was anachronistic and adrift, desperate to go far without letting desperation define me. But that only lasts for so long.

So when I saw a Craigslist want ad for an entertainment reporter position at an undisclosed publication, I figured I should at least give them a chance to disregard me:

> los angeles > westside-southbay > jobs > writing/editing
>
> ### Celebrity Reporter for Major Entertainment Magazine (Santa Monica)
>
> Established entertainment magazine seeks a journalist who is **PASSIONATE** about celebrity and pop culture, particularly film and television actors, pop stars, **RICH HUNKS**, and **GLAMOROUS CELEBUTANTES!!!!**
>
> Role requires an ability to break and report celebrity news and cultivate sources in the world of **HOLLYWOOD.** Do you regularly go out to clubs, parties, and bars with people in the **ENTERTAINMENT INDUSTRY**?
>
> Do you **LIVE AND BREATHE** pop culture and nightlife? Do you love the fast pace of weekly magazines, and are unfazed by the biggest stars in the world? If so, we're looking for you!!! ;)

Compensation: **negotiable based on experience**
Employment type: **part-time**

You should only lie to the police and your prospective employer. This time I was determined to procure an interview. If they wanted a Hollywood insider, I'd create a shiny mutant, a bottle service regular at all the clubs consecrated by celebrities. You should have seen the cover letter. Actually, no one should ever see that cover letter. To hear me tell it, I was a princeling of young Hollywood wisely keeping a low profile because of a sixth sense about the ravages of fame.

I was at Joseph's on Mondays and at Nacional on Tuesdays. You could find me at Concorde on Wednesday, White Lotus on Thursday, the Chateau on Friday. Only flagrantly bleached freeway pilgrims went out on Saturdays, so I usually enjoyed a low-key sushi dinner at Koi, followed by one drink (but no more) at the Whisky Bar. Sunday was typically a day to unwind, but if I felt classy and restless, there was always Danny Masterson's speakeasy jazz night at Guy's. Over the course of an adolescence in Los Angeles, I claimed to have forged unbreakable bonds with Mary-Kate and Ashley Olsen. And what a surprise, the "established entertainment magazine" called me in for an interview the following week.

No magazines are listed in the lobby directory. Nothing but advertising shops, law firms, and adjustable loan hammerheads. All I know is that the office is on the third floor of a charcoal glass rectangle in Santa Monica. I'm supposed to speak with "AVB," who has been firing off terse emails via an encrypted address.

There's no company signage for suite #321. Just dark walnut doors, frosted glass windows, and taupe walls. To enter, I need to buzz a plastic call box. Above it, there's a warning on a piece of printer paper:

> No solicitors or uninvited visitors
> allowed. Trespassers will be
> prosecuted.

I start to second-guess my decision. What kind of "established entertainment magazine" advertises on Craigslist? Was it being funded by the CIA? Why the Comic Sans? Then again, it was a pretty swanky building. I bet it paid well. And besides, I'd already risked overdraft charges to have my only suit dry-cleaned.

Over the intercom, a clipped voice asks, "Who are you?" and, "Who are you here to see?" Cracking open the door an inch, a hairy hand reaches out toward me. I hand over my driver's license. The door slams. I wait underneath buzzing fluorescent lights that make you feel like you're in an airport interrogation room.

When the door finally reopens, a bald and unshaven Armenian security officer in a big-and-tall suit waves me into a waiting area. He takes his job extremely seriously. Earpiece in, strip mall enforcer scowl. He grunts at a receptionist behind a glass partition, who doesn't pay

either of us any mind. The aluminum nameplate reveals
the company name: U.S. MEDIA.

Sitting on a stiff fabric couch, I notice a pile of magazines scattered on a fake-wood end table. Any illusions of
this being a respectable outlet are promptly dashed by
the latest editions of all the gossip rags, even the ones
where Bigfoot is always saving a baby from a flaming
camper. It dawns on me that I may have entered the western nerve center of Tabloid USA.

This isn't exactly familiar terrain. Sometimes, I'd
brainlessly flip through *People* at the dentist's office or
gawk at a tawdry headline while waiting to buy cigarettes
at a 7-Eleven. I'd never actually sat down and read any of
the slanderous captions and accusations. But at this
point, the gutter press might be my best bet to get paid
for creative writing.

The secretary is still philosophically opposed to my
presence. So I might as well educate myself on the issues
of the day. Timed to Arnold Schwarzenegger's first run
for California governor, the *Enquirer* has a cover exposé
on "The Gropinator's Filthy Sex Scandals." To ensure
civic responsibility, they include a "Who Would You
Vote For?" infographic with the other celebrity candidates in the recall: diminutive ex–child star Gary Cole-
man, *Hustler* publisher Larry Flynt, and porn star Mary
Carey—whose platform involves making lap dances
tax-deductible.

The Sun claims that if the government would interpret Nostradamus correctly they could catch Saddam.
Weekly World News chronicles a space alien's shocking

memoir about his "steamy nights" in a UFO love nest with Monica Lewinsky. *Globe* dedicates itself to the fallout from Kobe Bryant's rape arrest. In *Nova*, Demi Moore and Ashton Kutcher are moving in together (*BYE BYE, BACHELOR LIFE, ASHTON*).

"You Alice's guy?" The secretary acknowledges me like she'd rather be picking glass from an open wound.

"You mean AVB?"

Rolling her eyes, she curls two fingers for me to come closer. Her look is, let's say, rockabilly scrivener. Candy-apple cat-eye glasses match her lipstick and acrylics.

"Don't call her that."

"What should I call her, then?"

"She'll be here soon."

From the front desk, you can see into the newsroom. It's not exactly bustling. About twenty people clack away in a cubicle farm. Half the desks are empty. The blinds are closed, the lights are shrill, the Freon is numbing. A tombstone aroma of printer ink, burnt Folgers, and despair hangs in the air.

A woman in her midfifties approaches me.

"You're the one with the tip about Courteney Cox's pregnancy?"

Her hair is chopped short and embalmed into an amber crown. She's in a Hillary Clinton pantsuit from Nordstrom Rack.

"I think I'm who you're supposed to be interviewing."

"Oh, right," she says. "Well, if anyone asks, you don't know a thing about that."

As I follow her birdlike steps through the office, I'm

a little surprised. I'd expected fast-talking repartee and impassioned arguments. But "U.S. Media" has the broken-clock malaise of a state-line casino. Silences punctuated by tubercular coughs, clicking keyboards, and the occasional phone call—always dialing out, never coming in.

"The *Enquirer* is behind that door." My guide motions at an unmarked gray passage, guarded by security detail. A dehydrated and sallow man with a wilting mustache emerges.

"Hello, Jerry," AVB says unenthusiastically.

"Alice." He nods. Then he glances at me. "Is this the guy you were telling me about? Who knows Ryan Phillippe's drug dealer?"

"This is a potential new hire for *Nova*," she responds curtly.

"Stop by my office before you leave." He gives a wink. "I'm sure we can find some work for you."

As soon as we get out of earshot, AVB fixes her grenade-green eyes on me.

"You don't want *that* dead-end job. I was trapped there for a decade until I broke the story about Rush Limbaugh's pill popping." She takes a long pause. "The housekeeper is always your best friend."

"What's up with the security?" I ask. The guard's glare follows me around the room.

"Insurance."

"In case someone gets mad about a story and tries to break into the newsroom?"

"Corporate started requiring it two years ago. Some nutjob sent anthrax to headquarters in Florida."

"What happened?"

"Tragedy. A guy died. Don't worry, it was just a photo editor."

Inside her office, AVB bypasses all pleasantries.

"Why does a smart kid like you want to work here?" She's clearly scanning my résumé for the first time. Her placard reads: ALICE VAN BRONX, NEWS EDITOR.

"I'm hoping to meet Bat Boy." I try to match the condescension. "He ever come into the office?"

"He's a thousand years old. He prefers Boca Raton." She pauses, looking at me like I'm unripe produce.

"That your father's suit?"

"Not anymore."

It's clearly a hand-me-down: too roomy in the chest, too short in the arms. I'm barely old enough to legally drink. Prime cannon fodder. Professional enough to wear a suit to the interview, too broke for proper tailoring.

Despite my urgent need for employment, there are glaring concerns. For one, I can't see myself working for a tabloid. And even if I did, I won't let myself be clowned by a corny boss who looks like a human resources officer at a New England HMO. She has the cynicism and weariness of someone with nothing left to believe in. And while I might lack worldliness, growing up in LA gave me a natural bullshit radar. You always met people like Alice Van Bronx—Northeasterners pretending to be above the Hollywood vapidity. But look closer and there's a photo of her at the *Legally Blonde 2* premiere, posing next to a grimacing Reese Witherspoon.

"H. L. Mencken Award for journalistic excellence?

Impressive." She looks up and smiles tepidly. My college didn't even have a journalism school.

"We're looking for serious reporters without an elitist mentality," she continues. "Does that describe you?"

"Who's to say?" I stare at the oval moons on my fingernails. "What do you even mean by 'an elitist mentality'?"

She wants to hear that I'd be a pliant and loyal foot soldier for the sprawling U.S. Media empire. But I can't bring myself to say it. Maybe I should recuse myself by telling the whole truth: the cover letter was fiction; I'd actually been fired as the sports editor of my high school paper for "insubordination." My college lit mag dropped me as a culture columnist after a screed about the "campus safety Gestapo."

"I like your honesty." She leans closer. "Look, the magazine business is changing. These blogs make up whatever they want and people can read it instantly—for free. We want to bring in people with credibility and reporting chops."

"So you want to be more like *People* magazine?"

"Without the studio-planted crap." Her mouth curls in an awkward rictus. "I want our readers to feel like they're behind the velvet rope in all the hip clubs, rubbing elbows at all the VIP parties."

I'm getting fidgety now. My suit starts to itch. My necktie is a noose. She called the clubs "hip." I need to get out of this office, this city. *If I get in my car now, I can easily get to the desert before dark. I have enough gas money for that.* Before I can leave, there's a knock at the door. Alice Van Bronx opens it. A beautiful redhead walks into the room.

"Who's this cutie?" she asks Alice, giving me a once-over.

"He might be our new entertainment reporter," Van Bronx says, with slight antagonism. "Can I *help you*, Brenda?"

"Someone wants to speak to you and says it's urgent."

"The Courteney Cox tipper?"

"No, it's about the Bennifer wedding. He says he's got valuable info, but it'll be expensive."

"Fuck, okay." She scrambles to her feet and hands my résumé and cover letter to the redhead in the black sheer top and designer jeans.

"Brenda, do you mind finishing up the interview?"

Brenda nods. Alice tells me that it was wonderful to meet me. We'd be in touch very soon. Then she vanishes down the hallway.

"Welcome to *Nova*," Brenda says as she leads me down the hall to her own corner office. She has choppy bangs and a cow skull tattooed onto her pale freckled left bicep. "I bet they did that thing where they didn't tell you what magazine you were applying for, huh?"

"I was hoping for *Entertainment Weekly*."

"We all have big dreams," she says with a laugh that sounds lifesaving in this twilight zone. "It's not so bad." Staring out into the cubicle grid, she finishes her thought. "I mean, it could definitely be better."

She ushers me into a room decorated with handbills of Stone Temple Pilots and Hole concerts. The name on the desk reads BRENDA YOU, WEST COAST BUREAU CHIEF. She's so pretty and sharp that I start wondering what misdirection led her to this Gehenna. Perusing my résumé, she raises an eyebrow.

"You're *really* intimate associates with Mary-Kate and Ashley?"

"Can I be honest with you?" She nods. I'm already dazed by her limpid blue eyes. *Here I go again.* I can't lie to this woman. She must be incredible at this job.

"I've never met either of them," I say. "I mean, I know a guy who claimed to have smoked with them once, but almost everything in that letter is made-up."

"What do you *actually* want to do?" she says, completely unbothered by the original lie.

"Write books. Profile rappers, maybe an NBA player or two. Make enough money to travel and retire in a modestly priced forest."

She smiles. "Nobody reads books anymore. I mean, I'm writing a book, but, like, you need a job."

"What's it about?"

"It's an erotic thriller about a Hollywood actress who becomes a serial killer." She laughs.

On the desk, there's a framed photo of Brenda and a miniature look-alike, clearly her daughter. Goofing off in paper crowns at Medieval Times.

"Look, I know you probably think this is all a joke," she goes on. "And I get it, you won't win a Pulitzer here, but Capote wasn't wrong when he said that all literature is gossip. And you'll *never* be bored either. We're about to go glossy. No more tacky tabloid bullshit. *Nova* just stole the editorial director from *Us Weekly*."

When I look confused, Brenda briefly explains the backstory of her new boss, a Canadian mother of four who invented the modern celebrity weekly with columns like "Stars Like Us?" "The Buzzometer," and "Who Wore It Best?" She received a $1.5 million base salary to take over *Nova*, plus equity, and the agreement to relocate the magazine's headquarters from Florida to New York.

"We want *Nova* to be *Us*'s kid sister with a tongue ring," Brenda explains.

"I don't even really care about celebrities like that."

"That's why you'd be perfect." She flatters me with that alluring smile. "You won't be fazed."

I'm starting to realize why she looks so familiar. She's a doppelgänger for the redheaded femme fatale from *Melrose Place*. The one who eventually gets run over at her wedding reception by her former business partner's abusive father.

"Can I ask you a personal question?" she continues.

"Sure."

"Are you gay?"

"No . . . Is that, like, a selling point for the job?"

"I mean, we'd be best friends if you were. But it's better that you're not. Everyone that works here is either a woman, a gay man, or a graying British cock from Fleet Street. We need a trendy young guy to get into the clubs and meet all the stars and their girlfriends and their girlfriend's friends—those are the ones who always talk."

"I'm sorry. I'm probably not the right guy for this." I feel queasy at the whole proposition. "You seem cool, and I'd like to help if I could, but—"

"No need to be such a purist." She laughs. "Take a freelance assignment or two, try it out. You'll put money in the bank, and can always keep applying for other jobs."

"Just don't ask me to sift through Jessica Alba's trash."

"I'll take care of you. What about tonight? You free?"

"Like I said, I really don't—"

"I assume you're familiar with Britney Spears?" she interrupts.

I'm now obligated to tell her my ". . . Baby One More Time" video shoot story, which has become a big hit over the years. Her eyes come alive. I'm being reeled in.

"Well, tonight is the Teen Choice Awards. And we *really* need someone to go to the after-party at Privilege." She taps her long black fingernails on the desk. "That's where Britney's supposed to be. You've been before, yeah?"

"Of course," I say. This isn't exactly true. But I feel like I've been let into Brenda's inner sanctum and don't want to look like a loser who has never been to the hottest club in the city.

"I'll be on the list, right?"

She gives an *oh, sweetie* laugh.

"Of course not. But you seem smart and capable and I bet you can find your way in. And you can always expense your drinks, gas, and anything you need to grease the door. Plus two hundred for the night."

"I just write about whatever I see?"

"Who's there, what they're wearing, who they're talking to, what they're drinking, what they're blowing. But Britney should be the main focus."

This is my last chance to say no. But I've already begun to convince myself. I'll only be going to the club. Tomorrow morning, one hundred other people could theoretically recount the evening to *Nova* for cash. Why shouldn't I get paid? Besides, how can I justify to my future self that I turned down a chance to party with Britney? Maybe I won't even see a thing. She probably won't even show. It might be the easiest money I ever make.

I know. You're 100 percent sure that you'd have seen the abyss in advance. You, a paragon of virtue, would've recoiled at the amorality of tabloid stalking and walked straight out the door. Maybe you would have, but maybe not if you didn't have any better options. I tell Brenda that I'm up for the gig, but just this one time. We'll see how it goes. She tells me that I won't regret it—it'll be fun, I promise.

"Try to file your copy by 10:00 a.m." She hands me her business card, which has a black-and-white caricature of her drawn like an underground comic. "You can call me anytime. Don't do anything you're uncomfortable with, but don't be afraid either."

"Afraid of what?"

"Exactly. A photographer may call you later to join. His name is Oliver. You'll get used to him."

Booze! **BETRAYALS!** Breakups!

Madcap Thrills
Inside the **Mansion!!**

The *MUST-HAVE* Hats
of Summer!!!

Glide into this bent matrix. West Hollywood on a
Friday night, late in the summer of '03. Rolling
north on Robertson in the resentful August heat,
windows down, heading toward Privilege. "In da Club"
taunts from the trembling speakers of my run-down
4Runner: 50 popping champagne, offering birthday rubs,
reminding me that I'll never be rich enough.

This is gilded turf. A nip-tuck netherworld on the
border between Beverly Hills and West Hollywood.
At 9:00 p.m., paparazzi are still camped out on the sidewalk outside of the Ivy, capturing celebrities eating $30
salads. The tabloids publish these photos religiously each
week, which in turn magnetizes out-of-town pilgrims
to this cluster of organic cafés, Asiatic tonic pharmacies,

and couture boutiques. Who needs a map to the stars anymore?

I drive past Kitson, the one-stop clothier for every starlet, club girl, and fame seeker, where rhinestone chokers sell for one month's rent. If Al-Qaeda got serious about exposing the depravity of infidel excess, they would drop propaganda leaflets on the Coalition of the Willing, picturing the Hilton sisters vaingloriously strutting out of this store, holding hundreds of thousands of dollars in merchandise.

Kitson is Britney's preferred emporium for Juicy tracksuits and Uggs. The former provincial teenager in the Kmart skirt now sets mass trends. Even when a look theoretically shouldn't work—the matching Canadian tuxedo with Justin Timberlake at the '01 American Music Awards—it becomes the stuff of folklore. The A&R from the ". . . Baby One More Time" video shoot was pretty much right about everything. She wasn't just an icon; she'd become an idea.

It was impossible to ignore her in the phosphorescent helix between impeachment and implosion. At newsstands and airports, her eyes entranced you from the cover of *Vogue*, *Esquire*, and *Rolling Stone*. The raunchy men's magazines teased her as a jailbait temptress, the tween pubs played up her girl-next-door charm, and the pop-culture tribunes did a little bit of both (while recognizing her wealth of pop bangers). She was the face of McDonald's and Got Milk? There were Britney video games, sunglasses, and Skechers. For one Christmas,

Pepsi dressed Britney in a navy-blue Santa Claus dress with white fur trim, a matching blue Santa hat, and *fuck me* black boots.

Our relationship was similarly complicated. I couldn't help but feel a bit territorial. I was the first outsider to fathom the full extent of her magic, and now she was being worshiped in the middle of the mall. Beloved by everyone from prepubescent princess girls to arthritic old lechers lusting for their own Lolita. A childhood crush who leaves your school without saying goodbye, then one day, years later, you see them in a magazine or on TV. You feel an irrational connection to their success, as if you were somehow part of their story. *You knew them when.*

Even the most sanguine Jive executive could not have anticipated such cultural dominance. The debut, naturally titled . . . *Baby One More Time*, sold thirty million copies worldwide. The ancient Greek rhetoricians called it "kairos": "a passing instant when an opening appears which must be driven through with force if success is to be achieved." *Forbes* called her 2002's "Most Powerful Celebrity."

Spice World crumbled into the sea. Boy bands became bozos with silly-string goatees. Christina Aguilera, Jessica Simpson, and Mandy Moore all trailed in her wake, but it was the difference between a light bulb and lightning. Don't get me wrong. The other girls all had admirable charms and hits. But only one had the juice to make the guys on my college basketball team—not exactly Top 40 connoisseurs—act out a histrionic lip sync to the third-biggest song on that first album. "*Some-times I run, sometimes I hide.*"

After burning through a yellow light at the Melrose intersection, I hook a right onto Santa Monica, past ca-balleros sipping colorful drinks underneath rainbow flags and house music. This is the heart of LA's gay club-land, where the year before at the Halloween Carnaval, I saw no fewer than three drag Britneys wearing the latex catsuit from the "Oops! . . . I Did It Again" video.

Wheeling left on Crescent Heights. A beam of threat-ening light illuminates the mansions in the hills, lording over the commoners in the flats. Privilege won't open until ten. I still have time to squander, so I swerve west down Sunset, now packed with partygoers savoring one of the final weekends of summer. A boom time without ebbs, just swells of increased volume.

To my right, Dublin's breezes past. The brick-and-timber Irish pub, immortalized by a Jay-Z lyric about "bubblin'" there, has lost its cachet by becoming accessi-ble to the plebes. The Body Shop screams in gaudy lights: GIRLS GIRLS GIRLS!!! The marquee of the House of Blues touts Arthur Lee and Love, a faint reminder of the area's Aquarian past.

To my left, the Standard hotel with its upside-down signage and naked white lobby. Paid models lounge for hours inside a glass jail that doubles as an art installation. There's the minimalist domino-shaped hotel named after the Dutch painter who aspired to make "pure plastic art." Miyagi's, a sushi restaurant–slash-club designed to look like a Kyoto shrine. Saddle Ranch, an ersatz Western roadhouse where Great Plains vacationers get thrown from the mechanical bull.

I pass the Whisky a Go Go, now a pay-to-play ruin where local high school ska-punk bands shank Sublime covers for $5 a head. The mammoth Hustler store where a gubernatorial candidate sells porn discs and sex toys. At the Rainbow, Lemmy from Motörhead swills Jack and Cokes and plays video poker all night. The Viper Room, of course—the site of River Phoenix's fatal overdose. Ghosts everywhere, but the Strip is too self-consumed to allow itself to be haunted.

At Pink Dot, the late-night market drowned in lonely neon, I bust a U, now heading back east toward Privilege. On the radio, the Black Eyed Peas command me to free my "inner soul," "break away from tradition," and "get it started in here." It sounds like a commercial for a geriatric Caribbean cruise line. I switch the dial from Power 106 to KIIS-FM, but it's still the Black Eyed Peas. Only this time, Justin Timberlake joins them to ask, "Where Is the Love?"—a lobotomized update of "Imagine."

I should probably admit my bias right now. From the moment that I first saw Timberlake wearing a bandanna and Cross Colours on *MMC*, I knew he was a total poseur. A schmaltzy song-and-dance man with a talent for mimicry, but lacking originality, imagination, and the capacity to surprise.

Timberlake was shrewd enough to pick undeniable smashes from Pharrell, but then again *everyone* wanted to work with Pharrell. He was a medium talent lucky enough to have a big budget and the ability to perform a

passable Michael Jackson impression after the King of
Pop passed on the beats. The "nice boy" always clumsily
code-switching between a fake hood accent and a choir-
boy chirp. The type to flatter your friends' divorced
moms, but start air-humping about how bad he wanted
to "bone them" as soon as their backs were turned. His
true character was revealed in the story about the first
time he hooked up with Britney—when he reportedly ran
back to the *NSYNC tour bus begging his bandmates
to "smell my fingers."

When Britney and Justin broke up in the spring of
2002, it was like the DiMaggio and Marilyn divorce
for *Tiger Beat* subscribers. That November, Timberlake
dropped the "Cry Me a River" video, where he cast himself as a spurned hero betrayed by a wicked ex who
looked identical to Britney Spears. The media lapped up
his version, which tied nicely into the growing narrative
that Britney was a concubine masquerading as a vestal
virgin—the most corrosive influence since 2 Live Crew
taught American children to "Pop That Pussy."

Britney's minor slipups were treated as catastrophic
failures. And they were beginning to pile up. Her 2002
movie debut, *Crossroads*, grossed $60 million, more than
five times its budget, but the Razzies named her "Worst
Actress." She opened up Nyla, a New York Cajun restaurant with a catwalk, but when she cut ties with the failing
eatery after nine months, the press called it evidence of
her waning influence. A night partying at a Miami club
became a cocaine exposé. Even her parents' divorce was
fodder for the tabs.

It was all about narrative conflict. The good-girl routine didn't sell. Drama was necessary, and Britney was a
natural from her first *Rolling Stone* cover. That's when
a risqué bedroom photo shoot with a velvet Teletubby
caused the American Family Association to create a fake
scandal that boycotted stores selling Britney albums.
Her "disturbing mix of childhood innocence and adult
sexuality" was an affront to "God-Fearing Americans."
The similarly puritanical wife of Maryland's governor
declared that she would shoot Britney if she had the
chance. PETA was apoplectic too, after Britney performed
"I'm a Slave 4 U" at the 2001 VMAs with a twenty-five-
pound Burmese python named Banana draped around
her shoulders.

It had been two years since they broadcast that
Bronze Age fertility ritual on cable TV, but it had been
heat-transferred to my memory. I wasn't alone. You still
couldn't go out without hearing Britney's own Neptunes
collaboration bumping in clubs, bars, and six-CD chang-
ers. As I pull up at the light next to the yellow-red crayon
of Tower Records, a car full of blonde scene girls stops
next to me. They're dancing and screaming along to Britney's ode to obsession like it's giving them life.

> *I'm a slave for you*
> *I cannot hold it, I cannot control it*

In the last two years, the "not a girl, not yet a woman"
had become a sex goddess in a cosmic harem, batting
Cleopatra eyes over Neptunes beats. "I'm a Slave 4 U"

sounded like something Prince would've bestowed to one of his muses: nasty, no-safe-word space-funk, but with hip-hop drums to induce exotic dancing. Winter formal anthems swapped out for bondage and masturbation fantasies made for a club that didn't look twice at fake IDs.

The car crawls down Sunset, but my mind rewinds to the "Slave" MTV performance that aired five days before 9/11. A vestige of a dying world and a harbinger of the new. The hissing snake in the paradisal garden contrasted with the primitive ruins of a collapsed future. Britney breaking out of a cage where she's been trapped with a live tiger, wearing a jungle-green cutout bra top and glittering low-rise shorts, and precious gems affixed to a body like Aphrodite's. She hops on the back of a dancer dressed like a zebra and seductively waves her arms. You could cut the symbolism with a machete.

I watched it live with about a half dozen people at a friend's off-campus house. Outside of the Super Bowl—at which Britney had performed that year—the VMAs were practically the only thing left that warranted appointment viewing. And I can't tell you for certain about the reception that it received elsewhere, but in the narrow sample of that living room, every boy, girl, and mineral in front of that TV would have sold both kidneys for a chance with Britney. She was the hottest thing that any of us had ever seen. The sexuality, electricity, and control of her dance moves, the delirious cool with which she wielded the hissing snake. Afterward, we all went outside to smoke a spliff and try to figure out what midnight-in-the-garden voodoo we had just witnessed.

Privilege is a limestone-white and azure-blue fort situated at the crossroads of Crescent Heights and Sunset. I pay $20 to park in a strip mall paved atop the ruins of a hotel named after a lost paradise, where F. Scott Fitzgerald, Humphrey Bogart, and Errol Flynn drank themselves to death.

It's not even 10:00 p.m., but getting in seems hopeless. There's a line all the way to the Chateau, which towers above us like a Transylvanian castle. I'm standing beneath a *Freaky Friday* billboard with the tagline GET YOUR FREAK ON.

Trucker hats are everywhere: terry cloth and velvet; leather, denim, and imitation leopard; Von Dutch issue with faux dalmatian fur and camouflage. Hats of vintage Mexican playing cards bought at Barneys and foam-bill John Deere hats from thrift stores. They're worn straightforward, cocked to the side, and at geometric angles that neither Pythagoras nor T.I. could conceive.

Earlier that afternoon, I asked a few of my more obnoxious acquaintances how to get past the velvet rope. They just laughed. On a normal night, most males can only get into Privilege by bringing a few gorgeous girls, buying a table, or bribing the bouncer. For a Britney Spears–attended private party after the Teen Choice Awards? They wouldn't even give you odds.

Before I left home, I spent about an hour trying to figure out what to wear. The selection isn't exactly robust. The guys at clubs like Privilege look like they spend half their waking life and discretionary income at Fred Segal. I don't have that bank account. The only real option is to dress down and act so nonchalant that the doormen think that I'm a mild personage.

I go with a suede coat with plush fur trim, a recent purchase at a thrift store. Pair it with a white tee, jeans, and Chucks, and it's almost believable that I've appeared on *That '70s Show*. It's not ideal that the night is broiling, but as Pimp C once said, TV don't know no temperature.

Whenever I was dragged to these clubs, I hated them. The DJs think that they're eclectic Merlins for mixing Bon Jovi into Snoop. The doormen treat you like you have SARS. Anytime you talk to a girl, she's trying to see if that's really Pacey from *Dawson's Creek* at the bar, or just someone who *really* looks like him.

The secret is that you're supposed to act affected and disaffected at the same time. So as soon as I approach the front of Privilege, I spark a cigarette. It gives me something to do but, more importantly, allows for a grace period to scope the line's dimensions, the crowd's character, and the situation at the door. I can linger around the periphery until the tobacco reaches the filter, but if I hang around too long, the bouncer will order me to fuck off.

Am I nervous? Maybe a little. But part of me doesn't care if I fail, which lends a reckless strength. I toss my cigarette and stomp it out. Here it goes. Back arched. Posture counts. Don't strut, but swing your arms confidently.

Don't act like you own the place, but carry yourself like you can temporarily cover the mortgage.

The bouncers are retired nose tackles with funereal suits and contemptuous sunglasses. A swarthy promoter commands everyone around, twirling a black cane.

"Wait a minute, kid!"

The bouncer stiff-arms me to clear the path for Mini-Me from the *Austin Powers* movies. The little actor with a dangling earring grabs the promoter's cane and swings on it like a carousel. They laugh and fist-bump. Then the diminutive Dr. Evil saunters into Privilege, his arm wrapped around Miss San Clemente.

The promoter stares me down and sneers at my intemperate coat. "Isn't it a little early for Sundance?"

This is coming from an Oswald Cobblepot–looking-ass white dude in his late thirties, wearing a top hat, bandanna, and diamond heart pendant.

"I thought they killed the Penguin in *Batman Returns*?"

The promoter grips the eight ball atop his cane. His tight smile reveals bleached kernels.

"Funny . . . I almost like you, son," he spits. "You better be on the list."

"I wouldn't cut the line if I wasn't."

"Name?"

"Muniz."

"Muniz?"

"Frankie Muniz from *Malcolm in the Middle* and *Agent Cody Banks*. Up for Teen Choice Awards in both film and television. We got a table."

Having scanned the Teen Choice nominees, I'd nar-rowed it down to two semibelievable lies. Frankie Muniz and Elijah Wood were both nominated, and it seemed more logical that I'd be with one of them than, say, JC Chasez or Joe Millionaire. But Frodo Baggins seemed too Silver Lake to bother with Privilege. He was probably go-ing to go home after the event, quaff a goblet of fine mead, and savor Elliott Smith albums on vinyl.

"Your homie ain't on the list."

"He hit the owner's Treo a half hour ago. Sam should know."

Sam is Sam Nazarian, the owner of Privilege and the entrepreneur behind the burgeoning SBE nightlife em-pire. Name-dropping is essential.

"Aight, yo," the top hat squawks. "You need to wait for your mans and 'em."

"Frankie told me to get here early and make sure it's good for him when he pulls up." I inconspicuously slip him a $20.

"What am I supposed to do with this? Buy a party pack at Del Taco?" He waggles his cane at me to disappear.

"Bruh, you just let in Mini-Me. I know you can let me in a few minutes early."

"Verne is family at Privilege." He puffs out his chest. "Get to the back of the line. Vamoose!"

Girls in derby caps slink past me, swinging Louis V purses, inching closer to the entrance. I join a short VIP column along the side. I've done what I can. From here, I'll idle for an hour to catch the comings and goings.

Maybe catch a Britney sighting. File my observations in the morning, collect my $200, pass Go.

I overhear banal murmurs about who isn't texting back, scorn for rivals' outfits, and other plastic banter. A blonde in a blinding chain-mail top names the six after-parties tonight. I've been cut in line by Jack Osbourne, an exuberant Joey Fatone, a sweaty Andy Dick, Dave Navarro and Carmen Electra, and someone named Cindy Margolis. An ICM assistant in a porkpie hat and a bedazzled skull sport coat whispers to me, "She's the most downloaded woman on the internet. We rep her."

Before I left the office, Brenda lent me an extra Sidekick they had lying around. It was supposed to help me play the part and keep in touch if any news broke. Around 11:30 p.m., Brenda texted to say that Britney lost everything tonight. Beyoncé beat her out for "Choice Female Hottie." JLo topped her for "Choice Female Fashion Icon."

By midnight, Britney (and Muniz) have yet to enter the building. I've huffed another six cigs and told countless people, "I'm just waiting for my friends; you can go ahead of me." Time to go home. The report will be serviceable.

As I'm leaving, a black Escalade streaks into the valet parking area. The driver unrolls a tinted window. He's in his midtwenties with a long curtain of corkscrew hair, wolfish eyes, and a British accent.

"Aye, mate, come over here!" he hollers at me. "I know where she's at."

"Who are you?"

"No time to get into that. Brenda sent me. Hop in."

"How do you know who I am?"

"I looked you up on bloody Friendster."

Drumming on his steering wheel, he waves me over.

"Don't be a ponce. Do you want to go to Britney or not?"

The bouncer lumbers over to harangue the Escalade driver.

"You're going to have to get out of this lane, sir. This is the VIP-only valet."

The truck quakes from the bass of "Shake Ya Tail-feather." What choice do I have but to hop in? Who am I to contradict Nelly and Murphy Lee's anthem whispering: "We do it for fun, this is history baby"? The tires squeal. We peel out. But not before the driver flicks a middle finger at the bouncer and shouts, "Wanker!!"

The speedball at the steering wheel is breaking down Britney's migratory flight patterns while weaving in and out of traffic, doing sixty-five in a thirty-five zone, west on Sunset, blasting through the green light on Doheny into the jade opulence of Beverly Hills.

"Y'see, mate . . . she aimed to hit Privilege after the awards, but someone said that chump Fred Durst was finna pop out, so she switched plans because she wanted crispy tuna from Koi," the driver says with semiauto-matic intensity and a heavy Cockney accent. "But she decided it was too long of a drive, so she bolted to the In-N-Out on Cahuenga."

"How do you know all this?"

"Brenda didn't tell you about me?"

"Only that a photographer named Oliver might find me."

"Just a photographer?" He's aghast. "Dawg, peep this!!"

Oliver points to the navigation system on the dashboard. It's easily the most advanced piece of technology that I've ever seen in an automobile.

"That's three grand! Check this." He whips past the Candyland pastels of the Beverly Hills Hotel, not bothering to look at the road because he's too busy scrolling through the programmed celebrity targets on his mounted in-car computer. There are three different addresses for "Brit," one each for "Brit's Mom" and "Brit's Bro."

"Two hundred names! One touch and bam—straight to their house!" he says. "And let's say I recognize someone driving past us. I got four hundred different license plates in the computer too."

"So we're going to Britney's house?"

He ignores the question. "Brenda really didn't tell you about me? Not even the beef with Josh Hartnett?"

I shake my head. He slams his foot on the gas, flying through Sunset and Whittier into Bel Air, using his free hand to give me his business card: Oliver Bournemouth, CEO and head photographer for OB Pictures.

"The hottest pap agency in America," he says. "I've got nine photographers, each supplied with the best camera equipment and a Beamer, Benz, or Tahoe. Go to any hotel or restaurant in this town and the doormen, waiters, bellhops, desk jockeys, valets, and even the bloody sommeliers are gonna tell me everything. I've got personal assistants, bodyguards, private flight attendants, nurses, personal trainers, stylists, all on payroll. If Brit gets a tan, I know about it before they start spraying."

He's got cult leader charisma. A generational salesman pirouetting at the speed of light, wired with supernatural amperage and a natural opportunism built for this city. Human fish scale cocaine.

"Britney arrived an hour ago after Jared Leto texted her to come to the mansion," Oliver explains. "She's apparently in a pissy mood because she didn't win any of those stupid awards, which means she's been drinking. You know how she gets when she's smashed."

"The mansion?"

Oliver skims my face for stupidity. The car drifts into the next lane, eliciting a prolonged honk from an S-Class. He's unfazed.

"The mansion. It's the Midsummer Night's Dream party tonight." He turns up the volume of "Wanksta" on the stereo. "Brenda's going to be so jealous that you went. When she was producing for Jerry Springer, she posed for Playboy's Cyber Girl of the Week, but only online. Hef hates redheads in the actual mag."

"How the fuck are you going to get us into the Playboy Mansion?"

"There are things you learn when you can get a hundred grand a pic," he says. "Besides, you're rolling solo.
It's too hot for me in there."

I learned early to always act like you've been there
before. Treat this star-studded Dionysian reverie as *just
another* ho-hum Friday night in my life. Of course, there
are the delusions that you'd expect from a twenty-one-
year-old crashing this holy grail of American hedonism.
Playboy may be a dated artifact of Boomer fantasy that
no one in my generation reads. And a doddering seventy-
seven-year-old in a smoking jacket dating women my age
is downright gross. But I am a born sucker for the Los
Angeles of the platinum imagination, the quest to reach
the final room in a never-ending carousel of trapdoors
and false ceilings. Pull the candelabra, the wall rotates,
and you're in Shangri-la. Except this time it's Miss September frolicking naked in the grotto, hanging on to
every quip from David Spade.

"The front door's gonna be madness," Oliver rattles
on. The velocity of speech makes his gray eyes pop. "As
you enter, a couple birds on a laptop will be checking
people in. DO NOT MAKE EYE CONTACT WITH
THEM OR ANY SECURITY. You're on your phone the
entire time and ignoring anyone who approaches. If you
appear important, *you are* important to these muppets!
What if they accost you and you turn out to be Matthew
Perry's plus-one? It ain't worth the risk."

Careening off Sunset onto Charing Cross, a series of
speed bumps forces Oliver to finally slow down. This is
Holmby Hills, a different stratum of wealth, where the

Playboy Mansion is stashed up a complicated skein of narrow one-way streets that dead-end at tall iron gates sharp enough to impale any intruder.

You can live here your entire life and never know these roads existed, let alone interact with any of their inhabitants. The children attend Harvard-Westlake and Crossroads and have memorized the differences between a 4.0 and a 4.6 Range Rover like a catechism. For holidays, Gulfstream jets whisk them from Van Nuys Airport to Aspen, the south of France, and private resort islands in the Caribbean.

Oliver torches a Benson & Hedges. "Have one." He offers his pack. "Imported from London. Your American ciggies are rubbish."

We climb into more exclusive terrain, where the streetlights are spare because the residents want outsiders to remain that way. Black sycamore trees hunch in the darkness. Towering evergreen hedges shield baronial estates.

"Walk along the left side of the house along the shrubbery and count three doors," Oliver says. "One, two, three, and boom, you're at the side entrance. There, you'll find a tall bloke named Kerel. Tell him you're Oliver's mate and he'll let you in. Make sure no one is following you or sees. Got it?"

"And I'm supposed to keep an eye on Britney or just observe the whole party in general?"

"Yeah, you're getting paid to scarf shrimp cocktails and try to fuck the hot Czech exchange student from *American Pie*," he says as we blow past a sign warning all cars to turn around, except for limos dropping off party guests.

"Nah, mate, find Britney. She's in there somewhere with *Requiem for a Dream*. I'll wait down the hill, but when they're ready to dip, text me, so I can get in position to snap a pic of her and Leto. That's thirty grand."

"I thought Britney was dating Colin Farrell?"

"You're gonna need to catch up if you're going to survive. He ended things a few weeks ago by mailing her an I SLEPT WITH COLIN FARRELL AND ALL I GOT WAS THIS LOUSY T-SHIRT T-shirt."

I wasn't TiVo-ing *Access Hollywood*, but I'd stayed abreast of Britney's experiments in modern romance. First, there was the scandal with the choreographer Wade Robson—the "other man" who allegedly inspired "Cry Me a River." Next came a brief fling with a married dancer named Columbus Short. And then the apocalyptic revelations of earlier this year: when Fred Durst of Limp Bizkit went on Howard Stern to trumpet his wild night with Britney, down to sexual position and personal hygiene. It was around the same time that she announced a six-month sabbatical "to chill out and be a normal person."

Normalcy is relative. When you're the biggest pop star in the universe, a night at the most fabled masquerade of the moment is a matter of course. For someone who was attending low-rent college foam parties only six months prior, it is not regular.

I hop out of the Escalade, awestruck by the psychedelic tapestry of mint, lavender, and flamingo lights. The

mansion looks like a French dauphin's château that's
been renovated to shoot soft-core porn. The Playboy
bunny logo is projected above the doorway. Ivy and vines
smother the gray stone walls. Twinkling dream lights
snake through the trees. In the center of the driveway, a
nude cherub perches atop a burbling fountain, complete
with a wishing well to amplify the hopes of all who
enter.

Chaos reigns on the manicured front lawn. Security
guards and event staff entertain would-be attendees bar-
gaining to swing open the gates of Xanadu. Everyone is
always on the list, and yet there is always some mistake.
I'm pretty sure I see Owen Wilson avoid the crowd and
saunter in with four girls who look like they're the cen-
terfolds for the rest of the year.

I press the Sidekick to my ear to pretend that I'm an
esteemed guest who Hefner personally called to ensure
that I was coming. To my surprise, no one glances in my
direction as I execute a screen action toward the eastern
corner of the Gothic Tudor palace. I spot Kerel. He nods
and directs me down a lightless servant's path leading
into the backyard.

It's half past midnight and things are coming un-
glued. Tipsy older men in embroidered sport coats and
trilby hats stagger across the grounds with their arms
draped around surgically enhanced women in lingerie. A
photographer's flash explodes upon three nude platinum
blondes with body-painted tuxedos. During the last shot,
a wild black-and-white bunny rabbit scampers across the
frame.

Wiping the sweat off my forehead, I spark another cigarette and float across the grass toward a massive party tent. The air smells like tequila and jasmine. Less than twelve hours ago, I was auditioning in the *Nova* offices. Now my path is blocked by Leonardo DiCaprio and his "Pussy Posse," their arms interlinked with several Wilhelmina models. They're wasted and honking back at an albino peacock revealing a starburst plumage.

Inside the white tent, a dance party is underway. Giant silk roses and tulips droop from the ceiling. The bunny logo is everywhere. So are bombshells in bunny outfits bouncing to Sean Paul's "Gimme the Light," spun by a DJ who looks like a *Baywatch* lifeguard. She happens to be topless. I feel like I've landed on *Pinocchio*'s Pleasure Island, except that you don't turn into a donkey if you stay here too long—you just squabble with Kato Kaelin for the last skewer of grilled shrimp. He's here too, with two Playmates staring into his eyes like he's about to tell them the real secrets of the O.J. murder.

About two dozen girls resemble Britney, but the genuine article remains elusive. Might as well devour some sushi, tortellini, and miniature slices of pizza from the expansive buffet. Delicious. It's probably not a bad idea to grab a drink at the open bar either, where I wait in line behind Jermaine Dupri and a voluptuous girl in Victoria's Secret who I think I saw once in a Ja Rule video. He's explaining why LA's strip clubs are inferior to Atlanta's.

With a brimming glass of Black Label on ice, I resume my mission, crunching down pebbled pathways that extend into a thicket of redwoods and tree ferns. I'm only a few hundred yards from the tent, but it already feels like I'm in a rainforest. Toucans croak. An undisclosed primate screeches from the shadows.

"Yo, so you like cars, right?" I hear a familiar rasp lurking several feet away.

"Oh my god, a spider monkey!" shrieks a blonde woman with blue eyes that pierce the darkness.

She steps into a floodlight partially illuminating the animal cages. It's Tara Reid, and she's talking to Xzibit. It is, in fact, a large new-world primate leaping from branch to branch.

"I auditioned for *Planet of the Apes*," Xzibit says. "Fucking gave my part to the *Green Mile* guy."

Tara Reid is enraptured by the brown monkey doing trapeze swings from the tree limbs. A squawk rips from my direction. It's an African crane in the cage next door. Distracted, Tara Reid spins toward me and nearly spills her apple martini onto my shirt. Recovering her balance, she fondles the lapel of my coat.

"Oh my god, I love *love* this coat! Where did you get it?"

She's wearing a ruby floral dress, bright red lipstick, and matching heels. A shattered somewhere-over-the-rainbow vibe.

"Uh, this, like, vintage shop in Topanga Canyon."

"Don't you think this coat is bomb?" she asks Xzibit, box-braided and fitted in dark denim.

The man who wrote "Paparazzi" nods his head, annoyed that my stupid fucking coat has interrupted his conversation.

From up the hill, the dankest weed fragrance that I've ever inhaled floats toward us. Xzibit squints in that direction.

"Yo, I think I see Snoop. I'ma catch up with him." He smiles at the *Van Wilder* heroine. "My manager is gonna hit you about that video, though."

They exchange a big *let's do this again soon* hug. Xzibit gives me a polite nod and rambles toward the house. Then it's just me, Tara Reid, and the spider monkey.

"Did you know the Aztecs considered spider monkeys holy creatures connected to the arts?"

"Maybe that's why I've always felt such a deep connection to them." She draws closer to the cage.

"The males mate with three or four females at a time. But the females are incredibly selective. They reject a bunch before deciding on their chosen one."

"Are you a zoologist?" she asks.

"Just a big admirer of their work." I gesture at the monkeys. She giggles and grabs my bicep.

For three months in the third grade, I was obsessed with monkeys. This is the first time it's paid dividends. Things are vastly exceeding expectations. Bunny Lebowski is hanging on to me while I drink expensive liquor traipsing through a private zoo at San Simeon for "swingers."

My coat pocket buzzes. The text from Oliver reads, ????

I ask Tara if she's down to head back toward the party. She agrees if she can "bum a stog." On our stroll, we make small talk, with a few crucial details swapped for the truth. I'm a working novelist, here at the behest of Hugh Hefner, a family friend, who wants to collaborate with me on a memoir because he wants to tap into the perspective of the next generation. Anything is possible if you dream big.

Our excursion leads through the grotto, aglow in purple and rose like Sleeping Beauty's Spring Break Castle. In the coral-blue pool, three dozen girls in thongs and bikini tops frolic and caress one another, while photographers preserve the Ambers in amber. Underneath a rock waterfall, a soaked cover girl cries out, "Hiiyee, Tara!!!" Tara returns the greeting with a royal wave and pageant smile.

Ahead of us, a man and woman walk into the mansion holding hands. I can only see the backs of their heads. He's got rock-star dirty-blond hair and dresses the part. She's a short blonde in a shorter purple dress. Can it be? I take longer strides, careful not to look like I'm rushing. But before I get close enough to figure out their identities, they vanish upstairs.

"Let's check out the house," I tell Tara Reid, who is maybe a little more fucked-up than I had first realized.

"Do you party?" she asks.

Of course. She grips my hand tightly, leading us into a game room, where partygoers shoot pool and play *Space Invaders.*

At the foot of the stairs, Tara Reid flashes her wristband at a hulking bodyguard, who waves her up. When I try to follow, he throws a shoulder block.

"Can't come up here unless you've got a Bunny band."

"Oh, c'mon, Calvin, let him through!" Tara Reid bats her gumball eyes to no avail. *Ain't happening. Hef's orders. No exceptions.*

We gravitate toward a wall of Playboy pinball machines with illustrations of Hefner and his Playmates: the girls completely fungible, his hair graying with each model. *Getting older as they stay the same age.*

Between shots, I scan the room for evidence of what brought me here. For a second, I catch Jared Leto at the top of the stairs, looking like an Urban Outfitters Kurt Cobain. Then he retreats deeper into the estate. Britney is nowhere to be seen.

A rumor ripples through the game room. *Everyone needs to get back to the tent. Someone MAJOR is about to perform.* Tara Reid grabs my elbow with urgency. We practically sprint down the lawn into the glassy gray-pink night, past the near-orgy in the grotto, back toward the tent festooned with a trellis of pale balloons and all the pretty lights and all the beautiful people.

Hefner is onstage now and thanks the crowd for coming.

"Every night at the Playboy Mansion is a dream, but tonight is a fantasy," Hefner says, like a corny granddad. Everyone politely laughs. He's wearing velvet pajamas and that goofy sailor hat and doesn't look long for this world. The artificial orange tan gives him the look of a wrinkled lizard about to captain a regatta.

"The next performer has a special place in my heart

because when he first came out, he had the message 'let love rule.' And that's always been my philosophy too. And, might I add, love as often as possible."

Excruciating laughter.

"Without further ado, I want to bring to the stage one of the most soulful young poets in rock 'n' roll. A Mr. Lenny Kravitz."

Everyone loses their minds. Standing applause. Tara Reid looks like she's about to kiss the sky.

Behold Lenny Kravitz. He looks exactly like Lenny Kravitz. Nose stud and sunglasses, leather jacket and leather pants. He pauses for dramatic effect before pulling out a guitar and sitting atop a stool. Then he plays an acoustic rendition of "Are You Gonna Go My Way."

Tara Reid and several girls in tuxedo body paint are near tears, as if no guitar riff this gorgeous has ever descended from the heavens. Total strangers clink their drink glasses together to toast their fortune. Mini-Me is here with a different woman. Hefner is with his six girlfriends, arm in arm, swaying along, slightly off beat. For a minute I feel depressed, as if I've shown up to the party a little too late, right when things are starting to get sad. And still, I wasn't even invited.

From the shadows just outside the frame, the tricky light of celebrity can be transfixing. Adrenaline runs through me, a new world unlocked, the reflected glamour of trailing the earth's most famous inhabitants to the places that seemed off-limits only yesterday. The actress and I are still intertwined and a server in a sparkling camisole hands me a flute of Dom Pérignon and Lenny

Kravitz is imploring a euphoric room to "hug and rub-a-dub." What could possibly go wrong?

My phone vibrates. A text flurry from Oliver:

> Where R U MATE!?!?
> BRIT JUST LEFT!
> GET OUT HERE NOW!!!

Tara Reid is gone too. She's slipped off my arm and followed the music. Standing up front, wrapped in a love puddle with a dozen Playmates in next to nothing, singing every word like sacred psalms. There is no time to say goodbye. Besides, it would be too awkward. We'll always have the spider monkeys.

I rush back into the teeming night, past the raucous grotto, where clothes have become an unnecessary burden, crossing the laptop sentries and security at the entrance. Say goodbye to the mansion.

Oliver screeches into the valet area, hollering at one of the guards attempting to thwart this lunatic from driving onto the lawn. Spotting me, he waves furiously, and I leap into the car. Slaloming down the hill, the gas pedal stomped in fevered pursuit, the chase replenishes itself anew.

Britney! IN LOVE or OUT OF CONTROL?!?!

WHAT WAS SHE Thinking????

<u>DIVA</u> Las Vegas!!!!

It's time for our final descent into McCarran International. Somewhere in this vortex of eight billion bulbs, the monuments of Las Vegas fight for dollars and attention on New Year's Eve. If I sharpen my eyes, I can see them all from my window seat: the simulacra of the Eiffel Tower, King Arthur's Castle, the Empire State Building, a buccaneer's treasure galleon, and the 350-foot steel-and-glass pyramid pumping columns of light into a bone-bruise sky.

Up until a few hours ago, I planned to hit up a costume ball hosted by Dita Von Teese at a Skid Row warehouse in downtown LA. The promoters promised *Eyes Wide Shut* vibes and a midnight toast with a flute of economically priced champagne. I'd heard about it from a girl I'd met on assignment at a club called Prey. None of my high school friends want to go, but I successfully convinced a few because no one knew of anything better to do.

My phone rang around 5:00 p.m. It was Brenda and Alice Van Bronx on a conference call from *Nova* HQ. Rumor has it that Britney booked a last-second private jet from Louisiana to Vegas to ring in 2004 alongside her backup dancers and childhood friends. *Can I make it to Burbank in time to catch the last Southwest flight out?* Oliver is already lying in wait, just in case I can.

After my adventures at the Playboy Mansion, I became *Nova*'s Rookie of the Year. They bumped my daily rate to $250 and started throwing me sinecures: red-carpet interviews at movie premieres and charity events, dinners at Mr. Chow in the hopes that I might see Nicole Kidman. She didn't make her reservation, but I still got paid. The duck was exquisite.

For the first time in my life, I had real money, which allowed me to upgrade my wardrobe and save for a place of my own. Working nights allowed me to write or not write my book during the day. Secretly, I reveled in the choose-your-own-adventure possibilities of every assignment. I'd begun to subscribe to the classic bad-faith axiom: *If I don't do it, someone worse will.*

It wasn't like I could turn down an all-expenses-paid trip to Vegas. My friends had just spent an hour begging to let them join. Sorry, comrades, elite cavalry only. *Nova* booked me a suite at the Palms, the hotel-casino of the minute, where Britney is allegedly staying—at least until she gets bored and dips to shoot with David LaChapelle in Miami.

She's everywhere this fall. There's "The Kiss" with Madonna at the MTV Video Music Awards, which triggers gay panic and "awooga" chants across America. To me, it seemed like an obvious PR gimmick in a Skinemax kind of way, but I can't pretend that I wouldn't have ordered the channel. *USA Today* put it on the cover for two straight days. After the *Atlanta Journal-Constitution* put it on the front page, their outraged readership demanded an apology. Madonna kissed Christina Aguilera too, a few seconds after Britney. But do you remember the second person to walk on the moon?

There are no better ingredients for controversy than god, drugs, and sex. The chaste belle became the bad bitch. Britney dissection is a national obsession. She's topless on the cover of *Rolling Stone* and bottomless on the cover of *Esquire*—the latter dresses her up like Marilyn Monroe to clarify which archetype she has inherited. An internet hoax claims that Britney overdosed. Nah, she just puked in a Manhattan club. She's the musical guest on *SNL*, where Lorne Michaels and Jimmy Fallon spend the opening monologue trying to figure out how to get her to make out with the host, Halle Berry. Britney demurs. Her brilliance lies in the blanks unfilled, the projection of something left unsaid but not unmissed. She is a mystery half-solved, a teetering ideal.

Everyone wants a taste of the action—to figure her out, tear her down, or both. On CNN, Tucker Carlson, thirty-four, drools at Britney, twenty-one, asking when she decided to kiss Madonna, whether she'd ever kissed a woman before, and if she would do it again. This is the same interview where Britney says we should trust and support our president in every decision. But she's sweet and polite with a cherry Kool-Aid stripe in her hair, and no one is perfect.

On an ABC prime-time special, Diane Sawyer cross-examines Britney to tears. In a skintight, snow-white dress, Britney makes prayer hands on the cover of *Entertainment Weekly*. Headline: *Nobody's Angel: Wild Partying, Erratic Behavior, Canceled Events. EW Goes on the Rocky Road with Pop's Sexiest Bad Girl*. She cuts her European tour short, flicks off the paparazzi in Mexico City, and kinda gets into Kabbalah.

Every article asks the same question: Are the publicity stunts overshadowing the music? To be fair, the title of her new single, the Madonna duet "Me Against the Music," gestures at the same idea. No matter how good it is, the music can't win. Of course, Britney is still selling records. The full-length, November's *In the Zone*, debuts at #1, shifting over six hundred thousand copies in its first week. Four straight albums at the apex. But the celebration is short-lived. Two weeks later, Alicia Keys knocks her off the top of the charts.

"Me Against the Music" didn't reconfigure popular consciousness like Britney's previous first singles. A month ago, it peaked at #35, her least successful opening ever. Brenda says that Clear Channel radio is punishing her for not doing her last tour with them. But a Madonna collaboration in 2003 feels outdated. She's a legend, but forty-five years old. Most twentysomethings are not trying to hear their Neptunes-lite duet at the club when the place is aflame with actual Neptunes heaters. Who would put this on instead of "Milkshake"?

I'm part of the problem. I LimeWired Britney's record, listened a few times, and went back to *The Black Album*. And, look, I liked it. I appreciated how she'd completely switched from PG-13 prom pop to fucking at the intergalactic rave. This was a natural progression from "I'm a Slave 4 U." And it was smart to sever ties with Max Martin for a sleek fusion of chromatic techno, Middle Eastern ragas, and Atlanta hip-hop. But you could sense the label executives plotting awkward collabs to annex new audiences. No one really needed to know what Britney sounded like "soaking wet" alongside the Ying Yang Twins. R. Kelly wrote and produced "Outrageous," a Bollywood-accented song about her "outrageous . . . sex drive"; it's somehow less subtle than you'd think. There is also a Moby track, because soccer moms need to let loose too.

In an age of excess, *In the Zone* is considered something of a letdown. And yet Britney remains the center of the tabloid solar system. So if she opts for a New Year's in Vegas on a last-second whim, millions will be dying for the dirt. That is, if she's even in Vegas.

On the phone earlier, Brenda and Alice give fifty-fifty odds that Britney will stay home in Kentwood. One tipster says that she's still in the Bahamas. A spy in Times Square swears that Dick Clark is going to bring her out as a surprise guest, upstaging the scheduled headliners, Jessica Simpson, Nick Lachey, and 3 Doors Down.

Or maybe the prophecy will be fulfilled in Nevada? Britney sparkling across the club, a portal of light haloing above her head, a slow jam bumping from the speaker coffins. She swivels her head; a telepathic mind meld tethers us, summoning me to her private table. We fall madly in love over vodka Red Bulls and Marlboro Lights. And if she doesn't show, I'm playing with house money.

Stepping off the plane, I'm greeted by a greedy clack of slot machines and cranked levers, Frank Sinatra terminal Muzak, and the liminal hum of thousands feeding coin-operated voids. Tobacco clouds drift; red sirens flash. The customers' eyes are enameled and relentless.

I catch a cab to the Palms in a sedan driven by a middle-aged Pakistani immigrant. He feels compelled to explain that he's in support of what's happening "over there." I didn't ask, but offer vague assurance that I get it. After we exchange pleasantries and he tells me that he really loves Vegas—"so much opportunity"—we lapse into silence and I stare into the neon Sinai.

The impulse to sin coexists with antiseptic whole-someness. As we drive past the Mirage, I can see minimum-wage workers passing out glossy flyers for escorts, in front of an artificial volcano that families gather to watch erupt.

The Palms is shaped like a credit card. It's forty-two stories tall and located a few miles off the Strip. When it opened two years ago, the world's "ultimate party hotel" got a bunch of free publicity for hosting an MTV reality show. Now, the billionaire owners charge the haute bourgeoisie $10,000 a night to trash the "*Real World* suite." But the right celebrity can have it for free. And you can't buy better promotion than letting Britney Spears bless the spot on New Year's Eve.

At the front desk, the clerk tells me that someone has already checked into my room. Guess who? On the thirty-second floor, Oliver sprawls on my king-sized bed, Air Force 1s dirtying the comforter. A Manchester United game plays at max volume while he yells on a speakerphone. With his free hand, he fires off a text on a different device.

"Mate, you were supposed to be here two hours ago!" Oliver bellows. "You're gonna hafta catch up."

"I'm shocked you're not already down five grand at roulette."

"I'm up seven. But that ain't what I'm talking about."

He pulls open the nightstand drawer. Atop a Gideon Bible: sixteen cylinders of MDMA, a Ziploc bag of coke, a half ounce of chronic, and a drugstore swindle of Percs, Adderall, Xans, and a few Valium for the sake of traditionalism. Enough high-caliber narcotics to get six months in a Clark County jail—or several years of probation, depending on your attorney's connections.

"Isn't this all a little on the nose?"

"More for me, then."

"Is she even here?"

"Do you think my wife would let me go to Vegas on New Year's if she wasn't?"

"You're married?"

"Green card."

"Did Brenda and Alice tell you what we're supposed to be doing?"

"Brit is on one. She spent Christmas back home in Louisiana. Got smashed, broke her curfew to fuck some hick. Her mum found out about it and starts screaming, 'Not under my roof,' all 'at. Brit shouting, 'You can't control me, I paid for your house.' Papa Spears was pissed, too.

"Then Brit, her mum, sister, and aunts went to a Caribbean resort for holiday, but she was acting batty. The second the plane touched back down in the States, she had a private jet waiting to take her to Vegas. Who's gonna say no? She's registered under the name Alotta Warmheart, with her dancers and a few of her mates, and you're gonna need what's in that cubby."

"How did you find this all out?"

"C'mon, dawg. They've been getting massages, facials, and mani-pedis in the spa all afternoon. I'm basically paying the desk girl's tuition."

"Where are they going?"

"They got the twenty-eighth and fifty-second floors all to themselves, but they're hitting Rain. You ever been?"

◆

I've agreed to meet Oliver in the lobby at 10:30 p.m. It's pathologically early for Vegas, but admission to Rain is far from guaranteed. Of course, he's not here.

The line spills all the way to Las Vegas Boulevard. Girls with Chinese-character tattoos wear Saran-tight party dresses with tiaras, sparkling glitter, NYE 2004 glasses, and glow sticks. I overhear two people say that next year "has to be better." I'm thinking about the last six months: graduating college, the anxiety and under-employment, the demoralizing sensation of starting from zero. Now here I am, at the hottest club in an unfa-miliar city, getting paid to spend New Year's alongside Britney Spears. The sixteen-year-old version of me would expect a little more, but he'd appreciate the continuity.

Florid tourists sip melted margaritas from fluorescent bulbs. ASU sorority sisters stagger through the casino maze trailed by bros guzzling tallboys in backward hats. High rollers and low-rent locals leer on the midway. A burgundy Mustang hangs in the air for a giveaway. *Wheel of Fortune* and KISS games fizzle. The lights are bright and callous; the piped air is cold and abundant.

When Oliver finally arrives, he looks like he's about to drive an Ed Hardy art car. The guy is wearing a peri-winkle silk smoking jacket and a turquoise necktie worn over a rhinestoned Black Sabbath tee. Boot-cut jeans, a white belt, and earth-toned dress shoes. He waves me to follow him into the marble-and-steel bathroom.

We head into adjoining stalls. Within seconds, he slides a freezer bag of coke and molly underneath.

"I'm not your mule," I snap.

"Hide it and act normal."

"It's yours; you carry it."

"I have to smuggle a bloody camera in my pants."

"Give me the camera, then."

"Are you out of your fucking mind? I look like I'm running a transcontinental opium ring. You look like you're about to pledge Alpha Epsilon Abbot Kinney."

I'm dressed in a crisp striped blue dress shirt, slightly baggy jeans, and apple-and-gold Onitsuka Tiger sneakers. This is the season.

"What if I get caught?"

"This is all necessary to do the job proper."

This is tricky. The ideal hiding spot is nestled inside a pair of briefs, but I've worn boxers. The next-best option is underneath the tongue of your sneaker, where security almost never looks. But there's too much product. The baggie doesn't fit into my wallet, and there's no tape to attach it to my ribs.

Time is precious. It's almost eleven.

"You've got cash, right?" I ask Oliver as we step outside the stall.

His jeans are so billowing that he can conceal his camera in the folds, which gives me another idea. I ask Oliver for $200. He peels a wad of cash.

In the bathroom mirror, men primp oily snails of hair. You can smell the bitter aroma of CK One and Paul Mitchell mousse. I approach a Persian dude in a crooked orange camo Von Dutch hat.

"I'll give you a hundred fifty for the hat."

"Bruh, this is authentic," he snorts.

"Two hundred."

Rubbing his goatee, he hands it over.

In the stall, I empty my pockets, stuff the contraband

in the compartment above my forehead, and slip it on. I look like I just raided Nicole Richie's walk-in closet.

"You know that hat is fucking mesh?" Oliver snipes as we walk outside of the bathroom.

"You can't see shit," I counter. "Or do you want to drive around North Las Vegas on New Year's Eve to see if there's an open Walgreens with masking tape?"

Bypassing the wait, we approach a steroids-and-suits trio of bouncers in all black. Oliver daps a guard with *my man* familiarity. You can see security's gears churning to see if this is someone he should know. We're trying to enter through the regular VIP. The celebrity VIP is accessible through secret elevators or a concealed zip line connected to the *Real World* suite.

"You got a reservation?"

"We're here with Brit," Oliver says, like his secretary should have called ahead. He slides a few hundred into the guard's palm. "We're on her team at CAA."

The Goliath asks our names. Another sentry scans a clipboard to cross-check, but before he can inform us that no, we aren't on the list, a scuffle breaks out between two groups of Brads behind us.

Limbs flail. Someone calls someone a "bitch-ass motherfucking cocksucker!" One of the Brads gets shoved into me. I stagger back a few feet. Totally fine, but the collision has upset the delicate balancing act on my head.

"Bloody amateur night," Oliver cracks. The bouncers don't smile but instead give us the predictable spiel: y'all are not on the list; call the person who put you on to come out and vouch; you can linger for a few minutes, but if they don't answer, be gone.

Oliver spins a disorienting Kabuki of lies rooted in cred-enhancing specifics: the names of Britney's manager, her brother, and the president of CAA, who would be "gobsmacked to know of the pervasive incompetence at the Palms." The Maloofs will surely have their heads on a pike tomorrow morning if we aren't admitted.

Victory is ours. But first, the perfunctory search. We pay the entrance fee and take several steps toward the velvet drapes. Just as paradise awaits, a paw clasps the back of my shoulder.

"Hey, buddy, mind taking your hat off," a guard commands.

"Nah, I'm good."

He lurches toward me, and I step past him, speed-walking toward the entrance. But his goon squad seals off the route. Oliver is trapped too. As the Beatnuts said, there's no escaping this.

"This is all your fault," I whisper to Oliver.

"You wore a mesh fucking hat!" He shakes his head.

Security steers me through an unmarked door into a makeshift interrogation room with a Gateway computer and a *Stuff* 2003 calendar that hasn't been flipped in months. Stacy Keibler is Miss September. It appears to be an auxiliary penalty box for the Rain mafia to have fun with paying suckers who ran out of luck.

The man before us looks like a hit man for a chain of mob-run Providence pizzerias: silver eyes, a disappearing chin, and a shaved head.

"You gonna take that hat off, or am I gonna have to do it for you?"

I don't say a word. Might as well make it uncomfortable for him. Maybe you're wondering what was going through my head at the prospect of a bread-and-water New Year's celebration in the Las Vegas slammer. But it was totally empty: a wall of white clouds obscuring the edge of an embankment.

The security officer stands up and does a theatrical crack of the knuckles.

"Let's resolve this like adults." Oliver breaks the silence. "You know bloody well that you risk a civil suit for laying a single finger on my colleague. This is technically false imprisonment. Do you know how expensive the damages for a campaign of harassment and emotional terror can be? Do you know how good our lawyers are?"

"You can't bring drugs into our establishment, sir. It's against federal law."

"Who said anything about drugs? You don't know what kind of medical condition or prescriptions my friend has. What you mistake for drugs can be tested at any local laboratory and you'll look like a fool! The next morning, my direct boss, the president of CAA, will call George Maloof and scream at him for what he did to his best employees. Britney will be furious at you for fucking with her team. And you're fired. For what? Not letting us in?"

"Just get the fuck out of my sight." He shakes his head and nods at the door.

"It's not that easy, mate," Oliver says. "The biggest pop star in the world is expecting us tonight, and it's already

11:37 p.m. We need to get in there immediately or else. Fuck, mate, you know how Brit can get."

The guard nods his head gravely. Oliver takes out his wallet and starts counting out hundreds, one by one.

"No one should be forced to toil on a holiday." Oliver slips a thousand into his hand. "Here's a late Christmas gift. We'll even buy a ten-grand table, so long as you sit us in a posh spot next to our girl."

It's hard to forget a flamethrower. Arson machines spurt fire to the beat of Nelly's "Pimp Juice" as we strut through a gold-mirrored tunnel into Rain. The fog is so thick that I can barely see past the bill of my trucker hat. We emerge into a twenty-five-thousand-square-foot maze of gyrating bodies, dancing water fountains, and pagan hedonism. A Viking rave sponsored by Armani Exchange.

Bottle service girls guide us into a bronze elevator. On the third-floor VIP mezzanine, tables are covered with ice buckets, top-shelf liquor, and mixers. Ours overlooks the elevated stage and dance floor. On platforms suspended in midair, go-go dancers in leather corsets wrap themselves around stripper poles. On an IMAX screen, RAIN is projected, with a palm tree dotting the "i."

In her private skybox, Britney Spears sits right next to us. For the last five years, I've dreamed of a reunion. But this isn't how I planned it. I figured we'd meet as peers operating in parallel spheres of creativity. Something like Arthur Miller and Marilyn Monroe. She'd be a huge fan of one of my books. We'd be introduced at the club and settle down into domestic serenity. Two kids named Kaleb and Brayden, a mortgage, a white picket fence, and a phalanx of twenty-four-hour security guards to clothesline anyone who tries to hop the white picket fence.

I didn't expect such tangled emotions. My adolescent crush has been tainted by celebrity obsession. There she is, dressed down in a baby-doll tee and hip-hugging jeans, but a force field exists between us, between her and everyone. Barely old enough to drink, but worth eight figures, the most glimmering possibility that a glitching system can still produce. It's not midnight yet, but the future is starting to collect shadows, and this eclipse falls over me while I silently deliberate what it all could mean for my own prospects. If I nail this story, there will be bonuses, enhanced cachet, the rise of my own crossed star. A start.

Above the DJ booth, a "Countdown Until Midnight" clock comes on. I stumble to the railing, looking into Britney's suite. She's orbited by lithe backup dancers, a few blondes who look like cousins, a security guard, and a dead-eyed Bluto wrapping a creatine-enriched bicep around her.

Oliver jabs me.

"Take off that hat."

Security is sparse in the VIP. You pay for what you can get away with. No one blinks when out the Von Dutch comes enough powder to have the club sleepless until the Rose Bowl kickoff. Oliver does key bumps in plain sight. I pop an MDMA capsule of "the purest shit," allegedly bought off a London rave legend. A few girls in

Britney's booth notice us, but Britney is mesmerized by this beefhead with a Caesar cut.

At the stroke of midnight, 2004 is catcalled in by fourteen-foot jets of fire and a cascade of artificial rain. A disco ball shatters. The crowd whoops. The speakers growl; the whistle shrieks. The clubgoers yell in response . . . "aww skeet skeet skeet skeet skeet!"

Lil Jon bounces out to scream all the ad-libs for "Get Low." Too Short emerges to perform "Shake That Monkey." Oliver and I pound tequila sunrises and absorb the syncopated chaos. Britney furiously kisses the frat boy with the popped collar. Of all the Patrón joints in all the neon towns of the world, I had to walk into hers.

Britney might not even be the most famous name in the building. In another water box, Kobe Bryant and his wife, Vanessa, survey the realm. In the next, Sacramento Kings superstar Chris Webber rehabilitates a microfracture of the knee with liquid cures. For the first hour, I bob my head as Britney bounces, being adored by both the boy toy and a Salma Hayek doppelgänger.

Refills are summoned with a swirl of the arm. Part-time models stare because we have a table at Rain on NYE. No matter how humble you think you are, it's easy to slip into a pretense of superiority. Live long enough like a king and you start to lie to yourself that you are one.

Britney and her crew file out of their box. When I stand to follow, the molly wallops me. A series of flashes and levitations. Arteries flooded by Jacuzzi jets. Day-Glo color lighting up edges of my mind. I'm sweating diamonds. *Oh my god, are they playing "Stand Up"?*

The dance floor is a strobe-lit acre. Ludacris and Shawnna duet, "when I move you move," and thousands freak in sleazy harmony. Never before or since has the phrase "feels like a midget is hanging from my necklace" carried such purpose.

"We're about to have a legendary moment at Club Rain!! ARE . . . YOU . . . READY?!!!" The DJ suddenly shouts. "MISS BRITNEY SPEARS IS IN THE BUILD-ING! And this is her NEW SINGLE!!!"

Britney's troop parts the crowd. The DJ flips a switch. A river circling the dance floor turns green, yellow, and red. Flames shoot and smoke leaks from the walls. When the mist clears, four dancers encircle Britney. "Toxic" bangs from the loudspeakers, a comet of erotic Alpha Centauri funk. This is the second single, slated to drop next week, but already destined to ring off in every club until the last days of revelation.

The strings bleed like they were stabbed by a synthe-sized pickax. Britney's eyes are flammable. Whipping her blonde mane, she rubs her hands across her flat bare stomach, almost inducing mass fainting. Her hips swivel and vibrate. She caresses her face, laminated eyes rolling back in ecstasy. From the VIP rafters, Kobe and Vanessa gawk. In tune with a song about fatal lust, the dancers weave like furies, bobbing within centimeters of her body, the cold fog becoming a steam bath. "With a taste of a poison paradise . . . I'm addicted to you."

Britney controls everything, writhing with no worlds left to conquer. For the first time in her adult life, she's free. Her family is back in Louisiana. The tyrannical managers and agents and publicists and lawyers and accountants and label executives and spying minders are thousands of miles away. The minute-by-minute itineraries, the persistent demands of press, and the teen idol façade feel distant. No one is here to tell her what to do, and all she wants to do is be twenty-two. She's flagrantly wealthy, having already fulfilled impossible dreams—a life's work finished early.

I sip tequila dregs, mostly ice. Tropical waves overrun my veins. I blink hard, crystal sweat trickling. Fans mob Britney, asking her to autograph receipts and bar napkins. She seems overwhelmed, but honors the requests until her bodyguard, Big Rob, swoops in.

Amidst the commotion, Oliver whispers to a girl in her entourage. They peel off toward the unisex bathrooms. Taking Britney's departure as an affront, the DJ spins Justin Timberlake's "Rock Your Body."

In the refuge of the VIP, I chain-smoke Parliaments and empty the Patrón bottle. The molly throttles me for a few more swells, but the rush eventually dwindles. *Where exactly am I?* Three a.m. in Las Vegas, sputtering . . . the go-go dancers swinging from their stripper poles, body paint chipped, makeup smeared, ripped confetti and spilled champagne on the ground. The shock-and-awe explosions still roar at timed intervals to defibrillate anyone slipping away. 2004 is dawning with inflamed and distracted eyes.

Oliver remains at large. Only the early morning scavengers remain among the crowd. I look through the smeared Plexiglas. Britney's after-party stumbles out, mostly smiles and full cups. Swiveling my head toward the VIP exit, I see her, scarcely able to walk. Knees buckling. The bodyguard and the lummox catch her and clandestinely escort her out before anyone can ask for another autograph.

✦

An Incomplete List of Tattoos at the Palms Pool
and Dayclub at 1:37 p.m., January 1, 2004

Man, thirties, upper back, cursive script: YOUR ONLY AS STRONG AS THE DRINKS YOU MIX, THE TABLE YOU DANCE ON AND THE FRIENDS YOU PARTY WITH!

Woman, twenties, right shin: A martini glass with several olives

Man, twenties, right shoulder: Gollum from *Lord of the Rings* clutching a bottle of Jim Beam (full color)

Woman, twenties, small of her back: HIT IT

Man, late teens, right upper thigh: An outline of the Twin Towers with the American flag behind it

Man, thirties, left pec: Spider-Man's head with webs and lightning bolts and a comic strip bubble reading WTF

Woman, twenty-four or twenty-five, neck: TRICK DADDY

Woman, forties, right shoulder: Two oversized
green eyes, tribal design eyebrows, and in Old
English script: NEVER LIE.

Sixty degrees is not warm enough to bask half-naked by
the pool, but Vegas tests the limits of your imagination.
Oliver lounges shirtless in rose swim trunks and black
sunglasses. I haven't brought anything cabana appropriate, but even if I had, I wasn't about to freeze while a local
radio personality played Chingy. My hangover feels like
an off-Strip prop comic took a sledgehammer to my skull.

"My bad, dawg. I meant to text you goodbye last
night, but shit got critical." Oliver takes a swig of a blue
Hawaii.

"Did you go home with that girl?" I take a tentative
sip of scalding coffee.

"That ain't just any girl. That's Kelsey Fish!"

"Is she, like, a Nickelodeon actress or something?"

"Mate! That's Britney's BFF! They went to preschool
together, and now they're getting crunk and crazy in the
Real World suite."

"What happened?"

"Y'know, got freaky on the dance floor, did a little
blow, snogged. She promised she'd come party with us by
the pool today."

"Aren't you worried you'll lose her to *that* dude?"

I point to a guy in his thirties with a pair of red lips

tattooed on his deltoids, alongside the phrase SPREAD LOVE.

He ignores me. "Someone is always getting assed out on a trip like this. Brit can't keep her hands off the lumberjack. Kelsey's feeling left out and needs attention." He outstretches his arms, revealing the full extent of pasty British pallor and audacious confidence. "Besides, you can't beat free drugs, this accent, and this body,"

After three drinks and an unreturned text, we're certain that she's flaking, until suddenly, *c u in 5!* In 10, Kelsey is hovering above us in a newsboy cap, get low jeans, and a crop top. She looks like she was made in a Britney cloning device that had the plug pulled at 90 percent completion.

"I can't stay long; we're going to the Caesars mall in a few." That's where nine-foot-tall animatronic statues replicate the fall of Atlantis under an artificial sky. She slides on food court sunglasses and collapses into the deck chair.

"I'm *beat*."

"Things get too real in the *Real World* suite?" Oliver says, lighting a Benson & Hedges.

"You don't even wanna know." He lights her cigarette. "Britney was a hot mess."

"Was she?"

She takes a drag and stares blankly.

"Do you have any more," she continues, "ah, uh . . ."

Oliver nods knowingly, taking out a crystal, placing it on a key. She perks up.

"Who was that guy all over her?" I ask, a little jealous.

"Who's he?" Kelsey directly asks Oliver.

"My best mate . . . the one I was telling you about last night." He turns to me. "This is Kelsey."

"Kelse," she corrects him. "Oh, right! I remember Oliver telling me about you. You seem so young to be a director!"

Behind her, Oliver raises his eyebrows and flashes the *play along* face.

"Yeah, like, just music videos, and the occasional commercial. But ICM says there's a feature in my future."

"So cool . . . You should do something with Britney." I nod. She returns to the thread.

"That guy is Jason, by the way. He's this football boy who grew up with us. Do they have *Friends* in England? He's like our Joey. A chill dude, but, like, I don't get it."

"What ended up happening?" Oliver cuts back.

"I probably shouldn't talk about it." She motions toward the vial that Oliver has left out.

"Who am I going to tell?" He hands it to her.

"Okay, but, like, you have to swear that you can't tell anyone about this because it's pretty crazy and I can get in *trouble*," she says, fiddling with the gold crucifix around her neck. "Ugh, I need a mimosa."

Oliver waves over our waitress.

"So we get back to the room last night and Britney can barely stand," she goes on. "Big Rob and Jason had to basically carry her out of the club."

"Was she drunk?" Oliver asks.

"I mean, that and the E that we all ate last night."

"I could've got you the good shit . . . should've asked me."

"This *was* the good shit. That's why she was so fucked up. We tried to have some champagne in the room, but she kept passing out. Whenever she'd open her eyes, she'd be mumbling about how she wanted to go home."

"Oh, that's not too crazy," Oliver goaded.

"You don't even know. So, like, Jason took her to bed, and we kept drinking in the living room, and then like fifteen minutes later, he busts out, screaming, 'I THINK BRITNEY'S DEAD . . . I THINK BRITNEY'S DEAD.'"

"Fucking mental."

"Right." She motions to him for another bump. "We're like, 'What the fuck did you do to her?!!' He swears, 'Nothing.' He says that she's sweating and breathing slow, so he threw her in the shower and now she's not moving. We all run in there and she's lying on the tile, white as a ghost."

"Is she okay now?" I ask.

"Well, like, we were panicking because, right, like, you can't call 911 and be like, 'Britney is OD'ing on X.' And we can't call her parents because they'll go crazy. So we start splashing cold water on her, freaking out. Jason kept trying to pick her up, but she couldn't stand, and then she slipped and hit her head on the shower, so we were about to call them anyway because we couldn't just let her fucking die!"

"Did you get her help?" Oliver inquires, with unexpected concern.

"Well, that's the fucking crazy thing. Jason keeps slapping and shaking her and eventually, after like a couple of minutes, she opens her eyes and starts laughing, as though she was totally fine . . . like no big deal."

"So are y'all going home, then?"

Kelsey shakes her head. "Nah, I mean, we have the suite until the fourth, and I don't have to go back to LSU until the fifteenth, so fuck it, right?"

No one anticipates what happens next. Later that night, we try to meet up with Kelsey and Britney, but Oliver's texts go ignored. We pop into Ghostbar, on the roof, but apparently just miss them. Afterward, we play blackjack and drink mai tais until four.

The next day, we pinball around the casino. Oliver bribes all the valets, limo drivers, and bellhops to alert us if Britney leaves. But they have two floors to themselves; they're untouchable to outsiders. Fine by me. I need a hyperbaric chamber to recover what's left of my synapses.

But around 7:00 a.m., Saturday, January 3, my phone blows up. Oliver shakes me out of my stupor.

"She up and did it!"

"Who did what?"

"Britney! She married the fucking hick at four in the morning!"

My childhood dream is in ashes. Light a votive for baby Brayden, who never was. Britney is lawfully wedded to a backup college football player. Horoscopes often lie.

It's tabloid 9/11. They'll have to interrupt the nightly news for a very special *Access Hollywood*. We have to move fast. Within hours, every gossipmonger from here to London will have staff and stringers on the ground, scrounging every last morsel of information to sate the world's curiosity.

Within a half hour, Oliver and I are mainlining coffee in a seedy North Las Vegas IHOP. It's an Edward Hopper painting in a decaying desert strip mall. Tweakers stare, still wired from the last hit. Pimps and call girls eat Rooty Tooty Fresh 'N Fruity breakfasts after a long night. Young working-class fathers yell at unruly toddlers for trying to drink the maple syrup.

We're waiting for the man who claims to have the dirt on Britney's marriage. *Nova* tells us not to worry about the price. A six-two, 230-pound hurricane in a Hawaiian shirt and cargo shorts blows through the door. He looks like a naval cook on Caribbean shore leave, and tells us to call him "Gutierrez."

Here is our informant: a Palms night-shift bellhop used to dealing with the reckless mania of Vegas, where there is always one more destination. And if you stick around long enough, you will eventually find yourself at the Little White Wedding Chapel—the tabernacle that sanctioned the unions of Frank Sinatra and Mia Farrow, Bruce Willis and Demi Moore, Michael and Juanita Jordan, and Britney Jean Spears and Jason Nose Tackle.

"You said it was gonna be just you," Gutierrez says.

He slides into a vinyl booth and lights a Newport from an almost-empty pack.

"This is the reporter for the magazine," Oliver says. "This is how it goes."

"I need twenty."

"We have ten in cash in right now," Oliver says, gripping a Gucci duffel bag.

"I'm sure you can get another ten as soon as the bank opens."

The waitress interrupts.

"You can't smoke in here, sir. This is a family restaurant."

She nods her head at a family with two toddlers sitting two tables away.

"Is this because I'm Puerto Rican?"

She blinks hard and shakes her head with exasperation. He silently extinguishes the cigarette in a caddy of Splenda. She hands us three waters and walks off.

"This fucking town, man." Gutierrez rolls his eyes. "The crackers hate me because they think I'm Black. The Blacks think I'm Mexican. And the Mexicans don't fuck with me because I'm a Puerto Rican papí. Britney was cool, though."

Without the cigarette, his nervous energy has no outlet. He starts building a fortress of creamers.

"We need to know everything."

"Let me see the lechuga."

Underneath the table, Oliver unzips it, revealing a top layer of hundreds. Gutierrez nods nonchalantly.

"Just remember, you can't use my name."

"Even if we wanted to, I'd bet we don't know the real one."

Gutierrez raises his eyebrows, points his finger at Oliver, and mouths, *BINGO*.

"What do you wanna know?" He looks at me as if I'm going to be the one asking questions, which I suppose is in my job description.

"Tell me how the night began."

"So, like, the front desk people are my homies, and around 2:30 in the morning, one walks over and is like, 'Foo, you aren't gonna believe this, but Britney is staying in the *Real World* suite, and the Ghostbar bouncers called being like, 'Can we get her a limo?' But it's too late and all the drivers went home, so I'm like fuck it, I can drive. Wait, you're paying for breakfast, right?"

I nod. He flags down the waitress and orders a Denver omelet, blueberry pancakes, and a chocolate milkshake.

"Are you a limo driver?" I ask.

"Technically, no, but it don't matter. I tell Britney and her man to come down in ten, and when they finally do, bam, I'm waiting outside in the lime-green stretch. Some real pimp-type player shit, you know?

"I ask where they want to go. Another casino, the strip club, Mickey D's? But they're like, 'Fuck it! Take us to get married—we're trying to do something wild. It's Vegas!' I was about to tell them that this shit is not going to stay in Vegas, but you don't argue with Britney."

It's difficult to gauge how much I should trust. The details check out, but there's more than enough money in that bag to encourage Gutierrez's creativity.

"Did she seem normal? Was she drunk?"

"Was she, you know?" Oliver puts his finger to his nostril and sniffs.

"I dunno, but she was, uh, definitely, you know, like,

interested in getting some from me," he says, with considerably less conviction than everything prior. "But I was like 'Nah, you can't be doing that with your career.'"

"You either don't know or she definitely wanted to buy from you. Which is it?" I counter.

"My bad, my bad. She didn't ask that."

"Tell the truth, mate," Oliver insists. "Or you won't get paid."

"Okay, well, she *was* a little faded, but she wasn't WASTED, you know. Just a nice, sweet little girl in ripped jeans and one of those tiny black shirts where you can see her belly. And a hat that, uh, I think said, HUG A TREE? She didn't look like MTV Britney, but she's Britney, she's always gonna be banging!"

He reaches to give Oliver a high five, but gets left hanging.

"What about the dude?" I ask.

"Total fucking chode, bro. She deserves better."

"Get on with it." Oliver takes over. "Where did you take her?"

"We hit up two different spots, but both were closed. So I take them to that wedding chapel with the drivethrough tunnel, on the Strip, next to the tattoo parlor and that hooker motel. But they're like, 'Y'all need a marriage license.' So I have to fucking take them to the county bureau."

"What time is it at this point?"

"Three thirty. Graveyard shift. Only three people are in the place, and no one recognizes her. But then the clerk is like, 'Oh snap, you're Britney!' And they want a photo and she gets nervous and we all laugh and they rush it for us. Then it was time to get it cracking."

Gutierrez describes the chapel's "Michael Jordan" room, where he took Britney and Jason at 5:00 a.m. A small temple of neon lights, white benches, velvet cushions, roses, and votive candles. A ceiling covered in naked cherubs and Cupids shooting arrows. The ceremony cost $200, including the video.

"Isn't someone supposed to give her away?" I ask. He takes a huge slurp of his chocolate milkshake.

"That's the fucking funny thing. See, I made a joke like, 'Too bad no one's here to give you away.' And Britney looks at me with those Bambi eyes and goes, 'Yeah, yeah, yeah.' Then she looks at me all serious and goes, 'Can you do it?' Can you believe that, bro?"

He gives me an overly friendly punch in the arm. "How many times are you going to be the father of the bride to Britney Spears?!"

"Anyone else see the ceremony?" I ask.

"Nah. Nah. Wait, actually this one couple. They were bugging that they watched Britney get married. They all got a photo together."

Oliver looks like he's in one of those cartoons where an animated cash register cha-chings above the character's head.

"What was the ceremony like?

"The minister read a script. All that bullshit. The recipe for a happy marriage is two hearts full of love, two heaping cups of kindness. She cried and put her head on his chest, and he had his arm around her real tight."

I'd never conducted an interview that resembled what "real" journalists did. There had been a few red-carpet interactions where I asked celebrities some prefabricated questions. But this required alertness and intuition. How reliable was my source? What follow-up question would unlock the right anecdote to add necessary color—to get that one detail that no one else would have?

I won't lie. Shaking down Gutierrez felt as natural as shooting hoops in the park. That's not to say that rooting through the dirt felt *great*. My stomach turned at doing it to Britney. But wasn't I just attempting to get as close to the truth as anyone reasonably could? Was it worse than when respected reporters ghoulishly pried for details from freshly traumatized families after a murder? For the first time in my adult life, it felt like I was actually *good* at something. So I kept going.

"Did you get any sense of why she married him?" I ask.

"Look, they're kids, fucked up in Vegas. Maybe she's just rebelling. Being like, 'I can do whatever I want, when I want.' What is she, nineteen now?"

I tell him she's twenty-two. He shovels some omelet into his mouth and lights another Newport. Ketchup stains turn the filter red. The waitress doesn't even bother anymore.

"Do you think they were in love?"

He waves his hand dismissively.

"Dawg, this is Vegas."

"What did you take away from this experience?

"I mean"—he thinks hard for a few seconds—"I've been to worse weddings, bro."

His name was Jason Alexander. You couldn't forget it because he shared it with the actor who played George Costanza. Until this morning, nobody had heard of Britney's new beau, but by lunchtime, the LA and New York bureaus had assembled a vigorous intelligence dossier.

Jason Alexander was a good ol' boy from Kentwood, where football and Jesus were the only faiths, until the town produced a new Virgin Mary. He'd collected splinters as a linebacker at a Mississippi community college, got cut from the LSU team, and was still quixotically chasing NFL dreams. He was the guy Britney would've wound up with if she hadn't become famous. Her dad in slightly different form. A keg-standing, table-dancing redneck who still lived at home and worked part-time at Spud's Auto Repair.

Hollywood assholes had played Britney. The pop heartthrob cynically exploited their romance for record sales. The married dancer turned out to be a married dancer. And you couldn't expect much from a guy whose biggest hit was about doing "it all for the nookie." Jared Leto, Colin Farrell, and John Cusack (rumored, unconfirmed)? Losing out to them, I could handle. But Jason Alexander? This one actually hurt a little.

By the late afternoon, the AP wire broke the story. A

few hours later, CNN broadcast it on the nightly news. In the morning, the BBC and all the dailies ran with the drama. But no one knew much more than that Britney got married in Vegas to a longtime friend from her hometown. *Nova* has the exclusive details.

Oliver and I call Brenda and Alice from outside of the IHOP. The former is exuberant. "You're the Woodward and Bernstein of Britania," she raves. Alice is more subdued, asking how likely it is that we'll get the wedding photo that Gutierrez mentioned. She's heard that *Us* and *People* already have reporters on the next plane out. In the meantime, *Nova* will throw up a quick website teaser to spread the word that we'll have the full scoop in the next issue.

"You'll help us break our circulation record!" Brenda says.

"Just get to that chapel, quick!" Alice instructs. "The newsroom will bleed our contacts too."

At the Little White, I corral banal quotes from the minister and the owner. They insist that Britney was in sound mind and body, sober and having The Time of Her Life. They won't sell us the tape of the ceremony, even when we offer them a hundred grand. While I handle the interview, Oliver sneaks a glance at the registry book and bribes a clerk for the number of the other couple who got hitched.

From here, we ride through the lonely Saturday-morning streets to the Flamingo Hilton, where Mr. and Mrs. [Redacted] are enjoying their honeymoon. They receive $50,000 for the exclusive rights to the photo, which they will be promptly cropped out of.

After sixty hard hours in Vegas, the skin turns to leather, the intestines revolt, the teeth break down into dust. No concealer can mask the spiritual rot. The obligations of conventional life lose all sense of gravity. You are here, and there is nowhere else. The only real response is to push through the pain and light another cigarette, or retreat home as hastily as possible.

Even the wedding photo itself is Vegas cliché, discolored and grainy. Britney's eyes are sunken, dead-leaf brown, deserted. Pupils dilated. The white garter is worn over her ripped jeans. She smiles, but the wattage is faint.

The groom looks like a Hollister model born into the Addams Family. His meat-cleaver hand caresses her hip as he practically thrusts into her. Underneath dark beetle brows, his eyes are crude and possessive. For any other twenty-two-year-old on the planet, this momentary lapse of reason would be laughed off as the goofy prank that it was. The photo should've been stuck in a drawer as a keepsake of youthful indulgence, the marriage quietly annulled. But there is no such luxury when you're standing atop the twenty-first century.

The winter darkness of the desert descends quickly. A stinging Vegas cold after three days of chaos. Following their first and only breakfast as a married couple, Britney called her parents to break the news. Within the hour, the entire family chartered a private flight from New Orleans. Her manager altered his weekend plans too. Marriage without a prenup potentially entitles Alexander to half of Britney's fortune, and he has nothing to lose. The owner of the Palms hires the most powerful attorney in Vegas for the Spears family. In a city overrun with magicians, they retain the master of making shit disappear.

After chasing false leads all afternoon, we receive reliable information that her family and team are gathering for dinner at the Palms' N9NE Steakhouse. When we try to make a reservation, no one answers the phone. When we show up downstairs, the doors are locked. So we linger outside, smoking cigarettes, sipping screwdrivers, attempting to appear anonymous.

After an hour, Kelsey wanders out of the doors, wearing a black sleeveless dress with a slit up one leg. Oliver interrupts her search for a bathroom.

"Hey!!! What are y'all still doing here?"

"They comped us another night. High-roller shit," he replies breezily. "What have you been up to?"

"Oh, you haven't heard?" she says. "Thank god it's not in the news yet."

"What's not in the news?"

"You'll find out soon." Kelsey laughs. "Britney married Jason last night. And when she told her parents, they FREAKED THE FUCK OUT."

"What were they saying?"

"The usual stuff. 'I'm going to have you committed! You ain't gonna destroy yourself and this family.' Her brother was the maddest. He was gonna murder Jason."

"They're all here now?" Oliver asks.

"Oh yeah, her mom and dad, her bro, her manager,

the owner of the Palms, the lawyers, all these other big guys in black suits. And, like, Lance from *NSYNC. They're forcing them to get the marriage annulled."

"What?!"

"They don't have much choice. They sat Britney down and told her that she could lose everything. They'll take care of it, but they need to sign the annulment papers immediately or things'll get dark."

"How's Brit taking it?" Oliver asks.

"She's been crying a lot, and as soon as her mom and dad and the guys in suits came in, she just seemed really out of it," Kelsey says, a little shaken. "I've never seen her like this."

Three security guards escort Jason Alexander out of N9NE. He's not being forced to leave, but it doesn't look like it's entirely his choice either.

Kelsey waves, but he doesn't notice. One of his minders peels from the pack and approaches her.

"Do you need help with anything?"

"No, I'm good. I was just looking for the bathroom."

The guard offers to show her the way, but she declines. Saying goodbye, she wanders back into the labyrinth. He turns to us.

"Y'all can't be just hanging around here."

"It's all good, mate," Oliver says jovially. "We're just waiting for the restaurant to open for dinner."

"This is a private event." He scowls. "You need to leave."

By the next morning, reporters from across the globe flock to Kentwood, attempting to interview Alexander, his family, and any regular at Extra Innings—the sports bar where he'd recently been arrested for punching a patron who bought his ex a drink. Britney's record label, Jive, issues a statement that the marriage was a "joke that went too far."

In the coming weeks, Alexander repeatedly sells his story: how Britney proposed to him; the details of her near-death overdose, her sexual prowess, and the threesome he claims to have had with her and one of her dancers; the coke and ecstasy they used to stay up, and the Vicodin and Xanax to come down.

To anyone who will listen, Alexander insists that neither of them wanted the annulment. "I was tricked by her mom, dad and lawyers . . . I was told our marriage could hurt Britney's career. The men in black swooped in!" He claims that her team strung him along for thirty days until the agreement was finalized. Then they changed her number.

The marriage officially lasts fifty-five hours, from the *I do* to the paperwork that invalidates it. It's filed first thing Monday morning, January 5, 2004—on the grounds that Britney "lacked understanding of her actions to the extent that she was incapable of agreeing to the marriage."

5
Rhythm
Is a Backup Dancer?

THE _CURE_ for a Blue Monday? LA's Hottest Club!

Oops,
She Did It Again!!!!

The studio apartment was on the second floor of a ninety-year-old Spanish-pink building on Hollywood Boulevard. When I signed the lease, the office manager told me that one of the founders of Paramount built it because no one would rent to actors at the time. He claimed the basement had been Rudolph Valentino's speakeasy. But as anarchy overtook Hollywood, the complex crumbled into disrepair. For most of my life, squatters and crust punks claimed it, until an arsonist torched the place a few years before I moved in.

"The Hollywood Renaissance" was what they branded the new version. From La Brea to Western, ambitious city council members and avaricious developers talked about "revitalizing" the blighted area. A public-private partnership opened a $600 million outdoor mall with a theater to host the Oscars. Luxury condos were getting fast-tracked through the planning department to make it a lifestyle destination for "hipsters." The bustling sex and drug trade remained, but moved a few blocks east of a modern Japanese lounge owned by Ashton Kutcher and Wilmer Valderrama, which *Los Angeles Confidential* declared the "hottest new hangout of 2004."

I never took myself for the type to rent an apartment in Hollywood, but I was always there for work, so maybe it was inevitable. The options were either drive drunk, spend a fortune on taxis, or find a place in close proximity to the arrhythmia of LA nightlife. It was out of my price range, but I had to play the part. Besides, *Nova* gave me a $3,000 bonus for helping to break the wedding story. First and last months' rent.

Brenda was right. With the most extensively reported article and an exclusive photo from Britney and Jason's wedding, *Nova* sold well over a million copies that week, eclipsing previous circulation highs. It was the first issue of the new year, which coincided with the magazine's shift from tabloid to glossy. For the first time in its history, legitimate news outlets cited *Nova* as a credible source. An unsavory one, sure, but accurate enough to skirt libel suits.

What didn't change was how much I had to drink to do my job. It became a ritual to wander home late at night after my assignments, absolutely smashed out of my skull. I'd stagger into the kitchen to snatch a final beer from the lonely fridge, put on a melancholic record from the '60s, and chain-smoke spliffs out of the window, overlooking Hollywood. From twenty-five feet high, I'd memorize the strange apparitions on their nightly hustles.

The well-dressed dope dealer in all black, who wore his Rocawear beanie low even in the furnace summer— and who stealthily ferried his customers to the side streets, except when the LAPD squad car rolled up from the station on Wilcox. Wayfarers with fanny packs, over-zealous in their quest to discover where Hollywood terminates, now worrying whether their western adventure will end in a robbery. Club kids in designer clothes trying to remember where they left their Beamers. Taggers writing CBS on aluminum shutters and USC fraternity bros screaming stale *Chappelle's Show* lines to make their buddies cackle.

Bandaged bodies emerged from all-night tattoo parlors. Drunks dropped bacon-wrapped hot dogs onto the pavement. Every Sunday night without fail, a man who occasionally slept in my building's doorway would bump Art Laboe's oldies show from his boom box. He looked a little like Morgan Freeman and sang with a celestial wail.

The chiaroscuro of the streets below lent comfort and security; for all my failings, I was surviving. I had a place of my own with one of those cheesy vintage record players you buy at Target, Ikea furniture, and a jealous tortoiseshell cat named Donna. She was a stray rescued from the abandoned lot next door and made gargling meows whenever I refused to pay her enough attention. It didn't endear her much to female visitors.

Sometimes, Donna would join me by the window and stare out with her own wistful romantic blankness. All cats being poets who refuse the indignity of writing. And I could relate to the sentimental longing, listening to those albums made long before I was born—*Bringing It All Back Home*, *Forever Changes*, and *Everybody Knows This Is Nowhere*—meditating on my own alienation and displacement. Wishing I'd been born into a time where the excitement didn't feel so empty, with a life purpose that felt tangible, not laughable, and the money to disappear and never return.

Quite often, the view from my window terrified me. The tumult below underscored how thin of a membrane separated success and failure, to say nothing of the increasing estrangement from my literary ambitions. I lived in fear of a career-killing mishap, a freak accident, or even a large vet bill that might evict me from this makeshift sanctuary. The fact that I was from here somehow made it worse. If you were sucked in by the dazzling Hollywoodland illusion, you could blame your downfall on the savage exploitation and hollow greed of the locals. But I was supposed to have natural antibodies. The tap water was not supposed to make me sick.

You might read this and think that every gig was a roller coaster of Britney espionage and platinum decadence. But if that was the case, I wouldn't have lasted long. It was way too high-stress to do regularly. Save for true adrenaline junkies, most full-time celebrity bloodhounds eventually burn out. That is, if you don't feel serious moral pangs in the first place.

I mostly paid my rent by doing red-carpet interviews at charity fundraisers, awards parties, and movie premieres. No better scam existed on earth. It was all an operatic farce, full of the most self-important people alive being flattered by the least self-aware. From the first seconds of the charade, spidery clusters of photographers whimpered for the perfect payday look from anyone with a modest hint of notoriety.

In theory, I was supposed to ask celebrities questions concocted by the *Nova* editors. In February, they wanted to know "What was your sexiest Valentine's date?" For Oscars Week, I was supposed to ask about their favorite movies of the year. If Jennifer Lopez was newly single, they'd want me to corner Jennifer Love Hewitt to ask whether she had any love advice for the "other JLo."

Even if I was willing to debase myself like that, it wouldn't have mattered. Unless it was the most insignificant Turnips for Tots fundraiser, the event organizers stationed *Nova* at the far end of the carpet, next to German TV and the intern from the last-place adult contemporary station. No A-lister would ever blow that far off course. The marquee celebrities showed up fashionably last. They'd hug the heavily made-up mannequins from the entertainment newsmagazines and briefly answer anodyne questions before disappearing into the event.

Keeping my job required filing *something* compelling. If I played by the rules, I'd have turned in nothing

but banal tête-à-têtes with recurring *One Tree Hill* characters and the guy who played the original Eddie Mun-
ster. So as soon as no one was paying attention, I'd ditch
my assigned post and stick my tape recorder out alongside the more desirable outlets. As long as I could nick a
couple choice quips by the end of the night, *Nova* was
happy. My "interview" with the Wayans brothers at the
White Chicks premiere impressed Alice Van Bronx so
much that she told me that I deserved my own talk show.
If the same quote appeared in another outlet, you could
always say that some brazen thief stole your answer. But
it never came down to that. I have no idea whether any of
my work made print. And if it did, it was under my pen
name, Hannibal Moncrief.

The real spoils came from sneaking in under the
guise of being an actual guest. I'd convinced *Nova* to let
me expense a Hugo Boss suit, which paid for itself several
times over. Wearing a sensible German fabric showed
foresight and commitment; it automatically deterred vig-
ilant rent-a-cops from fucking with you. The hardest part
was getting onto the red carpet in the first place. From
there, it was just a hop and strut into the party. The next
thing you know, you're sipping top-shelf whiskey, gorg-
ing on jumbo shrimp, and watching Stevie Wonder sere-
nade Muhammad Ali at something called the Afghan
World Foundation ball.

My favorite work weekend involved a leisurely trip to
the Palm Springs International Film Festival, where I
ordered immoderate amounts of room service, caught
several indie tearjerkers, and awkwardly interviewed

Scarlett Johansson about Pink Floyd. At the awards gala, I ate a scrumptious five-course meal and drunkenly made out with a very sexy older woman (twenty-seven) who I had met about an hour before. She was there with a fiftysomething Italian producer whose English wasn't fantastic, but she told me that he really respected her.

Britney wasn't exactly an afterthought, but she no longer occupied a significant portion of my waking life. After the annulment, her management and family had staged an intervention, where she confessed to having "wild spells" because she couldn't live in a prison. She began going to therapy and told reporters that the marriage was just "me being silly, being rebellious."

A month on the road for the Onyx Hotel Tour made people begin to forget about the Vegas debacle. Britney earned rave reviews and boasted the best merch sales for any female artist in over a half decade. Apart from a few missed shows for a knee injury and one for an undisclosed illness, it was considered a massive success. Midway through the tour, "Toxic" became the biggest pop song in America, charting higher than anything from her since "Oops! . . . I Did It Again."

Spiritual concerns became a vehicle for image rehabilitation. Britney was spotted holding *Conversations with God* and the Kabbalist tome the Zohar. On one Sunday morning in Inglewood, the former Southern Baptist choir girl and her mother popped up on the main stage of a Black megachurch, sobbing and searching for salvation.

In a reversal of fortune, Justin Timberlake absorbed the media's wrath when he ripped off Janet Jackson's bustier at the Super Bowl halftime show—exposing her right breast to a live audience of eighty-eight million. He blamed it on a "wardrobe malfunction." What the press called "Nipplegate" was supposedly his plan to one-up Britney's Madonna kiss. Instead, he looked like a horny doofus, earning the derision of the FCC and the NFL. Worst of all, Timberlake abandoned Jackson to handle the brunt of the controversy.

You almost never see history coming. It's the iceberg below the surface, the glossed-over briefing that reads, *Bin Laden determined to strike in U.S.*, the backup dancer who takes you home on a Monday night from a Hollywood Greek restaurant–turned-club. Only after it all went down did I realize that I'd witnessed a strike-slip fracture of the San Andreas.

My most consistent responsibility those days was something called "Joseph's watch." If you were young, rich, and famous, Joseph's was *the* mandatory club destination on Monday nights.

It was supposed to be an ordinary evening in my double life. The route had become something of a ritual. I'd slip out of the apartment around ten, strolling the three long blocks east on Hollywood, past boarded-up theaters, bankrupt department stores, and chintzy souvenir shops selling fake Oscar statuettes and I LOVE LA shirts. I'd measure the distance by the stars on the Walk of Fame. Most were long dead and obscure, but they'd at least contributed something worth memorializing.

The path went from Bob Hope to Duke Ellington,

and when you got to John Belushi, it was time to make a left on Ivar. In a minute or two, you were at Joseph's. There was only one reason why the hottest club in Hollywood was an unassuming souvlaki-and-saganaki café off Yucca: a sober, thirtysomething ex-actor turned promoter named Brent Bolthouse. Only a few years before, Joseph's clientele had been mostly elderly Greeks rumored to be tied to the Athens mafia, but the owners slapped on a fresh blue-and-white coat of paint, installed a dance floor, and partnered with Bolthouse Productions, the undisputed emperors of the club scene. The next thing you knew Cameron Diaz, Mark Wahlberg, and Vince Vaughn were regulars.

The door was run by a woman named Jen with black bangs and no interest in niceties unless you had a Nielsen rating. But there were ways around the fame hustle, and I'd learned them all. Last summer's nervous amateur had become a seasoned pro. You couldn't just show up once and throw money around. You had to do it regularly. You had to have style. You had to make dinner reservations in advance and show up with two or three pretty girls. You had to buy an expensive bottle of wine, wildly overtip, and do it again next week. And it's not hard to find people willing to join you when they never see a bill.

I'd done it enough times with magazine money to where I was considered just another unmemorable rich LA kid squandering his parents' fortune out of noblesse oblige. To be honest, I probably wasn't considered much at all. But I was a familiar enough face, and if I showed up early, as I did on that Monday night in mid-April, it wasn't hard to slip past the door.

No matter how much you love to party, you eventually get used to it. Most nights at Joseph's were a blur of small-batch bourbon and forced conversations only half-heard. But I remember that warm April evening fairly well. I was sitting at a table in the courtyard with my friend Jason, the perfect person to bring to these things. He was an old basketball teammate who had played a year or two at Santa Monica College, and dropped out after booking a few modeling campaigns for Phat Farm. He was completely fearless, loved to meet strangers, and so good-looking that girls always approached him.

"Those girls over there think that your dad is, like, a dot-com billionaire." Jason sits down, impassively gesturing at a pair of cute brunettes with Gucci bags, smoking cigarettes on the periphery of the dance floor.

On some Monday or another, I bought them a few tequila sodas. One girl was named Ashley. I couldn't remember the other's name, but knew that she worked at Neiman Marcus. Earlier that month, she told me that Meg Ryan dropped $20,000 on Marc Jacobs dresses and confessed how much she still missed Dennis Quaid. I passed the tip on to *Nova* to earn my weekly keep.

"What did you tell them?" I ask.

"Said that I don't even know what your dad does. I just know that he has a bunch of offshore bank accounts."

For obvious reasons, I couldn't let my real purpose

for being here become public. If the promoters knew that I was a tabloid reporter, they'd put pictures of me up around the club saying, STONE THIS HERETIC IF YOU SEE HIM. Jason is the only person who actually knew the truth, and he wasn't about to snitch. Whenever anyone asked what I did, I told them that I was trying to be an actor, just like everyone else.

"I didn't tell them shit about my family," I say with surprise. "Did they tell you why they think that?"

"Nah, they just said that's what someone told them. Apparently, your trust fund mystique has spread."

I light up an American Spirit, having made the switch about a month ago because someone insisted that they were healthier. I could describe the vibe for you, but once you've been to one of these nights, you've been to them all. Everyone acts like they're a little above everything and looks like they stepped off a soap opera set, which is true for at least a couple people. A DJ named DJ Dave Orlando plays J-Kwon's "Tipsy," and everyone in the club complies. The décor and mood feels very drugged-out Mykonos disco.

"You don't think that Stifler's mom is going to show up here?"

"Bruh, I doubt it. She's probably at, like, a classy wine bar in Brentwood."

About two weeks earlier, Jason tagged along with me to an AIDS benefit. When I interviewed Jennifer Coolidge, she kept telling us, "You boys are really good-looking. I mean really good-looking." When we finally snuck in, she was nowhere to be found, and Jason died a thousand deaths.

Jason sighs, sipping a vodka cranberry. "I think I love her."

Speaking of which, Britney has just entered Joseph's in a tight white top and jeans, surrounded by her dancers, her bodyguard, and a claque of temporary best friends. The attention briefly diverts her way, but no one is about to stop and bow down. This is Joseph's, after all, where the whole appeal for celebrities is that they won't be seen as unicorns.

Britney and her entourage slide into the corner booth reserved for her whenever she's in town. It's not really a surprise. She's become such a Joseph's regular that *Variety* recently described it as "the most likely place to spot Britney and pals pop-locking on the dance floor." But in her post-Vegas quest to avoid the headlines, I've seen her here only once or twice this spring. Next week, the European leg of her Onyx Hotel Tour begins. She needs to let loose before the grind of the road.

I notice Britney pull an unfamiliar guy into her circle. He looks like he's a couple years older than us. He wears an XXL white tee, size forty-four jeans, and a tilted burgundy Dodgers fitted hat. I know the type well. Identical to every six-foot-tall white boy who tried to pattern his hoops game after Iverson's, who dreamed of being Eminem but was closer to Vanilla Ice, who switched up his style from Cross Colours to FUBU to Sean John. I guarantee he owns durags in every shade to match his Jordans. It looks like he and Britney already know each other. She invites him to sit down at her table, and they lock in: laughing, smiling, and smoking.

I don't think much of it. Plenty of other notables have packed in: the guy who plays E on *Entourage* and the Chicago finance guy named Bill who just won the first season of *The Apprentice*. Amanda Bynes turned eighteen two weeks ago, and is celebrating crossing the threshold to where she can be let into a twenty-one-and-over club. Rachel Bilson, Summer from *The O.C.*, is here too. It's the most popular TV show among the Joseph's clientele, and she's threatening to topple Britney for my number one celebrity crush.

"Let's get out of here," a blonde girl who I've taken out a few times that spring tells the table. "All my friends are at the Dime."

The girl's name is Jasper Lockheed. She's from the Palisades, and everyone thinks she's the heiress to the Lockheed Martin fortune. But on our first date she told me that it's only a rumor—her lineage actually traced back to Pío Pico, the last governor of Alta California under Mexican rule. Our date ended shortly after she came up to my apartment and Donna started caterwauling and Jasper quickly realized that my family didn't summer in St. Barts. Nonetheless, she insisted that we needed to stay friends because "locals need to stick together against the transplants."

It's me and Jason and Jasper and Ashley and her Neiman Marcus shopgirl friend. Everyone at our table wants to leave. It's 12:30, and the energy is stagnant. If we head out now, we'll have time to get to Fairfax before last call.

"We can hit Canter's afterward," Jason sells me.

"Yeah, sure, all right." I nod, swinging a look toward Britney and the object of her affection, gazing into each other's eyes with grievous lust.

"Who's the dude with Britney?" I ask the girls.

"He looks like one of the bad-guy dancers from *You Got Served*," Ashley says.

"Uh, I'm pretty sure I talked to him once and he *actually was* one of the bad-guy dancers in *You Got Served*," Neiman Marcus responds. "I think his name is Calvin."

"I think he's kind of hot," Jasper says. The other girls wrinkle their faces and say, "Eww."

It's our cue to leave. I'm not about to stay here alone, waiting until two to see what goes down. I've already obtained enough for a *Britney caught canoodling with mystery man* tidbit. That's what I file to the magazine the next morning, and I promptly forget all about it.

I keep having this one dream. It always starts with me walking alone in the desert. I never know quite where I am, but it looks like somewhere out near Joshua Tree. A gorgeous alien wasteland full of cactus and creosote, with snowcapped mountains looming in the distance. After a little bit of walking, I realize that I'm in a dream. And by nature of it being a dream, I can fly, which seems necessary to help me figure out whatever it is that I need to find out.

It's never clear how I'm flying. I don't have wings or a

jet pack, but it's effortless. There I am, just soaring out over this lunar infinity in search of some foreign transcendence. Eventually, I stumble upon an oasis—a psychedelic super-bloom of golden mariposa and desert dandelions and a little one-bedroom house with a big satellite dish on the roof.

I land in front of the house and walk in through the front door. It's always unlocked. Inside the cabin, there is a rollaway bed with a TV in front of it. I climb into the bed, click on the TV, and a black-and-white image comes onto the screen. Right at that second, I always wake up. For the life of me, I can never remember what's on the screen, but I know that I'm always strangely satisfied.

On this particular Wednesday morning, thirty-six hours after Joseph's, the dream is interrupted before I have the chance to turn on the TV. Donna is howling because someone is pounding at the door. From my bed, I yell to ask who's there. The muffled answer has a fake high pitch and a British accent: "Rise and shine, sweetheart!!!!"

I'm hungover again. Oliver is the last person who I want to deal with, but he's in the apartment before I can even finish opening the door. Ever since Vegas, he's made the unfortunate habit of dropping by my place unannounced whenever he's in Hollywood for work.

"What did you do last night?" he asks, opening the refrigerator to grab my last High Life. "You look fucking abominable."

The place is in shambles. An ashtray full of cigarette butts and roaches. Bedsheets curled to reveal the mattress.

The cold skeleton of a rotisserie chicken gutted on the dining room table that doubles as my desk. I probably still have BBQ sauce stains on my face.

"I went to Cinespace for that Dim Mak night, but one of the Good Charlotte brothers was DJing off his iPod and it got too wack, so I went to the Rock & Roll Ralphs and got a chicken."

The Dim Mak night belonged to Steve Aoki, who'd been bringing every buzzing UK postpunk band described as "angular" to his parties at a theater-turned-club on Hollywood. As it got more popular, the faction of the Joseph's crowd that described themselves as "alternative" started slumming it there on Tuesdays. Sometimes, you'd be watching the Kills rip up a set, but at other moments, it felt like you were living in a parallel dimension, where the desire for fame and notoriety was equally strong—only the red-carpet photographers were swapped out for the Cobrasnake.

"I need you to help me, mate," Oliver says. He lights a joint and grabs the only thing of any value in my apartment, a Shaq-and-Kobe-signed basketball. Chucking it at me, he tells me that "it's all cleared with Alice."

"What about Brenda?"

"No one told you?" Oliver raises an eyebrow. I shake my head and start to brush my teeth. "She got canned. Alice is bureau chief now."

"What?" I'm slightly in shock. I filed my report about Joseph's to Brenda only yesterday morning. I guess that's why I haven't heard back. "Do you know why they fired her? Have you spoken with her?"

"Mate." Oliver looks at me like I'm a fool. "It ain't a fucking charity they're running over there. It's just business."

"Can you just tell me why the hell you're here?" I ask, throwing on a pair of jeans and a Penguin polo.

Oliver ignores me and examines my walls. Above my bed, there's a psychedelic bricolage of old magazines I sliced up one night while very high. Mostly rappers, fashion and swimsuit models, and *SLAM* covers. Unframed posters of Day-Glo '60s concert handbills, brooding black-and-white writers, and vinyl record sleeves too.

"No wonder you don't have a girlfriend." He dribbles the basketball off his foot. "This place looks like a bloody boardinghouse."

Oliver is only twenty-five, but he already owns a luxury condo a few blocks from the beach in Santa Monica. It doesn't have a waterfront view, but he tells people that it does.

"Where are we going?"

"Oh, good, you're in." He flashes his coyote smile. "Beverly Hills. You'll get your day rate, don't worry."

I can guess where we're going. During this period, the gap between the American and European legs of her Onyx Hotel Tour, Britney has been living in one of the $3,300-a-night bungalows at the Beverly Hills Hotel. Last year, she sold her house above Sunset Plaza to Brittany Murphy because she claimed it was haunted by evil spirits.

About once a month, *Nova* sends me to the Polo Lounge to spy on celebrity trysts and eat $37 McCarthy salads. Whenever an A-List actor is going through a divorce, you find them there. And when Britney is in residence, Oliver has one of his men staking out the cookie-pink castle.

Oliver doesn't tell me our destination right away. He's too busy driving fifty-five on Sunset while screaming at *Us Weekly* on speaker. They're trying to lowball him on a photo of Penélope Cruz with an unknown man that he swears proves *once and for all* that she's "over Top Gun." But they're unmoved. He hangs up the phone by telling them that they'll be sorry when he sells it to *Nova*.

"Did I tell you that the *Enquirer* tried to hire me?" I asked him. I'd received that unexpected phone call yesterday afternoon.

Now that I know that Brenda has been fired, it makes more sense. They've probably figured that I might be in the market to switch to the other end of the U.S. Media Death Star.

"So is this it for you at *Nova*? Are you going to solve the Scott Peterson murder case?"

"Yeah, right after I find the Sasquatch for them."

"I bet you could get them to give you 120K, easy," Oliver says as he accelerates through a yellow light just past the Palladium.

"Don't they strike you as a little evil? Just straight-up lying?"

"You think what we're doing is so different?" He laughs, driving past Sunset Sound, the studio where they recorded the classic Doors and Zeppelin albums. "Anything is fair game, mate. Everyone wants the truth, but good luck getting anyone to agree. Just get paid while you're in demand."

"Man, I'm just going out to clubs, doing red carpets, and hitting parties. It's not straight making shit up," I insist.

"Whatever you say," he responds. "You can admit that you like the glamour of it all."

Oliver reads the sour expression on my face, hears Eminem and D12's "My Band" playing on Power 106, and cranks the volume. As a way of apology, Oliver starts histrionically lip-syncing and fake pelvic thrusting into the steering wheel at the part where Em goes "especially when I drop the beat and do my acapellas."

My mood perks back up by the time we've parked underneath the palm trees adjacent to the hotel. The weather is utopian: a bronze wealth of sun with a slight breeze.

"Something's up," Oliver tells me in the idling Escalade. "Brit told one of my men to tell me that I need to be here today."

"Why you?"

"That's the thing. I know that I'm her favorite pap and that I'm the only one she trusts, but I'm baffled," Oliver says.

It would be a stretch to call them friends, but in the aftermath of our Vegas trip, Oliver and Britney had developed a relationship more complicated than vampire and victim. With the paparazzi a permanent fixture of her LA life, she attempted a pragmatic compromise. Maybe if she gave them what they needed, they would reciprocate with periods of uninterrupted solace.

"You see her new video on MTV last week? Maybe she's trying to arrange a personal screening for you."

"That's about these ordinary geezers," he spits. "They're stalkers. She and I are basically business partners."

The video in question is "Everytime," an instant sad-girl classic as soon as it premieres on *TRL*. Everyone claims that Britney and her cowriter conceived the vulnerable piano ballad as a response to "Cry Me a River." But it's more of a remorseful apology than a caustic kiss-off. If Britney's visuals have always woven her conscious fantasies with the desires of the viewing public, the "Everytime" video is just a literal nightmare. An abusive lover trashes a rack of tabloids and hurls them at paparazzi. They break up violently. Britney slits her wrists in the bath. The man returns in horror to find her lifeless dripping body. In the final frame, it's revealed that it was all a morbid dream.

"You know I saw her Monday night, right?" I tell Oliver, unable to fully mask my high at being back on the Britney beat. Everything else was so comparatively pedestrian. "She was with some dude who looked like Justin Timberlake dressed as Eminem for Halloween."

"Dawg, where have you been?" Oliver scoffs. "After Joseph's, Brit took the party back to her place and he slept over. They had brunch together in the a.m. and went to White Lotus that night. She's back on the sauce.

Last night, she went to the club without him, but I guess he got the booty call, because they're having a fuckfest right now."

"Wait, she's dating the backup dancer from *You Got Served*?"

"K-Fed," Oliver corrects me. "That's why we're here. She probably wants me to take their first official pics together."

Despite his mercenary streak, Oliver adhered to a code of honor. He'd pay when Britney ran into a convenience store for Red Bulls and didn't have cash. They flirted sometimes too. He'd ask about her family and the music. If she brokered a deal for pics in exchange for privacy, he never violated it.

"Wait, who the fuck is K-Fed?" I ask.

Before Oliver can explain, he blurts out: "Fuck it, they're coming!"

Leaping out of his truck, he drops into the paparazzi crouch: hunched and leaning forward, one eye closed, lens trained like a rifle scope.

Oliver isn't the only one that's been apprised. Six additional photographers clump in the shadows.

"I can't believe she's giving it up this easy," I overhear one say.

Britney traipses through a garden path flanked by orange birds-of-paradise and bougainvillea, side by side with her new paramour, clutching a bag of Cheetos. Her eyes are shaded by a velvet-and-white Von Dutch hat. She walks barefoot in a gauzy white blouse, daisy dukes, and a choker necklace. Plush lavender earrings, a red string Kabbalah bracelet, and a diamond belly button ring. Spring is here.

You Got Served is still wearing the same clothes from Monday night. The same XXL white tee, crooked Dodgers cap, and Jordans unlaced with the tongue hanging out. He squints into the throng of shooters like a club-land Clint Eastwood.

At the valet, Britney raises her eyes, beaming pridefully to the pack: "What's up, y'all? This is Kevin." He nods impassively. Within seconds, they're in her white Benz SL500. He's at the wheel, heading west into the beating sun.

Who the fuck was K-Fed? He was the chosen one, which doesn't say much for divinity. Kevin Federline was a fringe Hollywood character voted "Most Likely to Appear on *America's Most Wanted*" at his junior high in the Fresno suburbs. The son of an auto mechanic, he dropped out in the ninth grade, and after a brief stint as a small-time hustler wound up in a dance empowerment initiative for wayward youth. A guy whose crew bestowed him with the nickname "Meat Pole." In 1998, when he was twenty, one of those friends convinced him to move to LA, floating the then–pizza deliveryman and RV detailer a thousand bucks to help make the journey. They dreamed of becoming professional dancers.

Before the century expired, Federline landed a gig

backing up LFO ("Lyte Funkie Ones"), one-hit wonders temporarily famous for their song "Summer Girls." By his twenty-second birthday in the spring of 2000, he was on tour hitting the Roger Rabbit behind Rich—the one who liked girls that wore Abercrombie & Fitch. The headliner was Britney Spears. After one arena performance, Team LFO and the Britney machine all went out, but she was barely legal and he barely registered to her.

In the intervening years, Federline experienced modest success. He danced behind Michael Jackson in the "You Rock My World" video and backed *NSYNC at the Grammys and Destiny's Child at the Soul Train Awards. He was one of the Suave Gang who glided out of a gargantuan boom box during Timberlake's set at the 2002 VMAs.

By '04, the industry had changed. Girl groups and boy bands were passé. No one was about to hire a white twenty-six-year-old from Clovis to pirouette behind snap music. Along the way, he impregnated his live-in girlfriend, the actress Shar Jackson, who played Brandy's best friend on *Moesha*. Their first daughter was born on July 31, 2002, which Federline honored with a massive tattoo on his right forearm.

"You know his girl is six months pregnant with baby number two?" Oliver says as we wriggle in slow pursuit past the lush estates of Bel Air. "The sheriff just evicted them from their house in bumfuck Yorba Linda last month. She should be with *me*, not this deadbeat chump."

"Does Britney know this?"

"She will soon. Alice told me that they sent a reporter

to interview the baby mama, and she said that he and Brit are perfect for each other because they both smoke, drink, and cheat."

K-Fed was the quintessential striver that you meet in a trendy LA club: well-connected enough to earn entrance, but not notable enough for active recruitment. He was there for mise-en-scène, to even out the ratio in case it got imbalanced—a handsome nobody floating along, waiting for something to hit. Then he did.

"He's even worse than George Costanza from Vegas," Oliver sneers.

"I dunno, bro. JV Jason would have tried to have her barefoot and pregnant in a trailer outside of Baton Rouge within six months."

"Just wait," Oliver says. "K-Fed's mates have already been trying to sell the story to all the tabloids. Apparently, the morning after, he was calling up the homies being like, 'Guess whose back I broke last night?'"

The paparazzi caravan multiplies to include fifteen dark late-model SUVs. When we reach Sepulveda and cross the 405, a news helicopter joins the Britney second line. Then another, then another.

"You ever seen it like this?"

"It's batshit," Oliver says. "When I moved to LA two years ago, there were only a couple of us. Those birds didn't even shoot at night because they'd already gotten what they needed during the day. I had the place all to myself. This . . ."

He waves his arm without taking his focus from

Britney's Mercedes, cruising a few car lengths ahead. "I don't think she understands what she's unleashing."

Britney and Federline lead the domestic media apparatus into a Santa Monica beach lot. By the time they collect their food and drink and cigs and blankets, another dozen cameras are coiled in wait on Santa Monica Beach. The doom clatter of five helicopters deafens.

Britney and Federline amble down a dirt path fringed with icicle plants and blooming magenta flowers. The snapdragons on the beach see dollar signs with each click. Overlooking the avalanche, I can hear Britney tell him: "If you want to be with me, you've got to get used to this."

In the angry noon sun, Britney walks barefoot on the sand. She shrieks, "Eeh! It's too hot, it's too hot!!"

Hopping on Federline's back, Britney rides piggyback to the water's edge. She laughs gleefully. Her lips part to reveal the millions-sold smile. It's the first beach day of her twenty-second year. She has found someone who makes her feel alive after the emptiness and heartbreak of the last two years. This was their first real date, what should've been a quiet moment to cherish even if things didn't work out. In her short adult life, she had rarely been alone, and never able to walk into a mall without security. Maybe he could be the protector, the only one who wasn't being paid a salary.

They plop onto a blanket to have a Subway picnic. Britney reveals a lemonade-yellow bikini top. Some photographers shoot from the wet sand; others hover above the lovebirds. I'm happy for her, whatever it is that she's found. But I can't take my eyes off the novel variant of paparazzi evolving before us, chasing gold with obliterating greed.

After a few minutes, I hear her plea: "You got your pictures . . . can y'all go away now?"

The request sounds like a child asking to ride their bike for an extra half hour at dusk. Oliver slips his camera into his backpack and turns to me: "I've got plenty. These knobs could be out here all day and never get a single good shot."

We wander from the scrum in silence, lingering to the side, just in case anything crazier occurs. Teenage girls gawk in disbelief. By three, they've smoked all the cigarettes and sipped all the Aquafina. Chivalrously, Federline offers Britney his Nikes to avoid burning her feet on the magma sand. They return to the Beverly Hills Hotel, where they order strawberries and champagne in seclusion.

In twenty-four hours, Britney will be on a plane to London with her entourage. As for me, I can't help but feel a slightly perceptible but unmistakable change. A dark, tumorous cloud is slowly gathering mass, a soliloquy of chaos starting to thunder. The next day, Oliver tells me that on the way to the airport, he sees Britney crying in the back of the chauffeured SUV, but no one is exactly sure which answered prayers she's shedding tears over.

Hitch Me, Baby, One More Time!

NEED for SPEED:
San Fernando Valley

Pimps vs. Maids:
A Fairy Tale?!?!

It was supposed to be a state secret. A shell game of counterfeit invitations, fraudulent locations, and incorrect dates were unleashed to hoodwink the press. But no one fell for it. Santa Monica's Fairmont Miramar Hotel is a scene straight from Fellini. In the open-air lobby courtyard, every celebrity magazine rules its own fiefdom amidst the marble, fig trees, and plush sectionals. In the parking garages, paparazzi howl whenever the elevator doors open. We are gathered here today, September 18, 2004, to witness or wiretap, the holy union between Britney Jean Spears and Kevin Earl Federline.

In one corner is *People*, the undisputed heavyweight champions of the gossip world. Their reporters sip cosmos in Gucci sunglasses and sigh with regal superiority.

They know that whenever Britney deigns to tell her version of the truth, she'll call them. They're here for due diligence: to absorb stray ambience and take advantage of exorbitant expense accounts. In the other corner is *Us Weekly*: a sorority of scheming blondes savoring espresso martinis, clutching their Louis Vuitton Murakami bags, and currying favor with the bellhops and waiters. By the bar, *In Touch* and *Life & Style* slouch, the last picked on the playground.

I shouldn't even be here. Tonight's original itinerary called for indulging in the open bar and buffet of *Entertainment Weekly*'s pre-Emmy party, while attempting to interview the casts of *The Simple Life*, *Arrested Development*, and *Curb Your Enthusiasm*. But Alice Van Bronx rang the alarm about two hours ago:

"Cancel your plans and be at the Fairmont by four!" she ordered. "Britney's freaking out! We published when and where she was planning to get married, and now they think that they can throw us off if they get hitched a month early. What a silly idea!"

Allow me to backtrack. This past spring, within a week of heading off to Europe, Britney's heartsickness grew so severe that she sent for Federline on a private jet. Without any deliberation, he abandoned his deeply pregnant now-ex-girlfriend and nine-month-old infant daughter back in the States. If I remember correctly, the *Nova* headline was *LUSTY BRITNEY Flies Lover to Her BED!*

For one month, Britney and Federline toured Europe alongside a hundred dancers, set designers, management factotums, and security guards. After her last show in Dublin, they got matching dice tattoos on their wrists. Then on the plane ride home, Britney proposed in a high-altitude fog of sex and mimosas. Federline demurred for a few minutes, to instill doubt and insecurity, to make sure he *had* her. And right when she began to think it was a terrible idea, he insisted that, as the gentleman, he should do the asking. It had been six weeks since their stars collided at Joseph's.

There is no time to relax with her fiancé. "Everytime" enters the *Billboard* Top 20, accelerating the momentum of "Toxic." She's atop Olympus again. And now a three-month, fifty-four-city arena marathon awaits. Tour stops in secondary spots like the Indianapolis suburbs and Bakersfield. You can't skip the heartland when you're marketed as the American dream.

But first, a few days in New York to shoot the music video for "Outrageous," the theme song for the new Halle Berry *Catwoman* movie. What's supposed to be an afterthought—a fourth single where Britney and Snoop Dogg play basketball as sparks fly—goes awry. During a dance scene, Britney slips and falls on the pavement. She's rushed to the hospital at midnight, where doctors discover floating cartilage and immediately schedule arthroscopic knee surgery. It requires six weeks in a thigh brace and months of rehab. The tour is canceled, the *Catwoman* producers find a different single to convey the character's outrageousness, and the Britney Spears industrial complex grinds to a halt.

Between ticket sales and merchandise, the fifty-four

canceled shows translate to over $30 million in lost revenue—not only for Britney but for the entirety of Britney Spears Inc. For the last six years, all personal autonomy has been subsumed to the brand, whether it means punishing tours, promotional meet and greets, or marketing campaigns. She is both ruler and servant, fed orders and aspirations by a consortium of interested parties. Everyone is eager for a taste or a cut.

With the remaining half of her tour left on the operating table, record executives worry that radio will lose interest and record sales will decline. Multiple managers and booking agents are reliant on her tithes. Assistants, personal chefs, lawyers, bodyguards. Mortgages in New York, Louisiana, and Florida. Hotel bills are easily $100,000 a month. And she's supporting her whole family too. Britney foots her father's thirty-day stay at a Malibu rehab for his drinking problem. When he checks out, she helps him open a smoothie shop on Venice Beach called JJ Chill. Her brother, mother, and sister all rent apartments nearby. It's unclear whether it's to help her recover or to keep watch.

Expensive tastes are easily acquired and almost impossible to abandon. For her engagement, Britney buys herself a platinum-and-diamond engagement ring as big as the Ritz—which is where she and Federline are temporarily living. She buys him a $50,000 ring too. After years of being bicoastal, she puts her 4,200-square-foot New York apartment on the market for $5.7 million. Time for a 9,000-square-foot, $7 million Malibu mansion. Of course, plenty of upgrades must be done before they can even consider moving in.

The paparazzi are the true beneficiaries of Britney's hiatus. She'd given up wild club nights to live a lazy and extravagant life in Santa Monica, but they're practically popping up in her cereal. Even a trip to pick up a Maltese puppy with her mom and sister ends in disaster. During an attempt to leave the pet shop, a photographer leapt onto the back of her mother's SUV. Lynne Spears reversed while he was still hanging on. The pap shrieked, fell off the car, and claimed that she ran over his foot. The X-rays were negative. He sued anyway.

Oliver, meanwhile, was getting rich. Those iconic photos of Britney in graphic tees—I'M A VIRGIN, BUT THIS IS AN OLD SHIRT, MILF IN TRAINING, I AM THE AMERICAN DREAM—that was all him. When Britney and Federline rented a luxury boat, Oliver rented a helicopter and pilot and snapped $20,000 worth of photos while dangling from the chopper. Britney waved.

The thing is, Oliver's endearing qualities outweighed the amorality. No favor was too big for a friend. He'd take you out, buy you drinks until you were on the brink of passing out, then pay for your taxi home. It was a stretch to call him an honest man living outside the law, but he understood human limits. The unscrupulousness was offset by modest professionalism. Oliver had manners, never bullied or harassed, and sincerely wished for Britney's best, even if he was willing to profit off her worst. When a stalker started tracking Britney's movements that summer, her security team turned to Oliver to help them build a photographic casebook for the police.

I steered clear whenever possible. After I made my preferences known, *Nova*'s editors mostly assigned me the prestige gigs: the red carpet at the season premiere of *America's Next Top Model* and the BET Awards, where I gorged on chicken fingers as Jay-Z waxed philosophical. There was the *Spider-Man 2* premiere and going-away parties for Paris Hilton's "best friend," a promoter leaving to shoot a reality show in Vegas. At a soiree for Andy Dick's reality farce, *The Assistant*, a man emerged in a chicken suit to protest KFC, and Hugh Hefner arrived with a half dozen girlfriends and Kato Kaelin told me that "Andy is the best guy in the world." Jennifer Coolidge reappeared on the Sony back lot to celebrate the release of *Superbabies: Baby Geniuses 2*, but she didn't remember me.

Sometimes, I couldn't opt out. A staffer would get sick or take a vacation and I'd find myself shadowing Federline with Oliver, attempting to suss out whether the engagement was canceled. And despite the rampant speculation, it never was—which is why I'm at the Fairmont on Gossip D-Day. All able-bodied reporters are subject to impressment. Positions must be entrenched, a chain of command established. There are millions to be made or lost.

"Okay, let's make this interesting," Oliver addresses the motley oddballs of *Nova*'s editorial staff. They've snatched several couches in the center of the lounge—a

power move to ensure that the competition must acknowledge their presence. "How long do we think this
marriage is going to last? I've got five hundred dollars
that it doesn't make it a year."

"It's hard to say. Considering that his friends and
family have been desperate to sell us stories since their
first rendezvous, I see it lasting eighteen months," says
Alice Van Bronx. She's brought along her husband, Hud-
son, a retired engineer with multiple sclerosis, which
forces him to use forearm crutches. "But then again, I'll
hate to see it end. They're both so sloppy and trashy that
they're perfect for each other. The redneck *Romeo and
Juliet*!"

"What cynics, what cynics," tut-tuts the new manag-
ing editor, Nigel Nottingham, a Fleet Street veteran
slouching past fifty who has caromed through all the
stops at U.S. Media. He has a shock of silver hair, a Scot-
tish accent, and the coarse reflexive charm of someone
who has long needed it to escape unpleasant situations.

"You heard the girl in *People*. She wants to have *four
or five* kids with this anthropomorphic fedora," Nottingham continues. "If I recall correctly, the exact quote
was 'I kissed a bunch of frogs and finally found my
prince—my happily ever after!'" He bet three years.

About two months ago, Britney and Federline confirmed their engagement to *People* with an exclusive interview and photo shoot. It was a sore subject around
Nova. Everyone knew that they couldn't match *People*'s
stature or Time Warner's budget, but every time they got

scooped by the industry titan, thunderbolts clapped from the higher-ups in New York.

"I wonder how much *People* paid for that," snorts the effete senior reporter Neil David, a prematurely balding cipher from Brentwood whose last name isn't actually David, but he insists that it should be pronounced "Daveed" like the painter from the French Revolution.

"God knows that K-Fed has encouraged such obscene tackiness," David says, with his aftershave smirk. "Shopping with dirty hair and an unwashed face? Wearing the same jean shorts every day? Emptying the ashtray off a hotel balcony? I think it's a huge fuck you to us fans. Hopefully, her parents get this one annulled too. I give it four more months."

"I think fourteen months," says the staff reporter, Jessica Appleford. She's a Yoplait-plain blonde in her early thirties who wears Old Navy and speaks with a meek *OK Computer* monotone.

Everyone looks to me for my prediction.

"I know it sounds stupid and no Hollywood marriage ever lasts, especially not when you get married at twenty-two"—I try to sound convincing—"but I saw them meet and think they really do love each other. And it seems like she appreciates that he's an average bro and all she wants is a way to somehow be normal. They just want to light candles, play Phil Collins's *Greatest Hits*, and fuck. I'd say, um . . . seven years."

Everyone cackles. You'd have thought that I was up here describing their eternal flame with Pablo Neruda quotes.

"I love you, mate, but have you gone mental?" Oliver shakes his fusilli curls energetically, draining his third mojito of the afternoon. "Give it six months and Playboy Feddy will be back doing the cabbage patch in the clubs—except now he'll be famous, and every skank from Laguna Beach to Chatsworth is gonna try to shag Brit's boy toy to see what it's all about. He left his baby's mum for her when she was pregnant with their second Federletus. That's all you need to know. Chester Cheater ain't gonna change his spots."

"Where exactly are they right now?" I ask.

"After they switched the wedding date, one of his mates called to tell me the new plans," Oliver responds. "They flew out twenty-seven guests last night and told 'em that it was for an engagement party. He took his boys to Houston's and out golfing. She took her girls to the spa. No one actually knows where the ceremony will be."

"They're in one of the two-story bungalows," Alice says, gripping her husband's arm affectionately. "Oh, you should see it. They gave me a tour once and it's exquisite. Beds made of Shetland wool, silk, and cashmere bamboo. A hot tub, an art collection, and a gorgeous view of the rose gardens. Marilyn would be rolling in her grave if she knew that her favorite room by the water was being inhabited by . . . K-Fed."

"Her parents don't even know this is the real wedding yet, but we can't be the only mag who his chums have sold the info to. Look around you," Nigel Nottingham adds.

The reporters roam the grounds like feral hogs. Bum-rushing the bar, nervously pacing near the check-in, practically swinging from the chandeliers. The entertainment TV shows have arrived and inundate the waitstaff with orders. Outside, you can hear the droning thwack of news helicopters.

An impish *Us Weekly* reporter in a sport jacket scurries past us. On red carpets, he always refuses to exchange even mundane pleasantries with me. Spotting Oliver sitting with the *Nova* reporters, he cruelly curls his lips.

"Never too late to join the winning team, Oliver," *Us Weekly* says, purposely loud enough for all of us to hear it. He sounds like a yapping schnauzer. "I hope they're paying you well enough to slum it."

"With one photo, I make what you make in a month, you polyester cockwomble," Oliver snaps. "Now piss off before I tell everyone the real truth about why Tobey Maguire refuses to talk to your rag!"

He scampers away. The excruciating conversation continues. Alice shows off pictures of her fluffy white bichons frises, Jayne and Mamie. Nigel goes on about how it all reminds him of Princess Di mania. Neil David talks about the trip to Thailand he's going to take over the holidays. Jessica Appleford yawns. The sun is starting its surrender into the Pacific. It's time for Oliver and me to slide to the valet to retrieve his Escalade, and prepare for the race.

Three dozen all-black SUVs with tinted windows line up along Wilshire Boulevard and California and Ocean

Avenues. At 6:30 p.m., a column of Sprinter vans—the wedding party—bolt out of the Fairmont garage, bound for the 10 freeway. Zigzagging through Saturday beach traffic, the paps follow in lawless pursuit. Every second matters. At most, they'll get a one-minute window from when the guests exit their cars and enter the venue. Whoever arrives first gets the money shot.

Tourists leap out of the way, shouting obscenities at the photographers, who are concerned only with victory. To our right, there's one of those plum-and-tangerine sunsets that lured everyone here in the first place, but no one cares. The last car in Britney's caravan ekes past a light. We're sixth to make a left on red; the crush of oncoming traffic honks an *eat shit and die* opera in our direction, but we're now traveling east on the Christopher Columbus Highway.

Oliver whips the Escalade like it was a toothpick, switching lanes at ninety and slipping past terrified motorists. He's in a séance: eyes like black pearls, teeth grinding, hunched forward. The other paparazzi are aggressive but less nimble, swinging recklessly, nearly causing accidents. If this is the way that I go, torched and mangled in a fiery crash while chasing Britney Spears on the way to her wedding, I deserve it.

The 405 bleeds into the 101, and we're in pole position. The final car in the wedding train zips ahead of us, but there's competition. A stripped-down Tahoe veers into our lane, forcing us to either hit him or swerve onto the shoulder.

"Shit! It's the chucklefuck from X17!" Oliver swears,

shoving the wheel right and hitting the brakes. Several other paps exploit our weakness and zoom ahead. "Watch this!" he whoops.

In hyperdrive, he zaps to the far left lane at a hundred miles an hour. Almost there. That is, until we hear the nauseating whine of sirens.

"PULL OVER."

Oliver unleashes twelve "FUCK!!"s. He pounds the steering wheel, slamming his head forward, steering the truck to the side. Dozens of paparazzi dash past, laughing at the sacrificial dopes who took the heat as they breeze to the final destination.

Grabbing his license and registration, Oliver holds it out to the LAPD officer, who approaches with mirrored sunglasses and a stun-gun sneer.

"Just give me a ticket. I don't have time!!"

"Now, wait just a minute here, son," snarls the heavy-set cop, who has a crisp clipped mustache and the mouth of a saltwater trout.

"My wife is giving birth! I need to get to the hospital. Just give me the fucking ticket, mate!"

He's heard this one before. Chuckling, the cop bobs his head in my direction.

"This your wife, here?"

"Her water just broke! This is my mate. There was no time, so he had to come with."

He looks at the cameras and lenses scattered behind us.

"You some kind of movie producer?"

"I'm the director of photography for *Law & Order*," Oliver tells the officer.

"Shit, I love that show," the cop says, impressed. "That Ice-T is a son of a bitch, but he nails it."

"I'll tell him you said that. Please, sir! It's an emergency!" He says it with such conviction that I'm almost starting to believe.

"All right, then," the patrolman says, chicken-scratching the ticket, giving a truncated lecture on public safety, and sending us on our way.

By the time we're back on the road, Oliver gets a ring from one of his men. Slightly behind us in the chase, they kept pace and have already made it to the location. It's only two blocks from here, just off the Tujunga Wash in Studio City, the place where all the helicopters are skulking in the smoke blue dusk.

The street's name is Farmdale Avenue. I know that sounds completely made-up, but it's actually her wedding planner's home. A milk-colored, Georgian two-story in the same neighborhood as the *Brady Bunch* house. She offered it as a backup locale after Britney nixed the five-star hotel in Santa Barbara at the last minute.

By the time that we arrive, all the guests are inside. Thirty paparazzi hungrily fan out across the usually drowsy cul-de-sac. With each minute, they multiply exponentially. *Access Hollywood* and *Entertainment Tonight* and *E! News* and *Extra* and *The Insider* arrive. All the local TV news stations too.

Britney attempted to avoid a circus by switching the date, but failed to realize how easily it would backfire if the secret was discovered. She's now getting married a short freeway cruise away from thousands of enterprising paparazzi, journalists, and curious onlookers. It has become a town-square spectacle, broadcast worldwide.

Savvy neighborhood children set up little stands to sell Coke and Cheetos. To my left, a correspondent from one of the local network affiliates does an on-the-ground news hit:

"We're coming to you live from Studio City, where it appears that Britney Spears is about to get married . . . one more time," says the cheery blow-dried blonde woman, who looks like a *Sex and the City* stunt double.

"Yes, that's right, America's sweetheart is tying the knot with bad-boy backup dancer Kevin Federline, a match that many people say is more *Beverly Hillbillies* than Beverly Hills. Despite the pleas from millions of fans and a barrage of jokes from late-night hosts, the twenty-two-year-old superstar is about to get hitched to the twenty-six-year-old father of two, in a relationship that many say feels a little . . . toxic. We'll keep you updated from our spot here . . . in the zone. Back to you, Charles."

The reporter is right: there is a volcanic anger below the surface of this wedding that cannot be easily explained. Britney was a corporation before she was fully corporeal. The fans think they're stockholders, projecting their own desires onto her, the helpless victim of false perceptions. There are those angry that she's dating someone perceived to be beneath her. Others are infuriated that she no longer sought to uphold the conservative values ascribed to her—the sepia mirage of chaste perfection and the antebellum myth of the dainty Southern belle. Some just want to feel better about themselves by getting off some cheap jokes at a soft target.

"Snap the fuck out of it, mate," Oliver says, rousing me from my daze. "Do you think we're going to just sit here and do nothing?"

"Did you bring a grappling hook and rope?" I reply. "You trying to go full Spider-Man to watch the nuptials?"

"Let's go around the block and see if we can watch from one of the neighbors' houses. For twenty thousand quid, I guarantee someone will let us have a viewing party."

Anything seems better than watching paparazzi try to bargain sodas from $2 to $1. Oliver ensures that his men will capture anyone who emerges from the party. No one notices us strolling around the block, knocking on the doors of a quiet street directly behind the wedding house. The first person is disgusted and tells us to go find Jesus or a real job. The second person isn't home. But the third person, well, this is LA, and the mortgage ain't cheap.

Our hosts are an affable married couple in their midthirties with two kids. He's a best boy on commercial shoots, and she works at a casting agency. Their daughter is about seven, a towhead with a Barbie princess castle. Her blue eyes expand when her dad tells her that Britney Spears is getting married at their neighbor's house. "Can I watch?" No, time for bed. She sulks. The little boy looks at Oliver and me like we're Martian invaders.

The father leads us through the living room with its fake fireplace and overstuffed couch filled with children's toys. A lacquered-frame poster advertises the LACMA Van Gogh exhibition from a few years back. Upstairs, he brings us to a small balcony and sets up two folding chairs.

"I'm doing this on two conditions: my name never appears in anything to do with this story. Ever. The second is that you show me any pictures you take."

"I can't let you delete anything—that's part of the whole exchange," Oliver responds.

"I don't want to vet them," he says. "I just want to see what Britney looks like on her wedding day. I know my wife will too. Who's she marrying this time?"

Britney's wedding was designed for a princess bride, but the actuarial tables didn't appear as promising as they once did. This was supposed to be the makeup. A palimpsest to erase the chemical folly of Vegas and give her the respectability and redemption she craved—no matter how much she enjoyed tearing down the expectations of others. But then the tabloids told the entire world, and it robbed her of the privacy she sought but probably never really could have.

This is a hastily conceived improvisation, in which Britney's family is floored to discover that the event is no engagement party. Her mom is stunned. Her dad is concerned about how he doesn't even have his tux here, grumbling, "Don't do this shit to me!" But everything has been taken care of. The formal wear is waiting upstairs.

Things could still look like Cinderella, though. The planners emptied greenhouses for hundreds of garlands of hot pink and red roses, purple and pink hydrangeas. Nearly every inch of real estate is draped in ivory tulle. A normal Valley home, twinkling and glistening, tricked out into a Disney vale.

An hour before the ceremony, the bridegroom swaggers in his white undershirt. The guests are baffled at first, but begin to beam. Someone jokes, "Where's Ashton at?" The groomsmen look like lost members of 98 Degrees, wearing squiggly goatees and gummy-worm braids. At any given moment, they might break out into a synchronized electric slide.

Britney's bridesmaids are her hometown girls, holding magnolias in elegant burgundy gowns: her cousin Laura Lynne; the rest of the crew from the Vegas trip; her sister, Jamie Lynn; and her loyal chambermaid, Fe. The Hollywood pretense and spectacle have been substituted for what might have been if Britney had never made it west of Mississippi. *People* pays a fortune for the exclusive rights to publish all photos from the ceremony. A video crew documents the festivities. Oliver tells me that he's heard it's for a reality show.

Under a crescent moon, the soft blur of slowly dancing images. From our partially shielded promontory, we watch her father kiss her on the cheek, lifting the illusion veil modeled after the "Like a Virgin" video. We are close enough to see the tears. Britney is blinding, her skin radiant, tresses returned to a natural brunette, a Hans Christian Andersen vision for the age of "Hot in Herre."

She descends a stairwell covered in a cascade of roses, wearing a strapless dress of all-white satin and lace, a princess tiara, and a crocheted choker. The long train trails in her wake.

The ceremony is brief, maybe fifteen minutes. The maid of honor drops the groom's wedding band. The nondenominational minister assures her that it's good luck. Britney's mother weeps. Her father's face is waxen and expressionless.

I'm floating through a hostile hallucination, where a phantom silhouette replaces me in my own teenage fantasies. I have a rude epiphany that my infatuation with Britney Spears was never really about Britney Spears, but the symbol of brilliant possibilities sparkling on the other side of the one-way mirror. Watching from the balcony, I am struck by an unshakeable sadness. The realization that even providence is very much provisional.

It's much later when I will interpret this moment as the real beginning of Britney's desire to escape a life that she doesn't want. In the process, she made an easy error: she believed in the timeless lie that angel's-trumpets will always flower, that tomorrow is a logical extension of today, that destiny can appear in the double-jointed limbs and fertile loins of an unemployed dancer.

The vows are largely inaudible, but you can hear Federline say how proud he is to be her husband. There is talk of love and souls. Underneath the floral altar, they gaze into each other's eyes with evangelical certitude, Heloise and Abelard consumed by a lust that neither reverend nor warden could deter. They do. They're gently pelted with flower petals. With the kiss, Federline practically bayonets her on the spot. The joy is transparent.

A white tent has been erected in the backyard for the reception, decorated with enough divans for a harem. A chandelier and candles drip from a gnarled tree made to look enchanted. Gold cloth atop every table. Their first dance is to Journey's "Lights." Their second, third, and fourth dance are to Journey's "Lights."

The guests feast on platters of ribs, chicken fingers, crab cakes, green bean salad, apple cobbler, ice cream, and white-chocolate wedding cake. Federline zealously removes Britney's garter belt with his teeth. By now, she has changed into a white skirt so short it can cause vertigo. Her dad keeps on trying to pull it down. Federline's friends and relatives leer. The bouquet is tossed, and the bodies veer closer, the music louder, the champagne defusing the inhibitions.

About midnight, the energy dwindles. Oliver and I creep through the house, showing a select few images to the dazzled owners. Back on Farmdale Avenue, there's barely room to stand. Oliver shoves his way to the front of the crowd.

When the entry door juts open, the pale street light is littered with popping flashes. A babbling roar crescendos: "BRITNEY, IS IT TRUE?" "KEVIN, DO YOU HAVE A COMMENT?" "ARE YOU NOW MRS. FEDERLINE?" "WHERE IS THE AFTER-PARTY!!??"

The stunned groomsmen beeline into a waiting black SUV. They're dressed in matching white tracksuits with PIMPS emblazoned in cursive on the back. Federline's father and stepdad are PIMP DADDY. In their pink Juicy sweats, the bridesmaids are MAIDS. Lynne Spears is HOT MAMA. Britney's announces MRS. FEDERLINE. His just reads, HERS.

Clutching their gift bags, the wedding party jumps into the getaway cars, squinting into the spastic lights of the cameras. Britney's jaw is wide-open, her eyes narrowed in disbelief, overcome with elation, one more accomplishment realized. Federline smiles confidently as if all of this was predestined. His fedora slants across his forehead like he's the star of a hip-hopera about the Maltese Falcon. They're on their way to a place called XES, pronounced "excess." The rest of the paparazzi are already waiting there.

Several days later, the tabloids reveal that the ceremony was not legally valid. With the prenuptial agreement still uncompleted, their lawyers had the couple sign a formal contract agreeing to what they called a "faux wedding." Until the requisite protections are in place, three weeks later, the union will not be official. But the vows are sincere and the tears are real and the cameras capture every movement, and for the millions who eventually witness it, this is what makes it binding.

7

Bob Saget's **BLOOD** Feud!

Grand Theft Paparazzo!!

A STAR IS BOURNEMOUTH!

People were running red lights at every intersection. Proverbs about virtue and humility felt paleolithic when everyone was trying to get ahead, get paid, and *push miracle whips*. It was *Laguna Beach* and *The Apprentice* and *Who Wants to Be a Millionaire. Home Improvement* became *Cribs.* Shock and awe as a cultural mandate. From every packed club and car, you could hear Usher, Lil Jon, and Luda's "Yeah!" The sky was balling.

Until you escape it, you rarely understand how much your environment affects you. I considered myself a cool-headed skeptic, but it's like living next to a power plant: only a Geiger counter can measure the extent of the radiation. What's the point of following the rules when the rule book is being shredded in real time? We were entering the famous-for-being-famous era, where the only currency was public recognition. Literary romanticism seemed laughable.

And still, I felt invincible. It's partially youth, sure. There were certainly paroxysms of anger and melancholy at an unrighteous world. But no reality check had yet counteracted my ability to dunk without stretching, wake up from a few hours of sleep with velvet in my vertebrae, and shrug off a hangover with an aspirin and a beer. Caution was for cowards. I was in a *Tom and Jerry* cartoon, where all injuries were painless and impermanent.

Humor me for a second and picture the left-hand path. A celebrity car chase scenario where I am barbecued in a Guernica of twisted steel and spewed gasoline. Imagine the scornful obituaries that would justifiably follow. The legacy of dishonor forever shrouding the family line. My parents forced to make up lies about my last minutes on earth.

Is there a more ignominious end than dying as a reporter or paparazzi in the line of stalking? You not only risk the lives of innocent pedestrians and motorists, you also potentially martyr a member of America's priestly caste. Picture the headline: *Fallen Star!! Crazed Tabloid Lunatic Cuts Down Josh Duhamel Outside of Jamba Juice!* I would have been a poltergeist who caused only damage and shame.

Oliver was the main reason why I believed in my own indestructibility. He had a chess master's ability to see three steps ahead and the lightning reflexes of an Andretti. For all of the terror wrought by his vehicular odysseys, I somehow felt plated with adamantine in his passenger seat. After sixteen months in this orbit, I believed that I'd absorbed his automotive sorcery by osmosis.

It was a Saturday morning in December. Three months after Britney married Federline. In the early evening, *Nova* booked me for a red carpet, but they always tried to squeeze as much action as possible into my now-$300-a-day rate. You never knew what they would ask. Sometimes, it would be a simple quest to find Britney and Federline's honeymoon suite at the Hotel Bel-Air, where I immediately abandoned my search to savor two highballs at the swanky piano bar. Other times, you'd ball out at the same Michelin-starred restaurant as Keira Knightley. But there is no such thing as a free sushi lunch. Because one day, it eventually lures you into agreeing to stake out Ben Affleck's Mediterranean villa.

Some context. After breaking up with JLo earlier in the year, Affleck fell for his *Daredevil* costar Jennifer Garner. They were blander than the first Bennifer incarnation, but operated comfortably in *Nova*'s 1B tier of coverage. And who knew, maybe a baby or affair would elevate them to the upper echelon. The magazine wanted me to lie in wait outside of his estate near Runyon Canyon to help secure a photo of him and Garner together. A fresh relationship meant more lucrative pictures.

I'd been on plenty of car chases as Oliver's passenger, but had never been asked to follow anyone myself. Until now, clear delineations existed between paparazzi and reporter. So I hesitated when Alice Van Bronx told me to

trail Affleck if he left, and immediately call Oliver to join
the pursuit. To sweeten the offer, she promised a cut if a
good photo came from it. I was assured not to worry: this
was a standard request; everyone did it. *Above all, be safe.*

I'm waiting outside Affleck's home at 9:30 a.m. My
call time was technically a half hour ago, but *Nova* can
only have my material presence, not my timeliness. Besides, I'd be willing to bet that Affleck is off filming a
movie or something. And even if he's here and wants to
go on a Dunkin' run, I can always claim that I didn't see
a thing. After all, the compound is totally secluded. This
whole thing is pointless. The only sensible move is to post
up on the hilly side street overlooking the entrance, kick
my feet up, and read about how the Dodgers are trying to
trade Shawn Green.

Around 10:00 a.m., the wrought iron gates swing
open. Crumpling my newspaper, I shift into first gear,
and creep from my hiding spot. It's Affleck, all right.
Rolling solo. I can see his voluminous coif through the
window of the S-Class Benz with dealer plates.

Be stealth, I tell myself. I can't let him know that he's
being tailed. Let him climb up the hill, slowly building
acceleration. I call Oliver. "We've got him? Where is he?
I'm coming!" Santa Monica is a solid half hour from the
Hollywood Hills without traffic. But conventional re-
straints or temporal barriers have never stopped Oliver
before.

I lurk a couple hundred feet behind Affleck as we as-
cend. He's unaware that he's being tailed. I turn on Power
106, and they're playing "Go D.J." I move like the coupe

through traffic, except it's a 4Runner. No traffic either. I'm just pretending to be another motorist savoring the powdered sugar sun of wintertime Los Angeles, completely naïve that the star of *Armageddon* is right before me. The plan is to keep contact with Oliver until we reach our final destination, where he'll get a picture that will at least triple my invoice. I'm going to do it big at the record store this week.

Everything changes when we hit Mulholland. Affleck's languid pace was a ploy to lull me into complacency. He's been expecting this. There are only a few cars on the road, and he wants to play the game. We blast past the palaces of producers and power brokers, bending serpentine curves at fifty miles an hour. Icicles of sweat drizzle down my back. My heart does cartwheels.

No time to admire the devil's punch bowl of the San Fernando Valley. As I drive, it feels like I'm spinning out of control atop the upper lip of the earth. My wobbling, elephantine car is no match for his agile V12 Mercedes, but I somehow keep up. Then, at the Cahuenga Pass, Affleck beats a red light by a breath, gracefully swerving left, smoking me.

There's only a fraction of a second to decide. If I get stranded at the light, the chase is over. I think: *What would Oliver do?* Without hitting the brakes or looking in either direction, I hit the left turn coming off Mulholland. Then I hear it: a slashing horn pounded by a champagne Range Rover barreling through the green light at 55 mph. It's about to plow into the passenger side of my car. I'd like to tell you that my life flashed before my eyes, but that's a lie. It was animal reflex. I slam the brakes and bust a U, heading back toward Hollywood. The Range misses me by millimeters.

Collecting my breath for a split second, the adrenaline chokes all cognition. I finish the 360 swoop. I'm heading west again down Cahuenga, reaching Affleck in his turbocharged Benz. He swivels his head in disbelief, trying to decipher the identity of this madman. I call Oliver to tell him that we're heading into the Valley. We're currently near the Lankershim exit on the 101. Somehow, he's not far off.

But Affleck has only begun. Catching me in his rearview, he swerves to the far left lane without signaling. I follow from two car lengths away. Saturday traffic starts to materialize, but he pays it no mind. As we hit Barham, he *Froggers* back across three lanes. Heart still bulging, I move more deliberately this time. Backup is on the way.

There's only so much that Affleck can do now. It's too crowded. Cars full of families are going out to breakfast. Semitrucks are hauling goods to the chain stores of Burbank. For the next few miles, he can only play the switching-lanes routine, but no opportunity exists for him to make a clean break without risking an accident. As for Oliver, I hear an aggrieved rain of honks before I see him, as he taunts the reaper in his own Mercedes coupe. Somehow, he makes it from the beach to the 101 to Barham in sixteen minutes flat.

With Affleck in his crosshairs, Oliver jets past me. I keep pace from a distance. And suddenly, it's over. The lead car heads into the parking lot of Bob's Big Boy, the old-school diner where Affleck has apparently decided to get coffee and eggs.

We slip into the upper level of the lot, parking a little bit away, still able to spot the target. Oliver peels his camera out of his bag to capture this suicidal early morning payday. But when the driver finally gets out of the Mercedes, visibly startled and shaken, it turns out to be Ben's brother, Casey.

I almost quit that afternoon. If you don't have a little clarity after nearly dying on a mistaken chase following the lesser-known brother of the star of *Gigli*, all the bulbs are broken. What was I doing with my life? With each degradation, I drifted further and further from my original desires. For most of that fall, I'd stopped writing my book. Instead, I surrendered to the ouroboros of getting fucked up every night, sleeping late, and spending most of the day marshaling my energy to do it again.

Even if I refused to admit it to myself, I still wanted what most of my peers wanted: wealth without risk or sacrifice. I wanted my voice heard, but lacked the ability to either restrain the volume or avoid cliché. I prayed for the superficial possibilities that fame promised to unlock: money, respect, and models. But I was playacting as a wealthy heir in a weird hinterland, offered a crystalline view of a world in which I was actually an untouchable.

For all of my ethical lapses since working for the magazine, I still considered myself vaguely dependable.

Tonight, I had agreed to cover a charity fundraiser for the Starlight Starbright Foundation, an organization co-founded by Steven Spielberg to entertain sick kids in children's hospitals. And thus, I wind up at the Beverly Hilton hotel in Beverly Hills, a space-age slab of mid-century futurism known for hosting the Golden Globes and countless JFK trysts.

The guest list is light. The event cohost, Pierce Brosnan, is asked about Bush beating Kerry in last month's presidential election, and James Bond tells us that "we must have harmony." The members of the fourth estate are sequestered in a lobby anteroom drowning in yuletide décor: artisanal wreaths, boughs of holly, and a fifteen-foot Christmas tree dripping with candy canes. It's Hollywood in the holiday season, ebullient from strokes of good fortune and eager to save the world through a rubber chicken dinner.

The guest of honor is a billionaire hair products and tequila CEO whose other passion is campaigning against a wealth tax. I schmooze with a buoyant ex-*Baywatch* starlet about her forthcoming reality show, *I'm an Exotic Car*. There's a short interview with a supporting actress from a USA channel dramedy. Then Bob Saget bounds into the cheery room.

The event's publicist doesn't know what's in store, or else she would've never made the introduction.

"Bob, this is *Nova* magazine," says the publicist, a prim woman with hollow cheeks and a wan smile. She flashes the *two minutes* fingers at me.

I was actually pretty excited to speak with Bob Saget.

I'd grown up watching him on *Full House* and *America's Funniest Home Videos*. His Danny Tanner was the most beloved, sensible, and cardiganed father of a generation. A mild-mannered and compassionate center of gravity. An ideal dad offering unstinting benevolence and lullaby piety. And, mind you, this is six months before *The Aristocrats* and the *Entourage* arc that rebranded him as a raunchy hedonist.

"*Nova* magazine?" He turns to the publicist and then to me. "You're *Nova* magazine?"

"At least for today." I laugh nervously. "I'm a big fan."

"You think that I'd talk to you? After what you did?" Saget growls. He's sneaky intimidating. About six four, an inch taller than me, and filled with ursine middle-aged paunch.

"I, uh, I don't know?" I mumble in confusion.

"It's one thing to make up lies about someone like me. I'm a grown man. I can handle it," he says, with an edge in his voice. "But your magazine did something malicious to two young people who I love. You nearly destroyed their lives."

His paternal eyes are now pyroclastic underneath gold rimless glasses. I can see his chest tensing in his gray sport coat and open dress shirt.

"I'm sorry, sir," I reply. "I genuinely don't know what you're talking about."

"I know you know what I'm referring to."

"Look, I'm just a freelancer," I explain. "I promise you that whatever was printed, I didn't play a part in it."

"But you're here, you're working for them," Saget

scoffs. "Take some accountability. Have some pride. What amount of money is worth losing all self-respect?"

"I'm really sorry if they hurt someone close to you."

"That's okay." He waves me off. "But you can pass on a message to your editors from me."

"Okay."

"Tell them that Bob Saget says that they can go fuck themselves with a rusty pink dildo."

The publicist steps in, mortified.

"Well, thank you for your time." She grabs Saget by the elbow, hurriedly leading him into the ballroom.

This is real life. Bob Saget has just publicly flogged me at a charity gala that he's cohosting. You can be assured that the publicist does not bring me any more stars hoping to spread the word about helping ailing children.

I search my helium brain to figure out who Saget was talking about. Within a few minutes, it's obvious. In the summer of 2004, *Nova* published several "exposés" about Mary-Kate Olsen's cocaine addiction, alleging that shortly after the box office and critical failure of *New York Minute*, she'd checked into a $1,000-a-night facility in Utah to treat anorexia. *Nova* slammed the waifish eighteen-year-old onto its cover, shrieking in bright colors:

IT'S NOT ANOREXIA
IT'S DRUGS!

Underneath: "Her Struggle with Cocaine Addiction; Her Family's Brave Intervention; Is Ashley in Trouble

Too?" Receiving significantly less attention, the magazine's top headline reported (almost) accurately:

BRITNEY'S BABY SHOCKER! SHE'LL MARRY IN NOVEMBER, BE PREGNANT BY JANUARY!

All year long, the magazine electrocuted Olsen. Even before the drugs, she was "all skin and bones." After she moved to New York to attend NYU, they charted her weight: *92 lbs & Gaining! Can It Last?* (September '04). Two months later, it was *Back to Rehab?? She's Skin and Bones Again!*

The other celebrity weeklies refused to sink that low (or risk the litigation) by pressing the accusations beyond an eating disorder. But *Nova* depicted Mary-Kate as the cocaine queenpin of Tribeca. Until now, I admit I rarely considered the human impact of the stories. I only felt obligated to make excuses for my own actions, which seemed relatively benign. Remove me from this inferno and nothing changed in any discernible way. But you could not dismiss Danny Tanner spraying Windex in my eyes. This was not Mr. Feeny, Mr. Cooper, or even Mr. Belvedere.

How many Friday nights in pajamas had I been in heaven with a pepperoni Domino's pizza, a big red two-liter bottle of Coke, and the vanilla syrup of *Full House*, with its half-hour bedtime resolutions? Sure, life may have thrown some thunderous blows at Danny Tanner, a widower at the age of thirty, left alone to raise three daughters, including a newborn. But it was nothing that

couldn't be solved by an idiosyncratic parenting arrangement in which his best friend and brother-in-law moved
into his reasonably priced San Francisco Victorian to
help form a new age nuclear family.

No obstacle or misunderstanding was so insurmount-
able that it couldn't be resolved by an impromptu Beach
Boys concert. A reassuring life in which not only will
you always win radio contest tickets, but you will also
be invited onstage to sing "Kokomo." Even if Jesse and
the Rippers don't take over the universe, they'll at least
be big in Japan. Abuse is alien, misfortune is a matter
of being patient enough for your luck to shift, and even
annoying-ass Kimmy Gibbler will turn out just fine.

The real Bob Saget was a forty-eight-year-old divorced father of three. The cherubic twin child actresses
who grew up before America's eyes may or may not have
been champions in the Medellín slalom, but there was no
way to ignore the visceral fury and dutiful concern in his
eyes. The stern but fair televised stand-in for a generation
of American absentee parents was telling me that I was a
failure. I had besmirched the honor of his brood and par-
ticipated in the destruction and public humiliation of a
defenseless child. Whatever happened to predictability?

On any other night, I would've snuck into the event,
stayed for the crème brûlée and coffee, and attempted to
meet someone who might contribute a story to my personal canon. But I couldn't handle it anymore. I was reel-
ing. So much that I forgot my plans to meet Oliver for a
drink. Which explains why right now, he's texting me to
meet him at Dan Tana's.

✦

It's after ten and Tana's is teeming with all phyla of Hollywood life. Actors, producers, directors, executives, musicians, every variety of fame barnacles. A gold-and-burgundy room of expensive scents, bold propositions, and old secrets.

Straw Chianti bottles and white Christmas lights dangle from the ceiling. The walls of the Italian restaurant are adorned with Lakers and Kings jerseys, European soccer uniforms, and a framed photo of an aged John Wayne riding a horse. He and Sinatra used to eat here all the time.

Oliver typically patronized the Red Rock, a pub on Sunset that attracted British exiles and downtrodden Strip riffraff. At Tana's, the paparazzi wait outside, hoping to catch Clooney or Leo wrecked after a veal cutlet and several Negronis.

I scan for Oliver in the marinara leather banquettes, finding faintly recognizable faces and Jerry Buss, the amber-haired Lakers owner. He's dining on shrimp scampi, surrounded by four pretty girls about my age who looked like they've just stepped out of an erotic thriller. It's the first year after Shaq left for Miami, and even though Kobe had a triple-double tonight, they lost to the "Seven Seconds or Less" Suns by three.

From the far end of the crowded bar, an arm waves at me. It's Oliver. He's sitting next to Harry Dean Stanton, who's smoking a cigarette in violation of California law. Tana's adheres to its own jurisprudence.

"We're celebrating, mate." Oliver grins.

He's got a ten-day beard the color of Mojave sand. His T-shirt reads, GRAPHIC SHIRTS ARE LAME. A bartender with avuncular eyes, a red coat, and a thick Slavic mustache hands him three whiskey sours.

"Who is 'we'?"

"Nigel was just here. Did he leave?"

He left. Oliver pushes the other drink to Harry Dean, who acknowledges it with a thankless grunt.

"What happened?"

"I'm going to be a dad!"

"Congratulations." I clink glasses and take a sip. "I thought you were in some sort of a green card marriage?"

"Circumstances can get complicated."

"Well, I'm happy for you. You'll be a great father," I tell him. "If we're doing the whole announcement thing, you might as well know that today's my last day at *Nova*."

"That's fantastic, mate." He smiles. "You get hired somewhere else?"

"Nah, it's a wrap. I'm not built for this shit. No more red carpets. No more car chases. No more Andy Dick."

"Do you know how many times I've trailed an actor and it turned out to be their bodyguard setting up a decoy? Happens to all of us."

"Man, it's not just that. You ever watch *Full House*?"

I try to explain the Saget situation, but Oliver's knowledge of the American father-figure firmament only extends so far.

"Dawg, you get used to this shit." Oliver slaps me on

the back. "I studied journalism at university, but you can't make a living as a writer. I was a kid getting smashed in London and bumping into the bloody Spice Girls and occasionally sending a tip to the *Daily Mail* to help pay the rent. Eventually, I met photographers in the pubs, and they told me how much money there was in this. Next thing you know, bam, I'm making three thousand pounds a day and I'm still eighteen. Youngest pap in the UK and I'm already famous because Liam Gallagher punched me outside of a pub and smashed my camera."

"Why did he do that?"

"Claimed I was stalking him." Oliver makes a fake-crying gesture. "He was just smashed. Wild fucking times. Later that week, some Virgin Radio knob gave out my digits and told all the Oasis fans to hound me until I went toes up. Do you know how many bloody Oasis fans there are in Britain? The government fined him ten thousand pounds, second-biggest penalty in history."

"What was the first?"

"Some DJ who got a nine-year-old girl to keep repeating 'soapy tit wank' over and over again."

Oliver turns to Harry Dean. He's wearing a shark-gray jacket and an indigo scarf and looks like he's been carved out of the Grand Canyon.

"Do you know if I can smoke in here too?"

A waiter comes to grab Harry Dean and take him to his table. He takes a giant drag, blows a cloud just past Oliver's face, and says, "No."

It's another half hour before we're seated under a poster of a movie about an elderly man who heads home to Yugoslavia to raise his orphaned grandchildren in a small farming village. Dan Tana himself cowrote and produced it. Beneath brothel-red lights, I take bites of a Caesar salad and continue to explain to Oliver why I'm getting out of the game.

I get about as far as: "I really appreciate all your help and generosity and it's not like you'll never see me again or—"

"So let me get this straight," he interrupts. "You have one off day where daddy dearest calls you a bad boy for being mean to his fake TV daughters—who are worth about a hundred million bucks apiece. At a charity event where he's supposed to be helping raise money for little Johnny in the hospital. And you have absolutely nothing to do with it! And *you're* the one who's living in a studio apartment with a cat named Donald. Oh, fuck off!"

"Yeah, I mean, if you had watched *Full House*, you might understand."

"Dawg, this is gonna lead to something for you." Oliver raises his glass. "Look at K-Fed. You're out here night after night, in the right places, with the right people. Who knows, maybe you'll wind up with some *Entourage* chick."

I sip the strong whiskey sour.

"I promise you, this is where you want to be right now!" Oliver insists. "We're at the center of the fucking universe. Check this shit out! I didn't even get the chance to tell you that the *Newsweek* article on me just dropped!"

On his BlackBerry, Oliver pulls up the article and insists that I read it now.

SHOOTING FOR THE STARS

*Paparazzi Like Oliver Bournemouth
Are Satisfying the Public's Insatiable Demand
For Celebrity Gossip. But at What Cost?*

By NICHOLAS BLAINE ON 12/8/04 AT 7:00 EST

Be very very quiet, we're hunting Britney. It's an autumn Wednesday during hunting season in rural northeastern Louisiana. Every September, these backwoods are traditionally filled with men and women in camouflage gear, clutching bolt-action rifles, aiming to take down rabbits and quail. But deep among the magnolia and live oak trees outside of Kentwood, Louisiana, we're chasing the biggest game in pop music, the newly married multiplatinum phenomenon Britney Spears.

Today, paparazzo extraordinaire Oliver Bournemouth traipses across the periphery of Serenity, the seven-acre estate that Spears, 22, purchased for her mother, Lynne. It's where the "Toxic" superstar has come to take her husband, Kevin Federline, to show him the hamlet where she was raised. But unlike the amateur sportsmen prowling these woods, Bournemouth's only weapon is a professional camera with a long lens.

"Any of these shots could be worth 30 grand," the London-born Bournemouth explains in his thick Cockney accent. "This is the first time Brit and K-Fed have visited her hometown. Their first trip as a married couple. The honeymoon before the honeymoon!"

The real honeymoon will take place the following week at Turtle Island, an exclusive hideaway in Fiji that promises privacy, seclusion, and most importantly, no paparazzi. However, photos will eventually be sold for publication in *Us Weekly*, after members of the resort staff allegedly violated a pact with Spears and Federline, having initially claimed the images were only for a personal scrapbook.

The incident speaks to the ravenous desire for celebrity gossip. If the tabloids were once on the fringes of pop culture, they're now international big business. The lines between news, sports, and entertainment have been erased. To the millions who faithfully read *People*, *Us Weekly*, *Nova*, and the latest addition to supermarket impulse buys, *In Touch*, there is no more entertaining figure than Spears, the former teen heartthrob who has been at the center of the fame hurricane for the last two turbulent years.

Overall magazine circulation may be down due to the World Wide Web, but sales of celebrity glossies have skyrocketed. According to *Adweek*, newsstand sales alone for the big four total over $1.3 billion per year. But the behavior of the paparazzi taking the photos that fill these magazines has attracted outrage across Hollywood.

Just last month, Justin Timberlake and his girlfriend, Cameron Diaz, were accused of battery and grand theft after engaging in a fracas with shutterbugs outside of West Hollywood's Chateau Marmont hotel. In the latest issue of *Details*, Spears called Jann Wenner, the publisher of *Us Weekly*, a "big old fat man."

"We're dealing with a new breed of stalkerazzi," says Hollywood publicist Bartlett Rosewater, whose client list includes Matthew McConaughey, Hilary Swank, and Josh Hartnett. "People hiding in bathroom stalls and starting violent altercations. It's the same type of behavior that killed Princess Di. There are no standards left."

But the high-paid editors at these magazines insist that rigorous standards do indeed apply: they don't "out" closeted celebrities; photos of people's backyards are verboten, and there are no pictures of children sans parents.

"We hear about miscarriages constantly, but we don't print that," says Alice Van Bronx, West Coast bureau chief for *Nova*. "Believe me, the types of personal things that we leave out of the magazine would make for at least two bestselling memoirs. The only alternative to this is endless puff pieces and studio-approved lies."

A few years ago, the actor George Clooney attempted to organize the Hollywood cognoscenti into boycotting publications that purchase paparazzi photos. Few peers joined the effort. Even his *Ocean's Eleven* costar Brad Pitt admits to the occasional guilty pleasure.

"I have a no-reading policy," Pitt told ABC News's Diane Sawyer earlier this month. "I like the pictures. You know, I found life much easier if you just abstain. You know, it was Julia [Roberts] who actually told me, 'Don't read.' She said, 'Don't read them.' Yeah, she was the first one to tell me that. 'Don't read them, just look at the pics.'"

The consensus holds that most high-level celebrities view paparazzi as parasites profiting off harassment, but the photographers insist that these relationships are symbiotic.

"They're playing the game. The same celebrities complaining about the paps are the ones always calling me up to tell me where they're going to go to lunch—and where they're going on holiday," Bournemouth says.

Bournemouth claims that he was recently paid $100,000 for the worldwide rights of Brad Pitt and Angelina Jolie posing as a married couple. The garrulous, long-haired photographer's biggest sale was $150,000 for documenting the Georgia reconciliation of Jennifer Lopez and Ben Affleck.

"You gotta love Ben's girls," Bournemouth says. "Really any celeb named Jennifer is a gold mine now. JLo, Jennifer Garner, or Jen Aniston."

◆

"Well, well, if it isn't my two favorite boys from my favorite old rag," a voice breaks my concentration. "What brings you down this country road?"

It's Brenda You. We haven't spoken since she was fired in the spring. That's how it was in this business. Someone would get dismissed and disappear off the face of the earth. She still looks like she's about to walk into a detective's office with a sensuous pout and a mysterious blackmail plot. Jessica Rabbit–red hair and alabaster skin. We each receive effusive hugs.

"He was just about to get to the part of the *Newsweek* article where I go to Brit's hometown and get photos of her buying lingerie at Victoria's Secret and K-Fed nearly blasting his foot off shooting guns in the forest," Oliver crows.

"How is our best friend? I worry about her."

"Norman Rockwell in the heart of fucking darkness," Oliver says. "She fired her manager and says she's taking a break from the industry. That chump husband thinks he's Slim Shady."

"And how are you?" Brenda turns to me. "Have you fully committed to the dark side yet?"

"He says he's going to quit! The best young reporter at *Nova* and he's going to piss it all away!"

"Okay, Oliver. First of all, you hate almost everyone there." Brenda rolls her eyes at him, then turns to me. "Are you going to work on your book?"

"I dunno, I hope so. I haven't really thought it through. Maybe go back to school. Maybe try to get another job in journalism. I need to get out before I get killed in a chase or the Coldplay guy tries to fight me."

"Honestly, I think you can take him." Oliver grabs my bicep.

"I think you should trust your instincts," Brenda says softly. There is something slightly different about her. The playful levity seems unnaturally subdued. "I'm shopping my book now. So if you see *Blood Red Carpet* out next year, I'll expect you both to buy it. But even if it doesn't sell, it was more fun than anything that I'd been doing for a long time."

"Oh, c'mon," Oliver says. "Tell him about all the fun times you had at the *Enquirer*. Like when you waited for six hours in the closet to get that photo of Oprah at her Christmas party."

"It *was* fun," Brenda responds. "But at a certain point, you realize that you're either helping or harming. You don't want to figure out the difference too late."

She turns to me like a concerned older sibling.

"I don't know if I ever told you this, but I started at the *Chicago Tribune*," she continues. "They had me reviewing grunge and rap albums and films and concerts. It was such a blast. But I was twenty-three, and it paid next to nothing, so I started selling stories to the *Globe*. And then one day—I had a kid by then—I gave the *Globe* a photo from the *Trib*'s archive. Somehow my bosses found out and fired me. And, look, I shouldn't have done it, but there were far worse things going on at that paper. But I was the one who got pink-slipped. And from there? The older you get, the more difficult it gets to dig yourself out. What we do isn't really all that different from what a lot of news reporters do. But it's the tabloid reputation that clings to you. Think about your own future. I promise you, they won't."

I nod and tell her how much I appreciate the advice. Oliver appears frustrated.

"We're giving people what they really want!" Oliver snaps. "Look how many magazines there are. Now, all the blogs! And all the customers love seeing the richest and best-looking people be miserable. It ain't wrong to meet the demand!"

"It's not that simple," I say, glancing around the bar. Jerry Buss slips on his aviators and stands with his seraglio. "You know the last people to say, 'Oh, I was just following orders'?"

Brenda's date, a handsome man in his late forties, who looks a little like the ghost of Cary Grant, gestures toward her. Their table is ready. She says that it's so wonderful to see us: "Keep in touch." But no numbers or emails are exchanged. Then she melts into the next room.

"If you think that everyone in this city, this whole damned fucking world, ain't trying to get ahead, you're lying to yourself." Oliver turns to me, slightly heated. "The banks are stealing from you, the colleges drown you in debt to build another rock-climbing gym, the valet alone here is fucking twenty dollars. You gonna go work for a 'respectable' media corporation just to get laid off during the next recession. No warning, no severance?"

"I don't have the answers, man." I finish my drink, feeling that glassy-eyed buzz right before you tip into the next realm, where even standing up becomes a sport. "It's corny, but, like, do you believe that there's such a thing as karma?"

"Take a look around you, mate." He lifts his eyebrows, nodding at the extravagance and indiscriminate luck that landed everyone here. "It don't exist."

Another round, another toast, a final cigarette under the smoky green light of the restaurant sign. With shaky drunken swears, we vow that our brotherhood will endure, and set off down Santa Monica in opposite directions.

BRITNEY and KEVIN:
Can *You* Handle Their **TRUTH?**

Reality Bites!
Brit Bombs on Boob Tube!

Just When He Thought He Was *Out* . . .

With the camera in her hands, all inhibitions dissolve. Her offstage shyness temporarily retreats. The detainee becomes interrogator, the object of obsession the voyeur. In this reversal, she finds an oblique freedom. Even since she was a teenager, she's been grilled about whether her breasts are real, whether she's still a virgin, whether she contributed to the degeneracy of American youth by posing in a bra alongside a purple Teletubby named Tinky-Winky. But now Britney has seized the means of production.

Questions are aimed at everyone in her immediate

orbit: *What are your thoughts on commitment? What's your favorite sexual position? Will you marry me?* She won't win any awards for cinematography. The footage is shaky, handheld, crude. A night vision miasma of burping, farting, snorting, teeth grinding, potato chip snarfing, and make-out sessions in Von Dutch beanies—so up close and intimate that you can almost see the cheddar cheese dust on their swirling tongues.

In the spring of 2005, UPN airs the reality show *Britney and Kevin: Chaotic*. The veil is removed to reveal a dead-eyed blooper reel of cottonmouthed musings, discombobulated lust, and untamed indigestion. The five episodes are culled from behind-the-scenes footage shot by Britney and Federline during last year's European tour, their wedding video, and semiprofessional interviews recently taped.

I watch every episode on its initial air date. My skin crawls from the first moments where Britney prowls around backstage, ruminating on her loneliness and how much she misses her family. And I know I'm not one to talk, but no tabloid could have ever dreamed about divulging this much. For once, she's scooped her tormentors, but it backfires disastrously. This is the most thorough celebrity demystification in pop-culture history.

Chaotic lives up to its name. Britney broadcasts her hurt when Federline initially rejects her profession of love. She moans to the camera about how ugly she feels. She laments how it seems like America is turning on her. She's afraid of falling for Federline and worried that life is passing her by. While running on a treadmill, she brags that she's had sex thrice today and describes herself as "wham, bam, thank you, ma'am." She puts her knees under her shirt and laughs hysterically. "Hey, they look just like boobs. But they're not. They're my knees!" He gets shots of B12 in his bare ass. She insists that time travel—as shown in the movie *Back to the Future*—is very much real.

At times, Britney seems eerily juvenile, affecting baby-doll voices, chanting playground songs, and repeatedly comparing real life to fairy tales. In other moments, she goes on lewd tangents, chain-smokes, and films Federline in a private train car while she's "butt-ass nekkid." But in the concert footage, the awkwardness and arrested maturity become irreconcilable with the swaggering self-assurance of the superstar.

Chaotic reminds me of one of those experimental Warhol films where an actor lounges on a sofa eating bananas for an hour—or the one called *Blow Job*, where you never actually see the act, just the self-consciousness, boredom, and blankness on the recipient's face. Maybe the more accurate comparison is Pamela Anderson and Tommy Lee's sex tape, the private moments of two lovers stolen and never intended for public consumption. You'd think *Chaotic* had been leaked to the world as a revenge plot, not sold after a "fierce bidding war" and shown in prime time.

I'd never seen anything like it, and neither had America. Popular celebrity reality shows existed before, but they'd been lightly scripted comic scenarios with past-their-peak stars like Ozzy Osbourne and Anna Nicole

Smith. Jessica Simpson's *Newlyweds* was huge, but you
could almost see the off-screen producers telling her to
ask whether Chicken of the Sea was chicken or fish.

In *Chaotic*, there is no polish or even a basic attempt
at image curation. It's the exact opposite of everything
that Britney has ever done. It's one of the first reality
shows of its kind, a harbinger of a panopticon future
where the unmediated realness makes you physically uncomfortable. In one scene, Britney lifts the tip of her nose
about an inch from the camera, making the type of snout
that you do in third grade, revealing the total abyss of her
nasal cavity. It isn't a metaphor, but it might be.

Britney is at the top of the mountain, and there
appears to be almost nothing there. Between her bodyguards, personal assistants, drivers, stylists, and dancers,
little from the regular altitudes ever seeps into her
bubble—until she meets Federline. And then she falls
madly in love, fires most of her minders, and decides to
"just chill and let all the other overexposed blondes on
the cover of *Us Weekly* be your entertainment."

Before it launched, *Chaotic* was arguably the most
anticipated celebrity reality show ever. Britney and Federline were reportedly paid $4 million for barely two
hours of footage. But it was supposed to be more than a
money grab. This was the opportunity to redirect the
personal narrative that had been hijacked by the media.
A press release quoted her saying that "last year, the tabloids ran my life. I am really excited about showing my
fans what really happened, rather than all the stories,
which have been misconstrued by journalists."

Even after all the negative attention, Britney still assumed that the world would love the authentic version of her—extensions out, manicure chipped, eyeliner smeared—as much as the carefully presented simulacrum. After all, she tells Federline that "everything I ever dreamt of, I put my mind to it and made it happen." But dreams can turn dark very quickly.

Upon the show's release in May, the tabloids, blogs, and mainstream outlets gleefully dismembered *Chaotic*. *The New York Times* called it "sleazy and boring" and observed that "[Britney] has the mind of a child trapped in the body of a blow-up doll." *Entertainment Weekly* described it as "career suicide by videocam." A little fewer than four million viewers watched the premiere—extremely popular by UPN standards, but a fraction of the audience of the Jim Belushi family sitcom running opposite on CBS. By the end of the fifth and final episode, the numbers had been halved. The network itself was off the air in six months.

I won't offer the contrarian opinion that it was a *good* show. *Chaotic* was amateur and sloppy, and the only moment of dramatic tension came when Britney freaked out over the possibility that border control might search their tour bus on the French and Spanish border. But no weed bust in the Pyrenees sustained the interest.

By the second episode, Britney's lingering spell on me was partially lifted, my adolescent crush left behind like a pinup on a high school locker. It was replaced by a sense of compassion. Until now, she had largely been shrouded in mystery. The girl next door who changes into a catsuit and becomes a superhero when the beat drops. Outside of her inner circle, no one knew the actual Britney. And so constant speculation abounded about whether she was an ingenious mastermind manipulating the culture or a savant completely lacking all self-awareness.

Chaotic neatly fit neither binary. She was a sad and lonely young girl deprived of an ordinary childhood, isolated by her success, aching for love. Without a management team to stop her, she bulldozed the gilded and filigreed pedestal so carefully built. She'd come to resent the idealized image that she'd been forced to inhabit since age sixteen, but fatally misunderstood the way that she would be perceived without filters.

I watched from afar. It was hard not to sympathize with her predicament and how real she kept it. Being a regular civilian again felt good—even if I missed the open bars and expense account. You might be wondering if I quit *Nova* with some grandiose Molotov goodbye, but I didn't have surplus bridges to burn. Instead, I gradually faded away. After rejecting four assignments, they stopped calling. Oliver periodically texted with updates about his high-paid exploits, always trying to sway me to return to what I was trying to forget. But slowly, the tabloid world became a memory.

Money became the immediate concern. *Nova*'s checks and lifestyle subsidies made my apartment possible, and now I needed a new revenue stream. I applied to every Craigslist writing job that looked halfway legit, but only the producers of a *Nickelodeon* sitcom responded. Without any television writing experience, a ridiculous cover letter and an impassioned phone interview somehow had me on the verge of getting staffed on a show about two wacky stepbrothers with *hilariously* opposite personalities. Or so I believed. But after submitting a spec script that involved a rapping genie, I never heard from them again. When I randomly bumped into the office secretary a few weeks later at Ralphs, she told me that I'd never actually had a chance. They were always going to promote the writers' assistant.

A life raft arrived when it turned out my mom's boss, the celebrity photographer, knew a guy who ran a movie trailer house. They were looking for someone to write the voice-over narratives. You know the type: "In a distant time, in a faraway land filled with danger, only one man can . . ." To be honest, it was the best job I ever had. I'd go into a cool and dark office in Hollywood with '80s action movie posters on the walls, and dream up ten-line summaries full of bad puns and pseudo-poetic epigrams. They were mostly straight-to-video horror films, which made it even more fun. I could be as bizarre as I wanted. But after two months, I got laid off because the DVD sector was in steep decline.

When things appeared desperate, I stumbled into a stable gig as a staff writer at a business paper in the San Gabriel Valley. Wool suit afternoons in the infernal sun interviewing ice cream distributors in Altadena, healthcare executives in Arcadia, and personal injury lawyers in Pomona. Early mornings, late nights, and the pay was roughly what I'd made working a few hours a week with the tabloids. It felt more honest, but barely. Most stories celebrated the laundering of white-collar wealth, or gave credence to Chamber of Commerce gripes about how my subjects would never be able to afford vacation homes because of government regulation. If only I'd been paid in the amount of times that someone told me that the world was flat.

I've never been one for routine, but the day job forced it on me. After forty-five soul-snuffing minutes on the freeway, I'd come home and collapse on my frameless mattress for an early evening nap. After exactly a cup and a half of coffee, I'd shake the grogginess to jog a 3.2-mile loop up to Franklin Village. Then it was frozen dinners from Trader Joe's, or if I felt extravagant, I'd order a family meal from Zankou Chicken, which could be economically conserved for up to three days. For my final act, I'd walk the mile to the Bourgeois Pig, order an iced coffee, and smoke a joint on the way back. Then I'd write from about nine until I passed out.

I abandoned my book in the hopes of creating something commercially viable. I fell into that classic Los Angeles cliché: I would make my living as a screenwriter. For months, I toiled on a sitcom pilot called *The Young and the Rested*, a parody of the rich club kids who lived like rajas in the fancy condos near the Grove. It landed me an agent at William Morris, who straight from stereotype told me that I was going to be the next big thing. He could *feel it*. All I needed were more samples.

So I wrote a period piece set in 1999 about a boy band

named Heat Wave and their Irish archrivals, the Lucky Charmz. The agent loved it. Said it was like "*Zoolander* on steroids." But he didn't think that he could sell it. There just wasn't a market for it. I needed to write another one, but this time, I needed to clear the pitch with him first. After forty different scenarios, he finally approved a reimagination of the life of Casanova set at a modern-day Malibu sex rehab. Shortly after giving me the go-ahead, he abruptly stopped returning my emails, and I never heard from him again.

I don't remember much about this period. I remember reading articles speculating about a draft and terror color codes being raised and lowered. I remember reading so many blog posts that I wound up at a bunch of forgettable indie rock concerts at small venues on the Eastside. I remember going to the supermarket and always hearing a Coldplay song and reflexively grabbing *Nova* and *Us Weekly* to see what Britney was up to—as though she were an old high school classmate who had settled down with the guy who wanted to skip civics to spit freestyles and smoke Newports in the alley.

Britney was now reportedly pregnant too, which created another layer of mania. According to my old employers, the pregnancy made her stop drinking, smoking, and partying. On BritneySpears.com, she claimed to be "taking a break from being told what to do." She said that she felt more in control than ever before. There was also a desire to write and direct a musical satire of the Hollywood scene called *Hollywood*.

The gossip complex grasped for melodrama. They

printed stories about how furious Federline's ex was that he was having another child and about how Britney and Kevin's sex life had grown stale and about how Britney's chihuahua "hates hubby." But without adultery, riotous partying, or visible instability, the narrative turned almost wholesome. The closest thing to scandal involved her walking barefoot into a gas station bathroom. So the tabloids pivoted to calling her a "hot mama," praising her "stylish" and "formfitting" outfits, and soliciting baby name suggestions from their readership ("Madison" wins). After years of being the main character, Britney finally becomes a featured part of the tabloid repertory.

Paris Hilton is dating a Greek shipping heir named Paris and Nicole Richie gets engaged to DJ AM and Justin Timberlake and Cameron Diaz are secretly betrothed too (maybe) and Christina Aguilera says "yes" to a music marketing executive and Demi Moore is seen sporting a yellow-gold ring from Ashton Kutcher and Drew Barrymore breaks up with the drummer from the Strokes and Joaquin Phoenix goes to rehab and *The Apprentice* star Donald Trump marries a Slovenian FHM model and Jessica Simpson and Nick Lachey are on the rocks and Lindsay Lohan may have gotten lip fillers and Ben pops the question to Jennifer Garner and Renée Zellweger elopes with Kenny Chesney (before it gets annulled for fraud) and Jude Law cheats on Sienna Miller with the nanny and Kirsten Dunst and Jake Gyllenhaal are back together and he's set to get down on one knee and she's set to say "yes" and Mary-Kate Olsen is dating a different

Greek shipping heir than Paris Hilton but after they break up Paris Hilton will date him too, and Tom Cruise, a forty-two-year-old man, is so madly in love with Joey from *Dawson's Creek* that he leaps on Oprah's couch in ecstasy and Lance Armstrong and Sheryl Crow may be "putting the brakes" on their relationship and Mischa Barton and Brandon Davis break up until he goes to Rome to win her back and her parents ARE FURIOUS and Johnny Knoxville is seen canoodling with Kate Moss even though he's married and she's linked with Pete Doherty of the Libertines and Ashlee Simpson is seeing Lindsay Lohan's ex Wilmer Valderrama and NOW IT'S WAR and Orlando Bloom and Kate Bosworth are engaged and Charlie Sheen and Denise Richards are divorcing until they are not, for now.

By midsummer, I'd convinced myself that saving enough from every paycheck could eventually purchase the freedom to travel, or help pursue a path that wasn't leading me off a different cliff. But my monthly banking statements swiftly corrected that miscalculation. It felt like there was no future, only a stale present of rent, weed, and bills, a nervous new breed of modern subsistence. And I was only getting older.

It was during this prolonged drift when Oliver called me for the first time in months.

"Mate, your boy came through again," he greeted me. "I just had a meeting with *People* magazine and they're looking to hire you."

"Why would they want me when there are hundreds

of people still working for the tabloids who would kill
for that job?"

"Because I told them that you were the best young
reporter that *Nova* had, but they were too stupid to use
you properly."

"What does that even *mean*?" I respond, slightly irritated, but not uninterested. "I'm not going back to stake
out Eva Longoria's birthday party."

"Dawg, this is *People* fucking magazine!" Oliver yells
over what appears to be the sound of a crying baby. "The
premier league. There ain't a party or opening night that
every publicist ain't begging them to appear at. You've
made it."

"Made what?" I say sarcastically.

"Listen, mate, just return the bureau chief's email. He
probably already sent it," Oliver says. The baby starts crying even louder. He tells me to hold on and I hear muffled
cursing. "Look, I gotta run. Don't be such a priss. I know
that business newsletter ain't paying you shit and you
need extra dough. It can't hurt to meet them!"

Yawning through a dinner for angel fund investors at a
Sierra Madre golf club the next night, the possibility of
working for *People* began to sound appealing. It wasn't
like I'd dreamed about writing for them, but this was a
quantum leap over *Nova*. *People* offered mainstream bona
fides and legitimacy, the perks with fewer indignities—or
at least different ones. Bureaus all over the globe and the
chance to publish complete sentences. I'd be welcomed at

restaurant openings and million-dollar video game console launch parties, formal charity affairs and radio station concerts. No more sneaking in. All it took was a different name tag.

People was Britney's favorite too. Celebrity gossip was balanced by interviews with popes and presidents, sanitized true crime stories, and human interest Hallmark tales. It was safe. And that's why she'd given them a pregnancy tell-all, where she revealed her cravings (pickles with ice cream) and epiphanies (pregnant sex is better, morning sickness is bad, being pregnant is empowering). Who knows? Maybe fate will finally assign my long-awaited face-to-face interview with her.

About a week later, I duck out of work for a "dentist's appointment" to drive to *People*'s West Coast offices. I'm being interviewed by the bureau chief on the twenty-fourth floor of a headstone-gray skyscraper on Wilshire, just past Westwood. He's a small but energetic intellectual type in his midforties, wearing black cool-nerd glasses and a Banana Republic dress shirt and slacks.

"Now tell me what you did at *Nova* that made Oliver say that you're indispensable," he says dryly.

"Little bit of everything," I reply. "Red carpets at all the awards shows and movie premieres. Too many last calls at all the clubs that all your reporters are probably at. And you know the rest of, uh, the stuff."

"Well." He clears his throat. "I should be *clear* that *People* is a different kind of publication than *Nova* or even *Us*. We never ask our photographers or reporters to

lie in wait for celebrities. We won't even publish a photograph with a long lens. We expect the stars to trust us,
and in turn, that way we can trust them."

"That's sort of why I stopped working for *Nova* in the
first place," I say, noticing the contrast in décor. It looks
like the office of an American Studies professor—framed
degrees, pop-culture history books, an autographed vinyl
of Elvis Costello's *Trust*.

"Good, because I know we're not *Time*, but that's our
sister publication, and we apply the same journalistic
rigor," he says.

Maybe this is where I should acknowledge what you
may have been wondering. It's what everyone asked me
all the time. How much of this shit is true? Of course
there was a hierarchy of truthiness. Push the line too far
and you were looking at a massive defamation suit. In my
direct experience, *Nova* never ran anything that was outright false. Whatever I filed would be massaged, exagger-
ated, rewritten with insinuations and innuendos that
may not have actually been there. But from what I witnessed, they were usually more right than wrong. For all
the heartlessness and irresponsibility, they strove for accuracy, or at least in its general direction.

Us Weekly rarely missed the big picture. If someone's
relationship was rocky, it generally was. They had the
best sources, but even the most reliable informants are
subject to human fallibility—let alone the difficulty of
conveying the inexplicable dynamics that govern every
intimate relationship. As for *In Touch* and *Life & Style*,
they were for the rubes who buy unregulated health

supplements off late-night infomercials. I can't tell you exactly how much the New York daily tabloids got correct, but they never let the facts get in the way of a good story. As for the blogs, they were a Greek chorus, proposing riddles and telling the audience who the murderer was. Usually, it was Kevin Federline.

But *People* always struck me as being of a different class. They seemed to have a traditional journalism school obligation toward accuracy. Besides, why take risks to sell copies when you can rely on deep coffers and spineless credibility?

"This can be a real stepping stone for a young writer," the editor continues. "I've written books with John Cougar Mellencamp, Clint Eastwood, and I shouldn't say this, but I'm supposed to be doing one with Lisa Kudrow. Something light."

"That's a relief." I slowly exhale, my tie digging into my neck. "I swore that I would never write the word 'canoodle' ever again. I'm not joking."

"Listen, I'll level with you." He lifts his hand dramatically, gesturing toward his floor-to-ceiling window with a view of another skyscraper. "Getting a Britney-is-engaged scoop? Sure, cool. That's how you get four million circulation. We need to do that. But me? I really do this because if you turn to page sixty of that same issue, that's where you'll find the diaries of a sergeant in the army—a kid about your age—taking you through his patrols in Sadr City. The hard-hitting shit that you don't expect to find."

I don't know if this is a lie to impress me or whether

he's convinced himself of the gotta-break-eggs-to-make-an-omelet trade-offs of the mission, but I know enough to nod my head with the solemnity that he wants. We talk for a little while longer. When he discovers that we went to the same college, his tone lightens noticeably. The job seems like a lock now. He asks me about the books I like to read, and the movies and shows I like to watch. Typical first-date banter. And as much as I hate to admit it, my cardinal flaw is that I like almost anyone who likes me first. This guy was talking as though if I played the game right, I would soon be profiling musicians, writing film and television reviews, and traveling all over the globe on Time Warner's open wallet. I started to envision a real route to escape.

It wasn't hard to see how much the editor appreciated all the ricochet glamour of the gig. He strutted around the office to introduce me to his gently alternative Gen X deputies, one with Jem and the Holograms hair and PJ Harvey and Sonic Youth posters in her cubicle. They scan about a thousand times cooler than the cadavers at *Nova*, and tell me twice how cute I look in my suit. They're who I'll wind up reporting to.

We all shake hands and they insist that they'll have the employment paperwork messengered within the next week. Shortly afterward, I'll be apprised of my first assignment. But things take longer than expected. A few days after my interview, the bureau chief abruptly departs the magazine. According to the *New York Post*, a staffer accused him of sexual harassment; *People* placed him on "indefinite book leave."

But the crisis is soon resolved. The bureau chief is replaced by the deputy with the *Goo* poster in her cubicle. *People* sent me on my first assignment: the *Dukes of Hazzard* movie premiere at a marine base near San Diego. Nothing too taxing. I'd interview Jessica Simpson, Johnny Knoxville, Willie Nelson, and Stifler about supporting the troops, the difficulties of getting into character as Confederate whiskey distillers, and the enduring power of daisy dukes. It was the most excited that I'd ever been for one of these jobs, mainly because for once, the talent would actually want to talk to me.

Come Friday afternoon, my boss at the business paper reneges on his promise to let me out early. It's a production day, and last-minute rewrites are required. I don't wind up leaving Pasadena until 3:00 p.m., which leaves two hours to trek the 110 miles to Camp Pendleton. I pray to the traffic deities to make the metal sea part. I tell myself that congestion is usually lighter in August. But never before or since have I seen gridlock that grotesque.

For six of the most panicked hours of my life, I chain-smoke on the 5, passing accident after accident. When I finally pull up to the guard tower, the event is almost over and the jarheads tell me to turn around and head home. I want to drive into the Pacific. The next morning, I discover that the *Dukes* premiere shared a date with a Pride parade and the San Diego Street Scene music festival. Traffic was so bad that the Black Eyed Peas nearly missed their set, and Fergie peed in her pants in the rush to make it onstage. You can Google the photos if you don't believe me.

In an attempt to salvage my relationship with *People*, I wrote a shameless apology that pledged total journalistic fidelity. These were *extenuating circumstances*. Like a simping R&B song, I pleaded for another chance. The editors said that they understood, but what else were they going to say? Just like that, my comeback bid came to an abrupt end before it even began.

9

EXCLUSIVE!
Beachside Bash
at *SECRET*
Love Nest!

The *MOST* Romantic Hikes
in Santa Barbara County!

2005: *Whoa!* What a Year

The sign says DO NOT TRESPASS. A dire warning to wandering surfers, lost hikers, and intruders staked into multimillion-dollar dirt. Clear as a coffin.

I'm standing at a crossroads underneath a steep cliff that guards Brad Pitt's beachfront pleasure dome. One trail leads up to the palatial Santa Barbara estate, but it looks too risky. Better to take the opposite path, bounding up a chaparral bluff that reveals a panorama of this 11.5-acre compound, a lunar fantasia of twisted boxes of translucent glass, teak wood, and sleek metal.

Stunned by this borrowed paradise, I grab a seat and

get comfortable. Stretching out on a thick carpet of salt grass, I stare dumbly at the palm trees, pristine sand, and lemon-blue water. The Southern California caricature made real, a Happy Meal Eden. From the hacienda, Angelina Jolie saunters outside in a black string bikini to soak up the August heat. I clutch my binoculars to ensure it's not a hallucination. Confirmed. A few hundred yards away, one of the centerpieces of my teenage bedroom collage, the plush-lipped enchantress herself, sunbathes on a chaise lounge.

How did I get here? Superb question. I was shocked when just yesterday, Friday afternoon, *People*'s editors called from a private number. If I was willing to leave town as soon as I got off work, they'd give me another shot. All I have to do is drop my plans to spend the next forty-eight hours monitoring the situation at Pitt's secluded fortress just off the 101. According to their sources, he and Jolie are throwing a fourth birthday party for her son this weekend. What's more, I'm instructed to captain a two-person paparazzi team. Oh, and I need to bring binoculars. I'm told that Rite Aid has them.

I say yes before even realizing what I've agreed to. Until now, I'd never been asked to command a paparazzi unit. Nor had I been sent off on a solo mission of such duration and magnitude. And I don't own any binoculars. Rest assured, there is plenty of cognitive dissonance in my being asked to do exactly what the magazine said that they would never ask me to do. But I know that if I ever want to work for *People* again, I need to pass the test.

It does seem a little strange. They offered little instruction other than Pitt's address and the contours of the mission. "Text the paparazzi when you arrive! Look for lights! Look for trucks! Write down license plate numbers! Book your own hotel! Happy hunting!"

I stop home just long enough to pack a weekend bag. Grab some weed, papers, and Adderall, and leave two days of food for the cat. I clutch a fistful of mushrooms too, because who knows how dull this might get. I'll probably spend 97 percent of the weekend waiting for nothing to happen.

In Friday rush hour traffic, I crawl past Camarillo and Oxnard, Carpinteria and Summerland. From the Pioneer speakers, Killa Cam raps about drinking sake on a Suzuki in Osaka Bay. I ruminate on my fate and vow not to fail. The *Dukes of Hazzard* debacle convinced me that I'd blown my best chance to segue into respectable journalism. My plan is to leverage *People* to crack a place like *Rolling Stone* or *Esquire*. Or maybe I'll meet a shrewd producer who will see something special in me and hire me to write his next blockbuster. Anything is possible again.

I make it to the central coast before the sun sets, staring into the soft purple twilight of the Santa Barbara littoral, smoking a joint from across the other side of the highway. There is no movement anywhere, so I retreat for the night to Solvang, the Danish tourist village. It's a solid forty-five-minute drive from Pitt's palace, but it turns out that this weekend is Santa Barbara's Old Spanish Days festival. Everything from baller suites to

broke-boy hovels has been booked for weeks. I sleep inside a windmill.

Waking up early, I turn the previous night's joint to
ash and peruse a copy of the *Los Angeles Times* over a
California omelet and coffee at a Viking-themed diner.
It's the forty-year anniversary of the Watts Riots, and the
"divisions are still there." Taliban guerillas have killed an
American soldier in Ghazni. A Baghdad bombing left
twenty-one dead, and the mayor is hiding after militants
ousted him at gunpoint. In Palos Verdes, Donald Trump
has announced that the Trump National Golf Club is on
pace to open by late September: "Getting the waterfalls
approved was no easy feat."

At 10:00 a.m., I'm parked just east of the 101. Pitt's
mansion lies directly on the opposite side of the interstate, largely invisible to the tens of thousands who
unknowingly zip past it every day. From my vantage
point, idled on a gentle incline next to a pasture, I can
observe the cars coming and going. There doesn't appear
to be much more for me to do. Nonetheless, *People*'s editors are growing impatient. They keep checking in every
half hour, emphasizing that no other magazine knows
about the birthday party. We need to *one-up them*. But
help is on the way. One of the paparazzi is coming to
meet me. We'll all devise a new strategy from here.

A British tabloid survivor in his midthirties pulls up
in a black Celica. A large Canon camera with a zoom lens
swings from his neck. Short greasy blond hair recedes at
his temples. His name is Neal Beagle, one of the Fleet

Street diaspora who flocked west around the turn of the century in search of mild weather and easy money. He's a freelancer for the paparazzi agency Splash News. My editor insists that we put her on speaker.

"They ain't making it easy," Beagle tells my editor and me. He looks like a hayseed tourist in khaki shorts and a T-shirt of a bear riding a bicycle with a surfboard on his back. "I couldn't see a blasted thing from the beach because it was still foggy. We swooped past the airport, but Angie's plane ain't in the hangar either. My partner is up the road, taking license plate photos of everyone entering, but it's still early. I'll send 'em over when the guests start arriving."

"Oh, drat," my editor says, with the tone of someone noticing a chipped nail. "How far did you make it on the beach?"

"Not very," Beagle says. "What we really need is someone to make it to Brad's place to let us know if it's possible to get any aerial shots. That might be our best bet."

My editor addresses me by name.

"Okay, so the house is next to El Capitán State Beach," she instructs. "Go for a nice long stroll on the sand, far enough to be able to get a glimpse of the house. If you can see inside, even better. Just take the binoculars so you don't need to get *too* close."

I was in no position to refuse their demands. In my mea culpa, I told them that I'd do anything short of getting *People* tatted on my forehead. And the paparazzi and the editor keep stressing the value of this new plan. My ability to get them an accurate grasp of the geography and terrain will determine every step that follows. If everything shakes out, it could mean millions of copies sold and my fate secured.

I'm on the verge of breaking open one of the decade's biggest stories. For the last six months, you haven't been able to buy a Snickers at the supermarket without missing the all-caps headlines about the love triangle between Brad Pitt, his *Mr. and Mrs. Smith* costar Angelina Jolie, and his now-jilted ex-wife, America's sweetheart, Jennifer Aniston.

It was all speculation until April, when *Us* paid six figures for a photo of Pitt and Jolie frolicking with her adopted toddler on a remote Kenyan beach—only a few weeks after he announced his divorce from Aniston. Jolie reportedly called in the tip herself. By month's end, *People* said that Pitt flew to London to pick up Lara Croft and whisk her to Morocco for a clandestine night on the set of *Babel*. Around then, some anonymous Prometheus coined the portmanteau "Brangelina."

Until now, neither Pitt nor Jolie have confirmed anything. The rumors change each week. They've moved in together. She's pregnant. They're already married—no, they're *about* to get married. No matter how lightly substantiated the allegations, their elusiveness and refusal to acknowledge the relationship only make the hysteria more intense. If I succeed, I'll be the one to confirm it.

A strange calm washes over me as I park in the public

lot at the state beach. Ambling onto the sand, I head south along the breaking waves and serrated rocks. It's one of those Southern California afternoons that gives you temporary amnesia. The sun, fixed at midday arrogance, turns the Pacific Ocean into a sheet of canary diamonds. A sparkling complacency sets in, the type of day where you can't help but get caught slipping.

It's such a picturesque afternoon that I put my binoculars in my back pocket and go for a jog. While I'm at it, I might as well take off my shirt and acquire a tan on the clock. It feels so soothing that there must be a catch. I'm getting paid by the most popular magazine in the world to exercise on this elysian beach. I'll scope out the scene, head back to my car, hang out for a few more hours, get high, and eat a gourmet feast on the company tab.

Weaving in and out of the coves, the tide keeps rising, and sand seeps into my socks. After about two miles, I reach my final destination. Pitt purchased this $4 million postmodern castle right after marrying Aniston, and it's patrolled by—well, it appears to be no one at the moment.

The first thing I notice is a quaint wooden picnic table on the beach. The DO NOT TRESPASS sign looms at the base of the cliff that leads up to the estate. In the other direction, another dirt path twists away from it, heading up toward the scenic bluff covered with a carpet of ice plants.

Without giving it much thought, I follow the path that doesn't promise a potential assault, criminal prosecution, and lifetime ban from AMC Theatres. After all,

I've just gone on a pleasant amble from the state park. I haven't hopped any fences or crossed any barriers. I'm just another shirtless taxpayer with every right to enjoy the charms of this seaside nirvana.

When I make it atop the bluff, I take out my binoculars to bear dazed witness to the golden dream. Just you, me, and Angelina Jolie, outstretched in the black string bikini on the chaise lounge. Even from five hundred feet away, there's no doubt that it's her. Her beauty is less classical and more evolutionary, as though this is what future aesthetic advancement will aspire toward. *Vogue* named her "The First Perfect Woman." *Esquire* crowned her "The Sexiest Woman Alive." Brad Pitt's first marriage never stood a chance.

I behold a trompe l'oeil that briefly deceives me into thinking that I am in possession of the millions required to purchase this patch of soil with a paradisal angle of the Pacific—to know what it would be like to walk out onto the sundeck on a lazy Saturday in late summer and find Angelina Jolie waiting for me like a complex empress. And it's at this exact moment that four goons on ATVs swarm me.

"GET DOWN!! HANDS UP!!"

A man with a Glock .22 tucked into his khaki shorts yells at me with a hacking Middle Eastern accent.

I leap up, swiveling my head to look to escape, but there's nowhere to run. I drop back down to the grass, hands to the sky, stomach sinking to my soles. I feel like dying.

The tightly wound man with the pistol seems to be

the leader. He has an aquiline nose, flat marble eyes, and cropped hair the color of apple cider vinegar. His henchmen grab me.

One torques my hands while the others strip me of wallet, keys, phone, and binoculars. They hand it over to the enraged man, who scans my driver's license, debit, gym, and discount cards.

"Where is your camera! Give me the camera!!!" he shouts at me.

"I don't have a camera!"

They shove me onto the ground and lift up my jeans, running their hands under my socks. He looks at his men and asks, "No weapons?" They shake their heads.

The security guards wear polos and khaki shorts. They have bulging muscles, black holes for eyes, and a whey protein blood type.

"You might as well tell the truth because we'll find out anyway." The security chief lowers his voice from first-degree murder to manslaughter.

"Look, man, I don't know what's going on. I was just hiking at the state park and took a rest up here."

"How do you explain this?" He holds up the fucking binoculars.

"I'm a bird-watcher."

"Cut out the bullshit—we know you. We've been watching you for months. We saw you across the highway with your accomplices!"

"Accomplices? Mister, I'm parked at El Capitán! I love birds. If you let me go to my car I can show you notebooks full of poems! This is what I do."

"I'm only going to ask you this once: Who do you work for?!"

I shake my head silently, terrified.

"Just let me put on my shirt first."

They nod. I can't believe this is actually happening. I keep ransacking my brain for things to say to possibly win my release.

"Please, sir, I don't know what's going on or whose house this is. I just want to go back to my car and leave and never come back."

"You show up here on a red alert day and expect us to believe you just stumbled in from the park? With binoculars? This is a load of shit!"

"This is a public beach. I walked here from the state park literally right next door. I'm being unlawfully detained, and I demand to be let go."

"You're past the mean high tide line and are trespassing on private property."

"You're making a big mistake."

"You are good liar." He laughs cruelly. "Maybe the authorities will believe you."

The Santa Barbara County sheriffs are not into poems or birds. But one thing that all cops are into is celebrities. They love busting them and getting their names in the papers and a commendation down at the station house. Taking the rich and famous down a peg, reminding them that only the law is above the law. A welcome interlude

from their usual repertoire of DUIs and casual harassment. Of course, the next best thing is saving a celebrity.
You're a hero now, doing your part to help nourish and
support America's most valuable resource. Maybe they'll
take a liking to you and give you a nonspeaking line in
a movie as a favor. Or at least hire you as off-duty
security.

Angelina Jolie has retreated back into her city-state
on the hill. She's replaced by a pair of deputies who arrive
within minutes. This is no regular 911 call. They strut
down the cliffside path with cowboy-cop swagger, mesmerized by the views afforded you when you play Achil-
les in $180 million adaptations of *The Iliad*. The house is
hedged in by palm trees that look like exploded fireworks.
The landscaping bill runs more than the cops make in a
year. Not bad, they nod.

I respectfully disagree. This is very bad. Unholy-
curse-placed-on-your-lineage bad. My skull feels like a
struck gong. My rotator cuffs are sore from being yanked.
I stare at the white-gold water, thinking about my refugee
ancestors cramped in the steerage quarters of leaky
transatlantic ships only for me to meet Joe Black under
such dire circumstances. It's the feeling of getting caught
cheating on a final exam and knowing you'll flunk the
entire class. I'm visualizing my mug shot on teasers leading into commercial breaks. People *paparazzi popped at
Pitt's palace. EX—TRAAAA!*

"So you're the bird-watcher." One of the sheriff's deputies approaches me after speaking with the head of
security.

"I like monarch butterflies too, but it's off-season."

"I don't think you'll be able to see them from the county jail."

He's in his early forties, with a shaved, bullet head, ruddy face, and storm-drain eyes. His chin flees into his neck.

"Listen, bro." The other deputy steers me from Pitt's security. "None of this needs to be a big deal. Cooperate and you'll probably avoid probation and only have to pay a fine. But you're going to need to tell us who you work for."

"I'm not working for anyone. I was hiking at the state park and had no idea that this is private property."

"You can tell your ridiculous story to a jury. See if they believe you," the mean one sneers. "Trespassing under Penal Code 602 is a misdemeanor and carries six months in County and a thousand-buck fine. But seeing as though you've got binoculars on you and there are multiple witnesses who caught you on the property of one of the biggest movie stars in the world when he's just trying to throw an innocent child's birthday party, well, shit, that's a 601, aggravated trespass. A felony means a three-year iron vacation from bird-watching. All expenses paid."

In these situations, you revert to instinct. Any sign of weakness can and will be used against you. Panicking only makes it worse.

"Am I under arrest or am I free to go?"

"We didn't say you're under arrest," says the one who keeps threatening to go human. The uniform tag reads,

QUISENBERRY. "We'll take you back to your ride soon enough."

His partner jokes a few minutes more with Pitt's people. His name tag reads, SALMON, which I hear him explain is really pronounced "Sal-Moan." They're periodically looking back at me with contempt. Quisenberry keeps gently trying to get me to tell him who I work for, insisting that he'll cut me a break, but I refuse to alter the story.

When Salmon returns, he announces, "We're going to get a statement from the gardener. He says he saw you across the highway, reading a book this morning."

"Are you not allowed to read past the mean high tide line?"

He digs his fingers into my arm, leading me toward the front. There are at least three or four different buildings on the property, each capable of being someone's dream home. The main dwelling looks like the fanciest shack for the world's wealthiest beach bum. Expensive toys line the expansive driveway: surfboards, Jet Skis, and dune buggies. Vending machines for soda and Guinness beer line the front entrance.

The gardener disembarks from a golf cart: a middle-aged man with a tidy mustache and plain baseball cap. Eyeing the Guinness machine greedily, Salmon pulls him off to the side.

"Yes, sir, that's him, that's the guy," I watch him say. Salmon scribbles notes and smiles with an undertaker's charm. Quisenberry keeps telling me that it'll be fine, but I should think about lawyers.

Who should appear then but none other than Mr. Smith, Tyler Durden, the Twelfth Monkey, who is actually more on his Floyd from *True Romance* game today, wearing a V-neck white tee, shorts, and flip-flops. Everyone halts at attention to salute el capitán. Salmon gives Pitt an *I got this* finger point.

At first, Pitt barely pays attention to the scene, heading to the beer dispenser for a cold one. Cracking it open, he appears to realize what's going on—that I'm the paparazzo diabolique. He removes his designer aviators and reveals the countenance that sold one hundred million magazines. The blond-haired, blue-eyed Mickey Mantle–as–shredded-matinee-idol. His skin is perfect. His expression is wrenched with disgust. He shakes his head slowly, confidently, letting me know that I've lost.

There are no handcuffs, no cross-examinations, no mug shot. The deputies escort me to their cruiser and drive me back to the state beach lot. No one says much. When we arrive at my battered 4Runner, they park diagonally, taking up three spots in the crowded August afternoon. Salmon turns on the cop car's flashers so that all the families gathered with their buckets, shovels, and coolers will take note of the very bad man emerging from the back seat.

"Can I get my keys back now?" I ask politely.

I'm attempting optimism: I've seen Brad Pitt and Angelina Jolie, gotten confirmation of the party, and

avoided a booking photo that would make me a permanent contestant on the summer jam screen. Current en-
tanglement aside, I've satisfied *People*'s requests.

"Not so fast, Annie Leibovitz." Salmon chuckles. "Seeing
as you were caught breaking and entering, we have prob-
able cause to search your vehicle."

"Trespassing and burglary are two different sections
of the legal code."

"Look, kid, the law is just a set of recommended
guidelines. You might have taken a prelaw course, but
that's all bullshit. The law is whatever we say it is. And
since you just gave us permission to search your car—"

"No, I didn't!"

"Sure you did."

With a weak smirk, Salmon nods at Quisenberry and
tosses him the keys.

"Take a look. I'll write the citation."

Quisenberry shrugs his shoulders and opens the passenger side door. He grabs an email printout from the
People editors that I brought in a fit of conscientiousness.
It's primarily directions to the compound, but also a few
choice things that I'm supposed to observe.

Salmon eagerly grabs the "evidence" from his partner.
Quisenberry continues his lackadaisical search. First, the
back seat, filled with books, magazines, CDs, and half-
empty water bottles. Then, the trunk full of broken head-
phones, old concert flyers, a basketball, and writing pads
filled with illegible scrawl. He finds my backpack, containing a few grams of weed and shrooms, and a dozen
Adderall that aren't prescribed to me. And now I'm going

to jail. A necklace of sweat beads my forehead. My back spasms. A funereal baritone breaks out in my head: *This is the end, my only friend, the end.*

"You've already got what you want," I mutter. "I've got an appointment in a few."

"Gotta report back to your editors at *People* magazine?" Salmon laughs, reading the emails.

I ignore him.

Quisenberry raises his eyebrows apologetically and opens up the backpack. But he fails to notice a second zippered compartment containing the contraband. Sealing it up, he slams the trunk, hands me back my keys, wallet, and phone. This is no break he's cutting me; he's just bad at his job. They keep the binoculars.

With a dramatic rip, Salmon tears the citation from his ticket book.

"You're a lucky fucking prick," he says. "No jail for you *today*. Just make sure you show up in court on the date listed at the bottom of the ticket. Because if you don't, they're gonna have a bench warrant out to eat your ass."

A nod. Head, body, and pulse convulsing. Opening the front door, I stab the keys in the ignition, and get the hell out of there as fast as possible.

The 101 gliding south across the Santa Barbara coast is among the most charismatic scenery in the world, but it could've been the city dump for all I cared. It took twenty miles to get my blood, brain, and vital organs to work at something resembling normal capacity. At State Street, I exit the freeway to get lunch in the downtown Old Mission–style district. I need some fish tacos, a margarita, and a place to plot what to tell *People*. Of course, I've forgotten that it's Old Spanish Days, the annual celebration where dizzy tourists and UCSB students drink too much tequila and memorialize the simpler times when the Franciscans used the Chumash as indentured servants.

Only one person can offer sound advice.

"You just hit the jackpot, mate," Oliver tells me after I call him from a low-lit Mexican restaurant way off the Strip, filled with hanging plants and fading posters of Tijuana bullfights. "Brad Pitt's security guards pushed you around like that? Falsely imprisoned you? That's gotta be $100K, easy! Screw finding you a lawyer to deal with the citation. You need to find one to file a massive civil suit. I know a guy."

I'm in no mood for more controversy. My only concern is how to finesse the situation to avoid getting fired. But how much to tell? I'm supposed to be on Pitt watch for at least another twenty-four hours.

We settle on a compromise. I'll tell *People* everything—except for the appearance of the sheriff. I'll retain my own lawyer, and who knows, maybe they can even get the ticket dismissed. As long as it's discreet, the magazine never will need to know that the law is involved. Besides, I don't even have to appear in court until October.

The editors are thrilled. What courage in standing up

to Pitt's carabinieri and escaping without a scar. *It's worth it for the reportage.* Confirmation that not only are Pitt and Jolie there, but that it's the child's birthday party—reconnaissance work that completely redeemed all previous blunders. *Oh, you think we can get a shot of the party from the helicopter? Let me call New York to see if we have the budget.*

I'm dreaming that they'll tell me to head back to LA. A *job well done.* But even though I've been roughed up, they want more. "Maybe just play it safe for the rest of the day. Have one of the photographers pick you up and hang out in the car with them. Come back tomorrow morning—say 9:00 a.m. again—and report back to us. We'll play it by ear!"

I slip back to my hotel in Solvang for a quiet dinner, smoking a spliff in front of my Danish novelty inn. The next morning, I'm up at 8:00. A quick scramble to buy a cup of coffee, a protein bar that tastes like peanut butter cement, and the Sunday paper.

If everything goes to plan, I'll be home by midafternoon. Take it nice and easy: park within eyesight but far enough away so that there can be no repeats of yesterday. Beagle will post up in front in his Celica, partially shielding me from visibility. I'll stay for a few hours, tell the editors that it's fruitless, and collect my thousand-dollar payday. More than enough to buy weed and psychedelics for self-medication.

For the first hour, I scan the *Los Angeles Times*. Two more suicide car bombs in Baghdad. A Mexican immigrant scours the Arizona desert for the bones of his daughter, abandoned by smugglers. There's a nationwide cement shortage, and two LAPD sergeants are suing the department for $10 million claiming that they were scapegoats in the Rampart scandal.

We're across the interstate, perched on a slight ridge next to a pasture where horses roam freely. Every five minutes, security stomps outside the citadel, staring at us with binoculars. Each time they do it, I get slightly more nervous, but I keep on telling myself that I'm safe on public land.

Around a quarter to eleven, a black Suburban with limo tints drives past, heading up a gravel road toward more big-money mansions carved out of old Spanish ranchlands. In my rearview mirror, I see him make an abrupt U-turn. He creeps parallel to my car and unrolls the window. It's Pitt's head of security, and he didn't bring doughnuts.

"YOU LIED, MOTHERFUCKER! YOU LIED!"

Imagine true possession. Popping veins, smoke-colored eyes bulging from a pink face, the vocal pyrotechnics of a professional wrestler in a promo sketch. I roll up my windows and lock the doors. He beats on the glass with simian rage, inches away from my face. This is probably what it feels like right before you get murdered.

"YOU'RE GOING TO JAIL, MOTHERFUCKER!"

Whipping out a camera, he starts snapping photos.

"HOW DO YOU LIKE YOUR PICTURE BEING TAKEN?! IT'S GOING TO BE ALL OVER THE NEWS!"

Before he can get a clean shot, I block my face with the paper. One of yesterday's janissaries, now sleeveless, with barbed-wire tattoos on both arms, joins on an ATV. They've boxed me in.

"MAYBE YOU CAN JOIN THE AUDUBON SOCI-ETY FROM BEHIND BARS!"

I lower the paper and flick him off.

"I'm leaving, I'm leaving! Just move the fuck away!"

"IT'S TOO LATE! THE COPS ARE ON THEIR WAY NOW! THIS IS A CITIZEN'S ARREST!"

I consider staying put. After all, this is public terrain, available to you, me, and the pack of brown horses eating grass about fifteen feet away. The cops ostensibly can't arrest you for being legally parked and reading the newspaper. But they can and will, for anything they want, which is whatever excuse they make up. I take another peek at the security head's face. He looks like the guy in a platoon "accidentally" killed by friendly fire.

I honk four times loudly. Neal Beagle has been watching the proceedings with curiosity, although not enough to get active. He spins his neck around, and I give him a *move up* nod. He starts the Celica and slides left to let me escape. I'm gone before the chief goon can even put his camera away, swerving toward the freeway a few hundred feet away. The Barbed-Wire Bro on the ATV follows in rabid pursuit.

I hit the freeway heading north at 60 mph, but the ATV is turbocharged and keeping pace. The Suburban isn't far behind and is gaining speed. They follow me onto the freeway without hesitation. They don't just want to catch me, they want to stick my scalp outside the fort for a warning.

Glancing in the mirror, I gamble toward the fast lane. The ATV struggles to top 70. No chance. The Suburban is a tank, but he's gunning at top speed and in a few minutes he's running even, veering inch by inch into my lane, trying to force me into the concrete median.

I pump on the brakes and dart behind him, then right, then right again. Before he can counterstrike, I merge onto the 1, outgunning all traffic on the way to Lompoc. No arrest today. He'll have to go home and kick his German shepherd for sport. On the off-grid highways, I start a roundabout detour back to Los Angeles, and by the time I reach Ventura I'm almost able to breathe.

◆

For two days, I'm *People*'s Sexiest New Hire. The editors rave over my report and profusely apologize for coaching me into a misdemeanor. "Big things are ahead . . . clear your future." I set a date to quit my day job.

The relief lasts until Tuesday at lunch, when a call from a blocked number interrupts my dalliance with a carne asada torta. It's probably *People*. The editors mentioned that as a token of gratitude they're going to try to list me for the Young Hollywood gala, a chance to introduce me to more of the staff and offer initiation into their exuberant family. Or maybe it's about my next assignment. Teen Choice Awards season is here again.

It's *People*'s interim bureau chief. She greets me with the tone of your third-favorite grammar school teacher, reluctant to mete out discipline but aware it's in the job description.

"Hey, uh . . . weird question to ask, but you didn't by chance get arrested on Brad Pitt's property last Saturday, did you?"

"No, I wasn't arrested." A pause. "Not technically."

"What do you mean, 'technically'?"

I explain the interaction with the cops and the citation. After she discovers my omission, the sympathy drains from her voice.

"Yeah, I'm going to need you to tell this to our lawyers. They'll have a better idea how to handle it than me."

"It's just a notice to appear before a judge. They didn't cuff me or take me to booking."

"Well, *Page Six* just called. They're reporting a story about your arrest and want comment."

"But I wasn't actually arrested!"

"It doesn't matter. They'll report what they want."

"What does that mean?"

"No one will know until tomorrow morning."

I can't eat or form a coherent thought. My skin turns cold as the abandoned sandwich. My head is tar. *Page Six* is the gossip rag as great destroyer. A vindictive, petty, seven-day-a-week ritual in the *New York Post*: it breaks sex scandals and divorces, places blind items that cause bicoastal speculation, and made Donald Trump and Paris Hilton famous. It's fanatically read by everyone in the media and entertainment industries, and the tens of millions who live for misfortune. An infraction as trifling as mine normally wouldn't be fit for print, but this involves Brad Pitt and Angelina Jolie, and most importantly, the opportunity to shade the reputation of their ostensibly sinless rival.

I'm in a shirt and tie in an Azusa strip mall, a chain-store suburb about fifteen miles east of Pasadena. In a half hour, I'm scheduled to interview the CEO of Naked Juice—recently appointed by the Connecticut venture capital firm that owns the company—about his plans to upgrade their product line to become a more valuable target for acquisition by a billion-dollar beverage multiconglomerate. But all I can do is stare at the yellow-and-red liquor-store sign across the street, deliberating buying a bottle of something brown.

Within ten minutes, I'm on the phone with a New York lawyer. He asks me to tell the story all over again, which I do, eliding no details. After I read him the information on the ticket, he offers encouragement. The trespassing charges won't stick because there's no proof of intent. The search of my car was likely illegal too. "Don't worry about responding to the notice to appear in court. Time Warner will take it from here."

I stagger into what might be the worst interview of my life. Pure hieroglyphic incoherence on my end. I'm sorry, Naked Juice CEO. Thank you for the Green Machine smoothie on the way out. It goes down less effectively than the half pint of Jack that I buy at the liquor store on the way home. There's no point in heading into work the rest of the day. The bottle is empty within the hour, chased with bong rips to blot out the nausea. Maybe I'll wake up tomorrow and it will be nothing. The story won't run and I'll be offered a third chance to sketch some shaky path forward. Or I might be twisted metal in the next demolition.

Half-drunk, I shoot hoops at the elementary school playground across the street from my apartment. Between the liquor and rust, my jumper is all bricks, and I get winded from the cigarettes that I keep trying to quit. I feel washed-up and possessed by a leaden nostalgia for childhood summers. The dread that consumed me each August, where I was unable to stop time and avoid having to return to school. But now I'd trade almost anything for a sense of a coherent future—one where if I sank my free throws, fate would handle the rest.

I'm twelve hours away from possible national humiliation, sweaty, and on the verge of puking. So I head back to the apartment, shower, change, and walk to the Frolic Room.

On the way there, I holler at Oliver to explain the latest developments. He wants to come through, but can't because his three-month-old daughter, Emma, has colic. I call a few of my high school friends, but no one is willing to come to Hollywood on a Tuesday night. So I keep ordering whiskeys on the rocks underneath the saucer-shaped red-and-yellow ceiling lights, staring mutely at the polished mirrors and the mural of Einstein, Clark Gable, the Marx Brothers, and Marilyn cavorting together. This was the last place anyone saw the Black Dahlia alive.

When the void is fully scrambled, I walk home feeling like I'm waiting for the lab results to explain why I'm vomiting blood. What follows is a free fall masquerading as sleep.

The next morning, my phone acts as my alarm clock. A granite light filters through my permanently tangled venetian blinds. I look at my caller ID. Oliver.

"Do I want to know?" I mumble, squinting at the collage in my room, suddenly struck with the urge to tear it all down.

"No, but you probably should."

"What's the headline?"

"'*People* Paparazzo Popped Trying to Snake Pitt.'"

"That's not very good. Read me the article?"

"Which one?"

"What do you mean?"

"You're at the top of *Page Six* and you're in the *LA Times*. B8."

"By name?"

"Your first, last, and middle name, age, everything on your driver's license down to your address, height, and weight. At least there's no photo."

"FUCK. They probably saved it for the *Daily Mail*."

This is what Oliver reads to me:

People Paparazzo Popped Trying to Snake Pitt

They may purport to always take the high road in the seamy gossip game, but anyone familiar with the industry knows that *People* isn't as spotless as it claims. On Saturday morning, a reporter for the dowdy grandmother of glossies was arrested for trespassing on **Brad Pitt's** sprawling Santa Barbara coastal estate, in an attempt to gate-crash the fourth birthday bash of **Angelina Jolie's** son, **Maddox**.

Xxxxxxx Xxxx Xxxxx, 23, of Los Angeles was taken in custody by the *Troy* hunk's security manager, **Ofer Shapiro**—who made a citizen's arrest—and will return to court next month to decide whether to press charges against this would-be paparazzo.

The intruder was spotted standing with binoculars on a bluff overlooking Pitt's property, said **Sergeant Erik Raney** of the Santa Barbara Sheriff's Department. The estate, which includes the bluff, was not fenced off but had a NO TRESPASSING sign, Raney said.

After escorting the uninvited guest back to his car, police found a printed email containing directions to Pitt's house—addressed from *People*'s LA bureau chief, **Samantha Sprague**.

"The correspondence gave him directions to the property and directed him to see what he could see—lights, trucks, parties—and report back," Raney said.

Pitt's publicist **Cindy Guagenti** says, "It's too bad that the media can't respect people's privacy. If the media continue to trespass on private property, they will be arrested. This is getting out of control."

A *People* editor insists that their "reporter" "inadvertently trespassed on the beach. He regrets it."

It looks like *People* are going to need more than people; they're going to need some good lawyers too.

"What does the *Times* say?" I ask.

"Basically the same shit, except they've got a quote from the cop saying that you didn't appear to be a photographer or staff writer for *People*. Just 'some kind of scout or forward guy.'"

"What do you think I should do?"

"Have you quit your day job?"

"Not yet."

"I'd say go to work and hope that your boss is sick and offline. If not, you might need to sabotage the office wireless."

I splash water on clammy skin, shave, throw on my suit and tie, and attempt to shovel a bagel and coffee into my stomach. My boss is neither unwell nor offline. His office door is closed, but through the glass window I notice an unread *Los Angeles Times* folded on his desk. We wave to each other, and I flash a faint smile.

I spend the next three hours refreshing Google every eight seconds, hoping that the story dies a rapid death. My answer comes at noon, when the AP blasts it to every major newspaper, radio station, and news channel. Then it goes international. The UK and the former Commonwealth run with it hard on a slow news day. It's a CNN news hit too—directly after a segment about Iraqi women afraid of the new constitution being too indebted to Islamic law—right before Pharrell is revealed as *Esquire*'s "Best-Dressed Man."

Errors abound in every version. For all the lies attributed to the tabloids, conventional media isn't much better. I'm called everything from a paparazzi photographer to a reporter to a binocular-toting rogue tangentially connected to *People*. No one knows that I wasn't actually arrested. In one version, I'm bailed out of jail. Others give an incorrect court date, where I'll be arraigned. In every retelling, the cops and security are unimpeachable voices of authority. No one asks for my explanation.

I become a piñata. There is, of course, a karmic irony in being forced to finally understand the spirit of celebrity arson that pervades the tabloids. But there is no numbing retreat into fame, fortune, or the adoration of millions. I just feel worthless.

The senior editor with the Alternative Nation posters sends a sincere apology for everything that happened, and says that she'll holler when people start to forget. It's fine. I forgive her. What is she supposed to say? *He was just some poor schmuck that we fired out of a cannon to see if he'd land standing up? He regrets doing it in a fire hazard zone?*

My editor at the business paper ignores me all day.

Around five, he gently calls me into his plaque-filled office and asks me to shut the door. You know how this goes. This is a very respectable and bespectacled journalist employed by a very respectable financial publication—one that prefers that its new hires avoid becoming targets of infamy. "What if they Google you?" I thank him for the opportunity and tell him that I understand. He'll write me a letter of recommendation if I ever need one. Now, if I'll excuse him, he has a few more things to attend to.

I drive home through clots of traffic on the 210. The sun is bright and hard, a bitter taunt, and my air-conditioning is coming out of only one vent, weakly. The downtown skyline is sheathed in smog. My phone rings, but I ignore it. Another call. This time, I can't help but look to see who it is. Alice Van Bronx of *Nova*.

She speaks in her sarcastic seen-it-all-before chime. "You didn't *tell me* you were going to be famous."

"It was a last-minute decision."

"When did you start working for *People*?"

"This was only my second time."

"And presumably your last?"

"I think my invitation to their Young Hollywood party was withdrawn."

"I could've told you never to trust anyone so self-consciously . . . cheerful."

"Did you know they operated like that?"

"Everyone does," she says. "Buck up. At least you broke the news that Brangelina are official. You making the news forced them to confirm."

"I'll add it to my résumé."

"Don't worry about the bad press," she says, a twinge of actual concern in her voice. "We'll all be chasing after another acorn tomorrow, and then another one the next day. By the weekend, no one will ever remember your name again."

10

While Kevin Parties, *Loneliness Is* **Killing** Britney!

This Love Is Toxic: <u>DIVORCE</u> Him!

READERS POLL: Is It *Acceptable* to Shoot Paparazzi?

All words fail me. Nothing can accurately distill the hexed combination of heartbreak and grief, depression and rage, self-loathing and guilt. Of course, lingo exists to convey the agony of defeat. I'm smoked, cooked, flatlined, and knocked the fuck out. I'm in the refrigerator, the lights are out, the eggs are cooling, the butter is getting hard, and the Jell-O is jiggling. I'm saturnine, woebegone, despondent, and disconsolate. But no thesaurus supplies an adequate match in the aftermath of my tarring and feathering.

I spent a full day trying to look up words in foreign languages, but even then, it appeared futile. Several viable candidates emerged from nation-states familiar with darkness and shame. The Germans contribute "weltschmerz" to my self-diagnosis, which *Encyclopedia Britannica* tells me is the feeling experienced by an individual who believes that "reality can never satisfy the expectations of the mind." Hence, the patient endures extreme world-weariness and sadness about life. From the Czech exile Milan Kundera, I wallow in litost: "a sudden insight into one's own miserable self . . . First, a state of torment then a desire for revenge."

We're getting closer. There is certainly weariness and sadness, misery and torment. And it's true that I'm rooting for *People* to have a precipitous circulation drop and for *Babel* to bomb. But it's clear that no one will answer my acrid prayers. I know that it's all my fault. It doesn't excuse *People* for setting me up and letting me take the fall. Pitt's security had all the humanity of hangmen, but I bumbled into their gallows. And the cops, well, they did what cops always do. I could have said no at any point, but I was willing to sacrifice myself on the dirty altar of my own ambition. And now the blade had fallen.

For a week, I barely left bed. Smoking what was left of my weed, I rewatched *Seinfeld* DVDs and developed a newfound empathy for the time that TV cameras caught George smeared in hot fudge at the U.S. Open. But my humiliation was more embarrassing than televised gluttony and more debilitating than mere job loss. My whole

future appeared stillborn. A reputation prematurely ru-
ined. An identity synonymous with laughter.

In a sense, Alice Van Bronx was right. No one will
remember my name, but Google results live forever. Even
my past became infected. Casual acquaintances, old
coaches, half-forgotten rivals had all caught me on the
news. A high school basketball teammate ran a GeoCities
website still read by a few hundred of our classmates. As
the joke of the day, he photoshopped me behind bars in a
prison jumpsuit. Friends texted asking if I needed help
with bail. Most messages went something like *wtf lol.*

About two weeks after my disgrace, Hurricane Katrina destroyed the Gulf Coast. An American city was
underwater, a legitimate apocalypse was unfolding, and
my own woes became inconsequential. By the time
Kanye went on that telethon to say that George Bush
doesn't care about Black people, I'd snapped out of my
fugue state.

I peeled myself off the mattress to survey the extent
of my radioactivity. Desperate for work, I applied to
every seemingly legit job opening for a writer. All background checks revealed the Pitt "arrest." The judge
dismissed the ticket before I even had to appear in court,
but no one cared. It turned out that to convict someone
of trespassing, you need to prove intent *and* the clear
breach of a barrier. But the actual truth couldn't compete
with the news reports.

By the fall, I accepted reality. I gave up my apartment
and moved back into my tiny childhood bedroom in

Venice. My mom wasn't pleased to relinquish her converted yoga room. My cat hated cohabitating with a Boston terrier that terrorized her for sport. But my bank account was depleted; my mood was a morgue. I needed a rebuild.

For a few weeks, some retro normalcy reemerged. I hooped a few times at the boardwalk, and the familiar patterns of strangers arguing about foul calls was almost as soothing as the crashing sea. With a few high school friends who stuck around, I got cheap burgers and beer at Hinano's, one of the last unreconstructed dives. Something was reassuring in watching them spark up conversations with randoms on Washington, bumping the first Game CD, and pretending that the last five years hadn't happened.

Until one morning in November when I woke up, checked the blogs, and discovered that my old editor Brenda You was dead at thirty-eight. According to *Page Six*, the coroner was calling it a suicide. Perez Hilton claimed that she'd intentionally overdosed on sleeping pills, then joked how *Nova*'s chief editorial director probably killed Brenda by putting a "voodoo curse on her former right-hand woman." Apparently, Brenda was about to enroll in med school and had been loudly criticizing our former boss in *Radar* magazine. They said that her unpublished novel was set to have been a *Devil Wears Prada* tell-all about the tabloids. She left behind a twelve-year-old daughter.

The news triggered a second wave of sorrow. Other

than Oliver, Brenda was the only one who looked out for me. She saw the absurdity of it all, but never seemed to let the job poison her. She was cool—not in the trendy sense, but with a timeless sophistication and remove. The kind of person born with a cigarette between her index and middle fingers. Now, she was another subterranean memory, a last bright spot snuffed out.

I texted Oliver to see if he had more information, but they hadn't spoken since Tana's. The funeral was private. All that was left to do was listen to Brenda's advice. For the next four months, I barely left the house to work monkishly by the glow of the laptop. Drinking pot after pot of coffee, I listened to melancholy instrumental hip-hop and thrashed at the novel that I thought that I'd discarded.

I've mentioned the book a few times by now, but haven't really elaborated. It was about what led me to start writing in the first place: the death of a college basketball friend, killed in a tragic car accident on a hazing trip. Ever since his funeral, I'd resolved to write a lasting testament to his existence.

A former college classmate's parent knew a literary agent, a thoughtful and kind septuagenarian who had once repped Jim Morrison and Jackie Robinson. He agreed to read it and meet up after. *This is going to be The Break*. But at a Brentwood Coffee Bean, he offered praise and encouragement, then told me straight-up that he couldn't sell it. No one was buying debut novels from unknown writers without MFA pedigrees.

I eventually landed a $13.50-an-hour job working the counter at Hear Music on the Promenade—a Starbucks-owned store that sold pumpkin spice lattes and over-priced acoustic Alanis Morissette CDs to older Gen Xers who didn't know how to illegally download. It was a pretty depressing gig, and my boss never let a shift go without telling me how his "progressive metal" band was going to be the next Tool. But I told myself that at least I was "closer to the music." Once or twice, I almost believed it.

After a year of dreamless sandstorm sleep, I started to have that same vision again. The one where I'd fly through the desert until I reached the oasis. But in this version, it was winter and all the doors of the cabin were locked and all the windows sealed shut. No matter how hard I tried, I couldn't enter. So I sat outside, cross-legged in the bone-chipping cold, until I woke up.

Venice changed too. The set that ran Oakwood was being slowly pushed out by real estate prices and court injunctions. Cheap bungalows along the canals became "fixer-uppers" bought by creative executives who built modern two-story glass monstrosities. Abbot Kinney might as well have been Beverly Hills. Dogtown spots became dog bakeries.

I felt trapped where I had begun. And just when I begin to abandon all hope, Alice Van Bronx called—from a private number, like always.

"Oh, hellooooo, I was worried you might still be in jail," she says, with an English-breakfast-tea-laced-with-ricin voice.

"I escaped. Surprised you didn't cover it at *Nova*," I respond.

"It sounds like you miss your old beat."

"I retired young. For the good of all involved."

"That's actually what I want to talk to you about." She raises her voice an octave. "I'm not at *Nova* anymore. And I could use your help."

"I'm sure plenty of recent college grads would sneak into Lindsay Lohan's hotel room to steal her hair for drug testing."

"Don't be cute. You know we'd pay the maids to do that." She pauses. "I'm at *HI!* magazine now. They've got tons of money and are looking to beef up their staff."

Last fall, the deep-pocketed, royal-family-obsessed British tabloid *HI!* launched a U.S. print edition. Founded by a pornographer-turned–media mogul, it was technically the largest weekly magazine in the world, publishing twenty-three separate editions from Australia to Azerbaijan, with a claimed global readership of thirty-one million. The goal was to conquer the American market by grossly overpaying for exclusives. Jessica Simpson appeared on the first cover as part of a multi-issue deal in which she got $200,000 and the right to approve everything. Paris Hilton was offered $2 million for the photos to her wedding with the Greek shipping heir, which never happened.

"What do you know about *HI!*?"

"Less than you'd expect."

"I don't want you out here risking probation . . ."

"The ticket was dismissed."

"I'm just joshing with you," Van Bronx says, with the tone of a soccer mom who would silently celebrate when a child on the opposing team got injured. "We're a kinder, gentler celebrity magazine. This is the legitimacy you pay for. Our relationships are far too expensive to blow up."

"Why do you even want me . . . after everything?"

"Are you kidding?" she snorts. "You're notorious. My bosses specifically asked for you when I mentioned that I knew you. Who could question your dedication?"

"I can't do that anymore."

"I want to offer you a retainer. Three thousand dollars a month, for let's say an average of four assignments. Red carpets at the Oscars, the ESPYs, summer blockbusters, after-parties, things like that. And if you do more than four, we'll pay extra."

From the other room, the dog barks loudly. My cat leaps up on my stomach, scared and shrieking. I stare up at my walls full of teenage fantasies: rap lyrics and *Maxim* models, movie posters with punch lines long played out, and NBA All-Stars now nearing retirement age. Everything suspended in amber since I was sixteen. When you're drowning, you can't be too picky about how you're rescued.

"No offense, Alice, but there's always something you're not saying."

"I do have one other tiny request."

"See? I'm sorry, Alice, but I just can't."

"Have you spoken to your friend Oliver lately?"

"Not in months."

"He's gotten a little, well, it's hard to say with Oliver."

She hesitates. "He's shooting Britney for us, but let's just say that he's not a reporter. And I need someone alongside him who can verify the facts. You'll never have to work with anyone else. And I know you and Britney have such a *special* connection."

"This is your sales pitch?"

"Do me a favor and think about it." She lowers her voice, as sincere and maternal as she can get. "I really would like to work with you again. It'll be fun."

I tell her that I'll think about it, and I try not to, but my hourly wage barely covers gas and weed. My mom keeps asking when I'm going to get a real job, and I can't pay off the credit card debt accumulated trying to keep my apartment. No one else wants to hire me, and this is a guaranteed payday. Before the week is over, I'm signing the contract in Alice's corner office in Beverly Hills. It's furnished with its own espresso machine and an autographed poster of *Miss Congeniality 2: Armed and Fabulous.*

Malibu's Serra Retreat is the most desirable zip code in America. Thirty zealously patrolled homes serenaded by postcard mountains and ocean panoramas. It's where Britney and Federline live, alongside their neighbors Matthew Perry, James Cameron, and Mel Gibson. And on a crisp February afternoon in 2006, they're joined by paparazzi stretching out a quarter mile—all the way from the enclave's black gates to the Malibu Village, a luxury open-air mall along the highway. I don't recognize any of them.

It's been six months since I've been out in the field. Seeing the competition reignites *what am I doing with my life?* dread, and the fear that Gibson will leap out of a bush, wave a butcher knife, and scream, "I am going to destroy your life and eat your soul."

Still, I can't deny that part of me is curious to witness the spectacle. In the front of his Escalade, Oliver and I wait for Britney. He insisted on my presence because she's rumored to be visiting her ob-gyn, and a photo of her walking into a medical building could confirm her second pregnancy. Oliver's problem is that thirty barbarians are wandering in the middle of the road, hurling cigarette butts and Burger King take-out boxes, waiting at the gates.

This isn't the first time that I've seen Britney since returning. Last weekend, I covered the red carpet at the Sony/BMG post-Grammy party, where she and Federline rushed through. They didn't talk to reporters other than one who asked who made the tight leather skirt that Britney was wearing. "I don't know, I designed it," Britney responded and kept moving. They made a show of constantly smiling and holding hands, which suggested either total happiness or a bad attempt at faking it.

"Oh, she's fucking miserable. Didn't you see the cover of *Nova* last month?" I shake my head. "They're claiming that he fucked a porn star named Kendra Jade in Vegas!"

"Did he?"

"He kicked it with her, but I bet he didn't. Too risky."

"So why does it matter?"

"Mate, anytime you have to explain to the mother of your newborn child about what *really happened* in Vegas between you and the star of *I'm a Dirty Filthy Cocksucking Cunt*, you've already fucking lost."

Their lives are a Möbius strip. A half-true tabloid story would get picked up by a reputable outlet, which would make it impossible to ignore. The paparazzi hounded the two of them from Malibu to Louisiana, hungry to capture them at unflattering angles and weak moments. The surveillance bred never-ending paranoia. Any awkward interaction became grist for the headlines. Then a friend or family member would sell secrets for a few thousand, causing more fights and distrust. It's hard enough to balance everyday partnership with the insomniac stress of having a newborn. Add in a constant churn of slander and it's practically impossible.

"Have you not seen *anything*? Not even the *Us* piece where she canceled his credit cards, took back the Ferrari, and spent her birthday alone in Hickville?"

Shaking my head, I tell him that I haven't read a tabloid since my one day as a main character.

"Oh, come off it. I know you heard 'PopoZão.' *PopoZão!! PopoZão!! PopoZão!!*"

That's Oliver's purposely bad imitation of Kevin Federline rapping.

"I mean, that's my ringtone."

Of course I've listened to Federline's debut rap single. Few songs were ever so swiftly and systematically maimed. In case you were unfamiliar with Brazilian slang, Federline loosely translated "PopoZão" on its first bars: "In Portuguese, it means 'bring your ass' / on the floor, and move it real fast." The social internet was young and just becoming aware of the heady power of communal hatred. And there was no softer target than a backup dancer–turned–white rapper appropriating Brazilian baile funk, rhyming "I want to see a kitty, with a little bit of titty / want to know, where I go, when I'm in the city."

YouTube became a clearinghouse of "PopoZão" parodies. The host of *Inside the Actors Studio*, James Lipton, declaimed its lyrics on Conan O'Brien. *Billboard* called it a "monument to mediocrity." Mind you, this was right after *GQ* named Federline one of their 2005 "Men of the Year" for fulfilling the id of the collective psyche, knocking up Britney Spears, and professionally living his best life. The headline read: *Meet the American Husband: Trophy Edition*. None of this helped the marriage.

"Everything was bloody hunky-dory until last fall. That's when it all started to get *really* berserk." Oliver catches me up on what I've missed. "You should've been at the baby bash, where one of the paps got popped with a pellet rifle outside the gate. Her security denied it, but those buggers definitely played a part. Lucky bastard. I bet he settles for six figures."

The *Los Angeles Times* had recently run an article about whether it was acceptable to shoot paparazzi. Opinions were mixed. In an *Elle* interview, Britney de-

scribed pregnancy as mind-blowing, healing, and thera-
peutic. Kabbalah was "feeding her soul." But a sense of
betrayal and manipulation was clear. Britney complained
to *Elle*: "Those closest to you . . . who might think they
have your best interests at heart . . . don't."

When the baby finally arrived in September, it was
bedlam. A police cruiser going ninety in Malibu attracted
the paparazzi teams permanently camped outside Britney's
gates. Before breakfast, the *National Enquirer* broke the
story, which caused UCLA Medical Center to be inundated
by entertainment reporters, paparazzi, and helicopters.

The globe devoured the news. *IT'S A BOY*. But for a
day or two, no one even knew his name. *Us* said it was
"Preston Michael." MTV News wagered it was "Christian
Michael." *Access Hollywood* won with "Sean Preston."
The next morning, Britney officially confirmed it in a
People exclusive. They acquired the first photos for a clean
million.

And if you believe the rumors, her second child is
already in utero.

"What the hell happened?" I ask Oliver, nodding my
head at the invasion currently occurring on this Malibu
street.

"You mean, who are these tossers?" He fiddles with
the radio, settling on a T-Pain paean to strip club love.

"They look like they escaped from a photography
workshop in San Quentin."

"One or two probably did," Oliver says, sparking up
his third joint of the hour, each chased by a Benson &
Hedges.

"Welcome back." He takes a long drag. "Everything is digital, mate. Who needs to know how to take a fucking pic? It's point and shoot. Any yabbo can do it. Most of the Brits bounced. X17 and TMZ are hiring the valet, the pizza boy, the hobo panhandling by the Old Spaghetti Factory. And if it don't work out, they just find another."

The analog world had begun to hollow out. The chief exception was what *The Washington Post* called "Print Media's Hot New Star"—tabloids. *People*'s circulation is up to almost four million. *Us Weekly* claims a 24 percent sales increase. *In Touch* and *Nova* enjoy "spectacular circulation gains." Just two months ago, a vicious new competitor entered the fray: TMZ, a joint venture funded by AOL and Warner Bros.

"This fucking up your business?" I take a hit of the joint.

"It's fucking up everyone's business." Oliver unrolls the window and spits. "The price of a good photo halved in the last six months. Online don't pay shit, and they jack all our photos. It's a race to the bottom. Three hundred paps in LA alone now—and they ain't minting real stars. Sure, there's more famous people than ever, but no one gives a fuck about the nitwit who wins *The Amazing Race*."

The shift is visible in the twitchy stares of the paparazzi. Small-minded mercenaries concentrating on the task at hand. The endearing-but-morally-adrift gallery had been replaced by the replicants.

"What are you going to do?" I ask.

"I had to let a few of my men go. I can't pay for tips as

much as I used to, but I'm still here." He runs his fingers through his clavicle-length curly hair, now thinning from stress and genetics.

Grabbing his binoculars, he tries to detect movement beyond the gate. "I'm the best, and quality wins, right?"

"You ever think you'll end up living in a place like this?"

"I used to think it was a no-brainer," he says, dragging deeply from the joint. "A few million-dollar years, some smart stock investments, and then I'd sell the business, buy a place on the water around here. Maybe a cottage on the coast of France for holiday. But, shit, I don't even know anymore. I moved to America because it seemed like the best place to live on your own terms, but you can't outmaneuver Time Warner—those are real fucking gangsters."

He catches himself in a moment of weakness and volleys it back.

"What about you?"

"Where else would I go?" I ask. An uncomfortable silence settles, and I change the topic. "Well, cheer up," I say with the little enthusiasm that I can muster. "Maybe Britney will finally realize that you're the one she's been waiting for."

"Shit, the way it's going, I don't think I'll have to wait long."

Oliver unspools more events from the last six months. A story about a Britney and Federline sex tape led them to file a $20 million libel suit against *Us Weekly*. But the judge tossed it from court because Britney "put her modern sexuality squarely, and profitably, before the public eye." Multiple nude scenes from *Chaotic* were used as evidence in the ruling.

He tells me about Britney's postpartum depression and fury at Federline's constant clubbing and weed smoking. When Britney visited her dying aunt Sandra in their small Louisiana hometown, Federline hit every bottle service club and craps table in Vegas. While she was at home with their newborn, he was spotted dancing with Ashlee Simpson at Element and flirting with a "pretty dark-haired girl in her late twenties" at a dungeon called Mood.

The tabloids count down the days until the divorce filing. They swear that Britney's up all night binge eating. Even a concerned Timberlake supposedly called a few weeks ago, urging her to ditch the marriage if she's unhappy. His people deny the report. Britney's PR person gives a particularly unconvincing denial of the rumors: "They're completely together . . . Just because they argue like a lot of married couples doesn't mean they're getting a divorce."

With a second pregnancy, the relationship is given a temporary reprieve. Maybe Federline will cut out the late nights. Maybe the Kabbalah will finally offer Britney the harmony and enlightenment she seeks.

The gates of the Serra Retreat finally open. Britney wheels out her silver convertible Mini Cooper, a leviathan bodyguard riding shotgun. In a sinister ballet, the paps toss their cigarettes, rappel into their cars, and walkie-talkie to the rest of their team. She's on the move and already stunned by the number of photographers.

But there's no chase. Instead of heading to the doctor, Britney hangs left into the shopping mall, intent on a Starbucks run. The paps double-park and leave their cars in the middle of the road.

Britney stops in a loading spot, then swivels and fumbles at unstrapping her four-month-old son from the car seat. The paps surround her like lions fighting over an antelope carcass. The three-hundred-pound bodyguard flings open the door, nearly knocking one of the paparazzi onto the ground, who screams, "I'll SUE."

We're a few breaths behind, but Oliver's minion, a graying *Daily Mail* veteran, is already snapping away, absorbing elbows. Photographers and videographers stack three deep, hopping on cars for a better vantage. The bodyguard—Big Mike I think—blocks a few of them, but he'd need an entire offensive line to hold the crowd off.

"They're going to kill her," I sneer as we hustle out of the Escalade.

"Never. She's the gift that keeps on giving," Oliver says, winded. "They may come close, though."

"BRITNEY! BRITNEY!"

"LOOK TO YOUR RIGHT, SWEETHEART!!!"

"C'MON, BRITNEY, SHOW US THE BABY!"

"JUST ONE PHOTO, BRIT, A QUICK LITTLE SMILE!"

On their way to Nobu, the idle rich of the land barely notice the mob. Mall security is nowhere. Britney looks petrified. She attempts to protect her child, but the exploding lights blind her. The baby wails.

Wrapping his arms around Britney, the bodyguard hurries into the coffee shop, guarding the door from paparazzi incursions. The paps splatter around the glass, pressing their lenses onto the frosted logo.

"Shouldn't we do something?" I ask Oliver, instantly ashamed at how naïve I sound.

"Mate, took a look around you: that's Bauer-Griffin, X17, Splash, TMZ, Finalpixx, and two dozen other freelancers attempting to sell these photos all over the world. Do you know how many people are paying their rent off of her? *You* tell them to stop. Maybe add a 'pretty please with nacho cheese on top.'"

The genteel British dirtbags are joined by hardened, unscrupulous men from Latin America, the Balkans, and the former Soviet republics. They hunch forward, these DSLR cyclopes, mumbling, "Yes, yes, good, good." Jackals sweating in cargo shorts and ill-fitting Ed Hardy tees, unkempt goatees, frowning unibrows, and jiggling rolls of flesh. Mirrored fake-designer sunglasses hide dispirited eyes.

When Britney orders her caramel frap, she freezes at the threatening storm. I can see her clearly. She's in a backless white blouse with a plunging neckline worn over a black bra, jeans, and flip-flops. Her pineapple-blonde hair is short and worn tied up, the roots just starting to show. Exhaustion and hopelessness crease her face. In the glass cage, she begins sobbing. An excited gasp erupts from the photographers who know that tears pay double.

A manager speaks to her but quickly drifts away. She continues weeping, burying her head into the infant. A worker in a green apron takes out a digital camera and starts shooting. Another employee indiscreetly joins. All alone, Britney burrows into her child, the customers pointing like toddlers at a zoo. The beach air is clean and cold and cluttered from the noise of the shutter clicks, the cackling of the paparazzi, and the motors of those escaping on the Pacific Coast Highway.

Oliver sizes up the angles and analyzes the winter light. Searching for a singular shot, he leaps catlike on the hood, sniping with precision. This has deteriorated beyond any single person's control. She's pregnant with her second child, fearful that she will never be able to protect either of them, let alone herself. What options does Britney have left? Disappear? Die?

Inside the coffee shop, she wipes the running mascara from her soft, wet skin. Her brown eyes are red and puffy. Nails chewed to nubs. The baby is oblivious and no longer crying. But there's only so long that she can hide. She scoops the child. Her bodyguard opens the door, forearming the paps out the way. They need to move fast.

Oliver descends from the roof to join the fray. Britney lowers her head into the top of the baby's skull. "Please stop, please stop!" she shrieks, her voice cracking. But her meekness, femininity, and Southern gentility only embolden the paparazzi. The bodyguard is outmanned.

Out of the mob, a soul-patched mercenary with a rooster tuft of black hair, skintight Affliction shirt, and ripped jeans aggressively shoves the paparazzi away from Britney's car. It seems like a chivalrous gesture, but he's making a show of it in the hope that she sees him—as though he's applying to be her protector. And even though Oliver isn't obstructing Britney's path, the would-be hero jostles him.

Oliver shouts back, "What the fuck, Adnan!" and pushes him hard. Once the paparazzo regains equilibrium, he lowers his shoulder and charges into Oliver's chest, knocking the wind out of him and breaking his camera strap. The lens shatters on the asphalt.

The skirmish offers Britney a window to slip into the vehicle. She and Oliver briefly exchange eye contact, but she no longer recognizes him. Hastily backing out, she holds tightly onto her son with the other arm. No time to put him in his car seat. The paparazzi sprint to their cars to follow—including the one that just slammed into Oliver. Who knows how much a photo of Britney driving with her infant on her lap might pay?

Staring at the broken camera on the floor, Oliver lets loose a string of "FUCK"s and "SHIT"s. But the paps are off on the next phase of the hunt, and his camera is wrecked, along with all of today's haul. We shake our heads silently, aware that something bigger than the camera has broken.

Looking at his Rolex, Oliver runs his fingers through his greasy hair and tries to give an unbothered smile. "It's drinking time in London."

He insists on going to Moonshadows, a fancy Malibu restaurant with a $40 million view. We stick to beers and whiskey shots and try to pretend that things will get better again soon. Disgusted by the devolution, I don't have much to say. You might think we witnessed something inhuman, but it's just humanity unleashed on a world where all the guardrails are actively being dismantled. A food chain where everyone happily consumes the product, but no one wants to take a visit to the abattoir that hides it. A cleansing and deboning occurring at each level, until the glossy images coax $3.49 impulse buys at the supermarkets from unbothered consumers who only *love to see the pictures.*

Tomorrow, the photos of Britney driving with Sean Preston on her lap will become an international scandal. The morning talk shows, nightly entertainment round-ups, blogs, tabloids, and PTA associations cluck their tongues at the sorry state of Britney Spears. The small-town teenage virgin was once a role model to their children, but they don't know *this Medusa*.

Britney offers *People* an exclusive about her "horrifying" encounter. "The paparazzi continued to stalk us, and took photos of us which were sold to the media," she says. "I love my child and would do anything to protect him." The statement is largely ignored. X17, who earned the biggest payday, claims that the pictures were snapped "in a very peaceful context, in which photographers exhibited no aggressive behavior."

Shortly thereafter, the Los Angeles County Sheriff's Department visits Malibu to interrogate Britney. It's the same week that Vice President Dick Cheney pumps his hunting partner full of lead. But the Transportation Secretary of the United States goes after the pop star, citing her as a textbook example of what not to do with children in the car.

"Recent photos of Britney Spears driving with her infant son on her lap are troubling," Norman Mineta says, while making Britney the honorary villain of Child Passenger Safety Week. "While Ms. Spears has acknowledged her mistake, her actions still send the wrong message to millions of her fans."

A <u>Baby</u>, One More Time!!

K-Fed BECOMES Fed-Ex!!

Bimbo Summit or Holy Trinity?

I live in someone else's dream. You can't fathom how many interchangeable Hollywood functions exist. Pre-parties and after-parties for the Grammys, Oscars, Golden Globes, Directors Guild, Screen Actors Guild, Kids' Choice, Teen Choice, and Young Hollywood Awards. Premieres and postscreening soirees. Album releases with free Hornitos. DVD drops at trendy nightclubs for the new season of *24*.

I'm at the 2006 Oscars. Stationed at the far border of the red carpet, past eight-foot-tall ersatz bronze statuettes, where no one outside of the Best Sound Mixing nominees can see me. Hundreds of starstruck acolytes, winners of a ticket giveaway, rock forward in bleachers erected on Hollywood Boulevard. They snatch at dark chocolates tossed by Wolfgang Puck, who tells everyone that the truffles alone cost $28,000. With each glamorous actor gliding into the auditorium—Jack Nicholson! Michelle Williams and Heath Ledger! Meryl Streep!—middle-aged fanatics and sucrose-eyed teens unleash Pentecostal swoons.

It is the year of "Make It Rain" as cultural manifesto. Venture capital wagers on the sticky machines becoming fastened to our palms. Obscene sums inundate Los Angeles, triggering brazen tax write-offs disguised as celebrations. The chasm between rich and poor expands in real time. *HI!* demands that I'm ubiquitous, and while it's not *People*, their sycophantic reputation ensures eager welcomes wherever I go. But the thrill is gone. It's just a job.

Mansion parties for the Helio Kickflip in the irrational altitudes just south of Mulholland, where minimum-wage attendants in red formal jackets retrieve Bentley coupes and Ferraris. Private Pharrell concerts in honor of the Samsung BlackJack, where Nicky Hilton, Kim Kardashian, and the Fall Out Boys drop it like it's hot.

At a launch party for the latest *Guitar Hero*, I briefly talk in a bar line with the internet's "it girl," Cory Kennedy, who has become a minor celebrity after her sleaze weegee boyfriend, the Cobrasnake, plastered her all over his blog. The Chloë Sevigny of the Sparks era is wondering why she's still here and where she's going next. *Do I know of anything better? I don't. Too bad.*

On the Fourth of July, a cosmetics company throws a party at a $32 million Malibu beach house on "Billionaire's Beach." It's two days after Lindsay Lohan's twentieth birthday, and she chain-smokes Parliament Lights and downs sea breezes in a stars-and-stripes bikini. The paparazzi snap photos from behind a literal line in the sand. She tries to light a sparkler in honor of the holiday, but it fizzles without exploding.

Another microgeneration emerges. *The O.C.*'s ratings ebb. Fox cancels *The Simple Life*. The latest phenomenon is MTV's *The Hills*, a spin-off of *Laguna Beach*, where the cameras follow a lightly scripted soap opera of young transplants drinking and fighting their way through Hollywood. The boundaries between television and real life start to blur.

Other stories vie for the bull's-eye—the expanding brood of Pitt and Jolie, Nick Lachey and Jessica Simpson's split, Jennifer Aniston and Vince Vaughn's romance, the thetan-spooked weirdness of Tom Cruise and Katie Holmes—but nothing can compete with the tribulations of Britney and K-Fed. Never before have a billion-dollar industry, millions of fans, and the gelatinous opinions of daytime talk show hosts been so focused on dynamiting a marriage—especially one involving young children.

Every day brings news that would seem patently insane if you tried to explain it to one of your ancestors. Fans launch DivorceKevin.com—for those "sick of seeing the train wreck"—where you digitally throw Federline over a fence and "put him back in his trailer." Another company releases a game where you pummel Federline until his skin flays. When Britney steps in as a human shield, you punch her until you eject the baby from her grasp.

Attacks escalate on Britney's weight, looks, talent, upbringing, work ethic, style, and parenting ability. *Nova*'s editor writes an open letter: "Look at what the last two years have done . . . The cheerful smiling face! The glittering career! The great body! They've all disappeared." A hit would automatically redirect the narrative, but she's pregnant and in no place to release new music or tour. But after two years off, she tells *People* that she's started to play piano in her home studio again, experimenting with live musicians and stripping down her sound.

Her PR team books her a segment on *Good Morning America* to visit young girls displaced by Hurricane Katrina; they describe meeting Britney as the best day of their lives. On *Will & Grace*, she parodies a blonde Fox News anchor who claims that "if you question our president, you're a dirty traitor." At the end, the character reveals herself as a "hard-core lesbian" named Peg, who is into "leather play, butch Black girls, and pulling the blinds."

TMZ makes its name on 24-7 Britney coverage. The tabloids sketch sine curves of breakups and makeups. Her lunch orders, vacation rentals, and attempts at decompression are dissected like the Dead Sea scrolls. There are fights on vacation, fights at gourmet dinners, fights at the club and about going to the club. Fights about his friends airing the couple's dirty laundry to the tabloids, fights about how he's spending all of his time in the studio, fights about buying a $300,000 watch without telling her, fights about how he neglected to mention ONCE AGAIN that he smoked weed at "the homie's crib."

More accidents. On the nanny's watch, her seven-month-old falls from his high chair, suffering a blood clot and minor skull fracture. Child services performs a "routine" investigation. The *New York Post* and *New York Daily News* publish front-page photos of Britney driving with the baby strapped the wrong way in his car seat. In May, she trips in New York and only a bodyguard's intervention stops the child from falling onto the concrete. A global assembly condemns her as an unfit mother.

The disarray leads to *Dateline*. She invites the NBC newsmagazine into her $10 million Malibu mansion for the most infamous interview of her career. The host, Matt Lauer, a quarter century older than Britney, calls her "sexy," "sexed up," and a "sexier version that the boys could like as well." Every tabloid rumor gets prime-time respectability.

In her jean skirt, flip-flop wedges, and three-month baby bump, Britney looks like she might have if none of this had happened, and she'd become a elementary school teacher as she sometimes dreamed. Instead, the hot television lights in Malibu leave her sweaty and flustered. Lauer probes about the shrieking headlines and marital woes, the paparazzi onslaught and the child-rearing mishaps, the constant accusations that she's a bad mother and what exactly she sees in Federline.

On screen, iconic clips from Britney's teenage videos are interpersed with tabloid images of her barefoot at the gas station or driving down Pacific Coast Highway with her baby on her lap. The producers are clearly aiming to depict a sweet Southern choir girl morphing into a trashy redneck swamp thing. Britney deflects ("I try not to respond to trash"), offers context ("Accidents happen with kids. Not everyone has eighty cameras on them"), and shrugs her shoulders at the celebrity bloodlust ("That's America for you"). As for her marriage, it has "no end in sight." Eventually, Lauer's condescension becomes too grating; Britney snaps at him, "You look at me like I'm a puppy."

No one calls it her finest hour. There is no on-site publicist, nor wardrobe, hair, or makeup. She isn't asking for pity, just a little understanding. But the more that Britney tries to locate her true self and exhibit it to the world, the more she's reviled. She tells Lauer that eighteen pregnant months have made her a hormonal wreck. Then she weeps and you can practically see Lauer calculate the ratings boost. Before signing off, he gazes into the camera and asks: "When it comes to Britney Spears, have the paparazzi gone too far? We want you to tell us by voting on our website."

The fallout is immediate. The tabloids mock her "rat's nest" extensions, her chipped nails, and the fake eyelash that falls out while she's sobbing. The Pittsburgh daily paper calls her outfit "ho gear." *Entertainment Weekly* chides Lauer for letting her off the hook too easy. In an essay on Trump University's website, Donald Trump writes that "Britney looked terrible. Her skirt was too short. Her makeup was messy. When she opened her mouth, it only got worse." He calls Federline "fantastic."

In an attempt to win back public approval, Britney does a nude pregnancy cover of *Harper's Bazaar*, a mom-life chronicle with *People*, and a banal back-and-forth with *HI!* where she talks about how much she loves "boo boos" (kids). When asked what she's learned about having a baby, she says that "nothing is what it seems." On her personal blog, Britney muses about how tigers are mysterious creatures on a constant quest for survival. Then she quotes William Blake.

On September 12, 2006, Britney enters Cedars-Sinai hospital for a scheduled C-section. The rumor is that she's expecting a girl, but Jayden James Federline, a healthy baby boy, exits the womb. Unlike with Britney's firstborn, the details are cloaked in mystery. For weeks, no one knows his real name. No photos are sold. A draw-bridge has been raised. People speculate that this might be the event that quiets everything down, a second familial addition to add gravity. This lasts for a month. Then, in a promotional appearance for his forthcoming debut rap album, Federline is ferociously body-slammed on *Monday Night Raw* by John Cena. The crowd thunders in approval.

◆

"You saw the video, right?" Oliver says, exhaling smoke out of his Escalade, knifing through Hollywood on a Saturday night. "It's like *Mortal Kombat* when you stick the harpoon through the bloke's chest and rip his head out the chest cavity!"

I tell him that I saw the video. Everyone saw it. About two weeks ago, it was YouTube's most popular clip of the day. While a camera crew filmed him for Canadian music television, Britney sent Federline the *I want a divorce* text. One second he's scrolling his Sidekick, the next his eyes became a total eclipse of the sun.

"I can't believe that I am saying this, but I almost feel bad for K-Fed," I say, lighting one of Oliver's Benson & Hedges. It's going to be a long night. "It's just getting sad."

"Oh, fuck me." He waves his arm as we pass the Amoeba on Sunset, billboards advertising the Gnarls Barkley debut and *The Beatles LOVE*. "He's a twenty-eight-year-old white rap wanker in a durag balling with wifey's money and talking shit like he's 'Pac. He's gonna get *paid*. He's asking for full custody and spousal support and I bet they pay him extra to sign an NDA."

I never had much positive to say about Federline, but didn't get any joy from his crucifixion. For all his flaws, the guy had a pretty good sense of humor about everything. He called himself the "luckiest man alive." The first song of his terrible rap album that no one bought was called "America's Most Hated." And for the last two years, he really owned the title. Even at George W. Bush's lowest approval rating, roughly a quarter of the country still loved him. Kevin Federline was the only villain that a divided nation could agree on. So he embraced it.

When TMZ broke the divorce news on November 7, 2006, the United States celebrated like it was Armistice Day. On *The View*, Rosie O'Donnell threw confetti into the air and declared, "Let me just say on behalf of a happy America, welcome back, Britney, we love you." *Gawker* hailed the end of "our long national nightmare . . . Cue the dancing in the streets! We're being serious here, actually." *Page Six* snarked that the divorce text probably read, "I H8 U, loser!"

For a week, Britney became America's sweetheart again. She rehired her original manager, Larry Rudolph, and on her first night as a single woman, they went ice-skating in Rockefeller Center. The PR spin reflected an obvious retreat to *you can go home again* traditionalism. She returned to the recording studio and showed off a freshly cut blonde bob in a surprise appearance on Letterman. The press hailed her "back to Britney body." Even her nemeses at *Us* wrote that "over a span of five days in the Big Apple, Britney turned one bitter split into a spectacular comeback."

The goodwill was tempered by a story in a British tabloid about how Federline was allegedly holding a four-hour sex tape for a $30 million ransom. The porn blog *Fleshbot* posted a nineteen-second clip purporting to be Britney going down on him. But within a few hours, it was revealed to be fake. Nonetheless, the report had legs. On CBS's *Early Show*, an *Us Weekly* reporter said that it couldn't damage Britney further because we'd already seen her at her lowest. Federline didn't deny the tape's existence for a week and a half.

"How's Britney doing?" I ask Oliver, who is currently steering the car with his knees, cigarette in one hand, slamming down a 5-hour Energy drink with the other.

We haven't seen each other much lately. Between parenthood and trying to keep his business afloat, his natural mania had morphed into a jittery flakiness.

"You ever read *Little Red Riding Hood*? The real version?" Oliver responds. I shake my head. "Well, the big bad wolf pops into the house and chows down on bony old grandma, then puts on the dress and bonnet, and scarfs Little Red Riding Hood when she walks in out of the woods. Ain't no happy ending."

"I'm not following the metaphor," I respond. "And I dunno if I trust a man drinking liquid speed from 7-Eleven."

"I'm saying we're all the wolf." He laughs and shakes one of the empty 5-hour Energy bottles. "Dawg, it's good for you. It's got vitamins."

"Is this Paris-and-Britney-best-friends thing real or just a PR stunt?"

"Paris Hilton don't have friends," he says, switching to a joint. "She calls Brit 'the animal,' because she never thinks before she acts. But Brit's valuable to Paris. Maybe they'll make a banger together. Maybe it just adds to the mystique."

"And Britney?"

"She's lost, mate. All alone, can't trust anyone, just wants to party and be deaf to the bullshit. And Paris is the queen. Problem is partying with her every night is like Keef in Tangier. You wind up in AA or buried in a Moroccan pauper's grave."

It's a quarter to ten on the weekend after Thanksgiving. Most of the *HI!* staff was back in their hometowns, which meant that Alice Van Bronx was destined to call. This time she wanted to send me to the hottest club of the minute, Hyde. I could say no, but there's never anything going on that week in LA. Besides, getting in on a Saturday would require the hand of god. I'd most likely be rejected at the door and check an assignment off my monthly quota.

They want me there in case of a Britney and Paris pilgrimage. For the last ten days, they've been inseparable. In the aftermath of the divorce, Britney took a trip to Kentwood to visit family. But on the way back to LA, she hit Vegas to record at the Palms Hotel studio with Dr. Luke. It's here that the resort's owner George Maloof formally reintroduced Gatekeeper to Keymaster.

The Britney and Paris honeymoon in Vegas included a $10,000 Britney blackjack victory at the Playboy club in a pink wig. Back in LA, Britney popped into Paris's American Music Award after-party, a few hours after presenting a crystal pyramid to Mary J. Blige. Reports described her as "inconsolable" after an opening sketch where the host Jimmy Kimmel lowered a Federline mannequin into a sealed crate, placed it onto a truck ("no damage will be done to his cornrows"), and dumped the fake corpse into the port of San Pedro. "PopoZão" played the entire time.

In one week, the paparazzi caught Britney stepping out of cars without panties four times. *Us* called them "Girls Gone Wild." *Nova* tried to make "Paritney Spilton" happen. The number of magazine spies embedded in nightclubs doubled. My own bottle service days had been replaced by formal parties and awards shows, where I didn't need to lie about my real reason for being there.

Back on Sunset again, the amphetamine reef of the Strip blinking to our immediate west, the spots always changing but never interrupting the insomniac rhythm. Oliver turns up the radio, booming "My Love," the interstellar valentine from Justin Timberlake, Timbaland, and T.I. It went #1 last week.

"This shit ain't helping," Oliver says. "Imagine you ain't put out a record in three years and your Mr. Marmalade sweater-vest ex becomes the biggest star in the fucking world. Again! Right as you split up! Brit can't escape him. People keep telling me she's bipolar and melting down, but leaving Fed-Ex is the smartest thing she's done in years."

The car sweeps past All American Burger. Same block where Hugh Grant was once busted for "lewd conduct" with a sex worker named Divine Brown.

"I need this," Oliver continues. "My wife keeps telling me we need to go back to London, and that this pap shit ain't working out anymore. For our girl, y'know. But if I can get in and talk to Brit, we can work out an exclusive deal. I was the only pap she ever rated."

"You really think that's gonna happen? At a loud-ass

club where everyone is one bump away from checking into Cedars?"

"Maybe not, but I ain't got more than ten grand for a photo in months. Payroll is due next week, and I need it to rain."

Hyde is on the same block as the Laugh Factory, advertising sets from Dane Cook and my old pal Bob Saget. Next door is Greenblatt's, where Marilyn always ordered the hot pastrami on mustard-brushed rye and where, several decades later, Southside Compton Crips claimed Puff Daddy ordered a hit on 2Pac. But the street belongs to the Brent Bolthouse–run lounge, give or take the two dozen paparazzi camped outside.

Within weeks of its formation in the spring of '06, Hyde became the throne room at the end of empire. Being basic cable famous didn't ensure admittance. This wasn't Studio 54; it was Andy Warhol's broom closet. Capacity was one hundred, and even that risked a visit from the fire marshal. It was the Hollywood club in final form, an ingenious leverage of supply and demand, where being snubbed at the door could mean public humiliation. No need for a VIP section when only VIPs can enter.

TMZ was headquartered across the street. Each day, they would faithfully broadcast the melodrama from the night before. Hyde was where Shanna Moakler socked Paris Hilton for kissing her husband and MTV costar, Travis Barker; in retaliation, a Greek shipping heir loyal to Hilton allegedly shoved the former Playmate down the stairs. Hyde was where Avril Lavigne spit on the paparazzi and where Nicole Richie collapsed before checking into a hospital.

The Fire Crotch Soliloquy of 2006 brought immortality. On a balmy night in May, Paris Hilton, Nicky Hilton, and Brandon Davis, scions of land, hotel, and petroleum fortunes, were tracked by TMZ and X17 from the Chateau to Hyde. The nightcrawlers bombarded Paris with questions about her rift with Lohan, who she was feuding with over a baron or two. The grandson of Marvin Davis, a porcine industrialist who once owned 20th Century Fox, acted as Paris's personal spokesperson.

Looking like a bloated and dying Elvis, Brandon Davis sweated and screamed into the camera: "Lindsay Lohan has the stinkiest, fucking sweaty orange vagina anyone has ever seen . . . She tastes like my Turkish father's ass . . . She's a whore . . . with a seven-foot-long clitoris."

In the background, Paris cackles and eggs him on. Two months later, she forgot to pay the bill for her storage locker, which contained multiple videos of her saying anti-Black, antisemitic, and antigay slurs. By then, she and Davis were beefing. To get revenge, he told the *Enquirer* that she was a racist. "Every Black person she referred to was a n****r."

Oliver parks the Escalade a few blocks from the club. I give him a ten-minute head start. It's left unsaid that we need to split up; two anonymous males trying to enter Hyde together on a Saturday is a suicide pact.

On the walk to the club, I'm shanked by déjà vu. This

is the block where it all started over three years ago. And now I'm a few weeks past twenty-five, still broke and slightly broken, bone weary. Wealth, celebrity, and youth are the only commodities on this corner, and even the latter is slipping away. Every attempt to escape the black hole failed. In the same span, Britney has been married and divorced twice, and birthed two children. We're back, like we never left. Everything happened, but nothing changed.

No self-respecting enfant terrible would pop up at 10:00 p.m., but my only hope is to leverage my lingering connections before the club fills up with A-listers. There are two entrances. Those seeking attention enter off Sunset, where the paparazzi take photos to be peddled to the highest bidder before bedtime. If you're searching for privacy, there is a second door in the back protected by glowering security and clipboard sentinels. That's the one we hit.

Even though it's a Saturday, there's no line yet. Most of the Hyde clientele are transplants and in Aspen, Tahoe, or Cabo for the long holiday weekend. A few people eye the door, but no one is shameless enough to go first. Lacking fear and restraint, Oliver makes a play. He stubs out his cigarette and saunters forward in a Burberry bucket hat, aviators, and a desert outlet mall sport coat.

I linger next to a trio of unbathed Australians. Von Dutch and trucker hats are out. The sleazy, pseudo-boho, trash-rock aesthetic is in. With long scraggly hair, blazers, and ripped vintage tees, it's hard to tell if they're homeless or received a 5.2 on Pitchfork. Near the entrance, Oliver yells at a bouncer, who leads him out by the arm.

"Listen, motherfucker, you got a lot of nerve trying to come in here owing me five racks," the bouncer spits venom, out of earshot from the other employees.

"Dawg, I've told you that you'll get paid when I get a big hit, which could be tonight if you let me in."

"You think I'm going to lose my job to let a pap in? You sure all that weed ain't laced?"

"I need to talk to Britney."

"Bitch, call her agent. I ain't got time for this shit. Get out my face until you have my money. Or else I'll find you."

With one hand, the bouncer violently shoves Oliver. The Australians give playful *didjaseethat* slaps to one another. Oliver storms off, rolling his eyes at me as he passes.

"You know that scumbag?" The bouncer looks at me, noticing the eye contact.

"Never seen him. What's his deal?"

"It don't matter. Oh, shit, I remember you. You used to go to Concorde all the time, right?"

I nod my head. Despite being six three, 250, the bouncer's name is Little D, a nickname acquired working next to Big D, a behemoth so supreme that he left to become Shaq's bodyguard in Miami. Over the years, I'd redistributed enough dirty tabloid money to pay for a semester or two of Little D's daughter's preschool tuition. It made me feel like Robin Hood.

At the front door, Jen, the incorruptible Checkpoint Charlie of Hyde, silently examines me.

"I should be on the list," I blurt before she can ask, having learned a long time ago that passivity implies that you don't belong.

She asks my name. Scans the clipboard.

"Who put you on?" she grills me, wearing a black skirt and gothic bangs.

"Don't you remember me?" I smile. "I used to be at Joseph's all the time."

"Never heard that one."

"My best friend said he handled it with Brent directly," I say, polite but firm.

"Who's your best friend?" She raises her eyebrows.

"Adam Brody."

"Seth Cohen?"

"He hates when people call him that."

"Where is he?"

"Wrapping up shooting. He'll be here by midnight."

"Shooting on a Saturday?"

Before I can answer, Little D interrupts. "It's cool, he's good people."

She frowns, eyebrows like slanted ski poles.

"Fine, someone has to be first inside. But don't even think about sitting in one of the banquettes."

Hyde is the city's most high-end haunt. Miniature crystal disco balls drip from a copper-leafed ceiling. Candles

flicker in iron sconces. The side tables are made of petrified wood. Ultrasuede walls dappled with pink-and-black
paisley. The unapologetically beautiful gaze at their reflection in smoked mirrors. All the perfumed unguents
and performative rituals of fame are present.

Stationed by the bar, I soak up industry gossip and
hubristic pickup attempts. I've been in these rooms so
many times that it feels strangely natural. The DJ, Samantha Ronson, spins "L.A. Woman." I order a third
whiskey on ice because I'm reminded of something Jim
Morrison once said: "Being drunk is a good disguise. It
means I can talk to assholes."

A Hungarian model with a Guess billboard humors
conversation, but mostly wants to know if I think she's
too old for "Leo." He's sitting in a crocodile leather ban-
quette with his *Blood Diamond* costar, Djimon Hounsou.
The model is twenty-four. I tell her that I think he's
dating an Israeli supermodel, but she just says, "So?"
Then she yawns and says that she's thinking about moving to Miami.

To my right is Colin Farrell, his facial scruff meticulously engineered at 4.6 days' growth. The Olsen twins
are here too. One dresses like a beatnik gymnast; the
other like a Romanian fortune teller. They greet Farrell
with a hug and kiss.

When Britney and Paris arrive, the music plays but
no one hears a note. The bartenders stop pouring, the
light smears into a soft crimson fog. It's slightly before
the stroke of midnight, perfectly timed for drama. Paris
floats ahead, tall, slim, and Sunset Tan bronzed. She's

wearing a ruffled white blouse over tight designer jeans, and a tiara headband. Her imperial blue contacts shield organically brown eyes. With a conqueror's gaze, Paris coolly weighs the situation.

All necks, male and female, curve in their direction as Paris flashes her fugitive smile. The baby-doll voice, the dumb-blonde schtick, create a requisite layer of fiction. She always knows the right angle and understands the cardinal rules of iconography. Being shrewdly attuned to the present allows her to see the future in which the only talent required is the ability to advertise yourself. The medium is the message, and the medium is a Carl's Jr. commercial where hamburgers are pornographically devoured by a platinum-blonde nymph writhing in a bikini.

Right now, there is no more divisive pop-culture figure than Paris, who's been attempting to go from a reality star to a renaissance woman. Her self-titled debut album was only a modest success, selling two hundred thousand copies in August, and landing a Top 20 single called "Stars Are Blind." She's the symbol of ugly entitlement: famous from a sex tape, parodied by P!nk on the hit "Stupid Girls," and recently arrested for a DUI in Hollywood.

Britney follows after Paris, skipping in slow motion. The Princess and Empress pursuing opposite ends of the same storybook, their paths perpendicular on Sunset Boulevard. If the Bel Air "celebutante" innately considered the entire world as her birthright, what was inside Britney awaited discovery. Her childhood was crawfish boils and auditions, not high-society balls and cotillions. The hidden majick glittered whenever she went onstage or into the studio.

The world Britney was raised in encouraged the fantasies, but the one she inherited was cold and confusing, filled with love and contempt to frightening extremes. Something, somewhere, had gone lethally askew, and she was chosen to be both weather system and weather vane.

Tonight, Britney wears a short black London-in-the-'60s dress, diamond earrings, and black high heels. Around her neck is a snake pendant representing sex, rebirth, and death. Her eyes are anxious but trusting. Her features are gentle, set off by a toothy and sincere smile. Paris escorts her to the bar, not far from me.

I overhear Colin Farrell ask his friend if that's really Britney. *It seems to be? Is it?* They haven't spoken in over three years—since he sent her that stupid gag gift. Better to play it cool, the friend says. They stay seated.

With purposeful volume, Paris tells Britney, "Who gives a fuck about Colin Farrell?! He's here every night trying to fuck a different model. He gets so wasted he probably can't even get hard."

Britney snorts like a slumber party. She's a creature of action, about to turn twenty-five and start fresh once more. Maybe she's a bit gullible, a little drunk, but not clueless. It isn't lost on her that the room always parts, the bartenders bolt in her direction. You don't just stop being Britney Spears.

Paris and Britney head outside to smoke cigarettes on the patio. The open-air space resembles a high school lunchroom hierarchy. Everyone here is a personage, but only these two are phenomena. A few clusters of the superlatively cool or well connected feint toward joining them, but Paris's contemptuous smile intimidates intruders. The few who know them personally—Mischa Barton's ex-boyfriend Cisco and a blond guy who may or may not be Rod Stewart's son—give them air-kisses on each cheek.

I'm smoking a cigarette so as not to seem like a total weirdo. From behind, a pair of arms wrap around my waist. I turn and face Jasper Lockheed, the girl who I used to hang with in my *Nova* days, but haven't seen in about two years.

"Where have you been all my life?" She puts the back of her hand to her forehead and gives a fake swoon.

"I threw all this away to become a yogic healer in Costa Rica. Call me Ocean now," I say.

She more or less looks the same. Her hair a little blonder, her jeans more low-rise, her eyes shadowed in the smoky raccoon makeup of the moment.

"Someone told me that you went to jail."

"Maybe spiritually."

"No, maybe it was like, just you were arrested?"

I shake my head. It's not worth getting into the whole story, because that would mean telling her that I'd been working for the tabloids the whole time that I'd known her. We were actually pretty close once, but she was too embedded in that life. By the time it felt like I could trust her, she would've seen my deception as a deep betrayal. So when I faded from the scene, we stopped speaking.

I ask what she's been doing.

"I dunno. Everything is so boring?" she says, gesturing to bum a cigarette from me. "My family went to Jackson Hole for Thanksgiving, but I just . . . *couldn't deal.*"

No one would've ever called Jasper easily impressed, but her eyes are a little harder than I remember. Her disposition has reached a final libertarian stage of jaded, where no one is to be trusted, everyone is out for themselves, and you might as well get as many free drugs as possible. She has existed in this underworld since she was seventeen.

"Are you still acting?" she asks me.

"Sort of."

"I did a Boost Mobile ad last year, and I was supposed to do a pilot for the WB, but then they shut down. Ugh, agents."

We talk for a little while about people that we used to know. Then the cherry reaches the filter, and it's clear that we don't have much to say to each other anymore.

"You know"—she looks at me with her glacier-blue eyes—"sometimes I think about something you told me once when we 'shroomed that one time."

I ask her what that was.

"You were pretty high." Jasper laughs. "I remember you telling me that no one could see what was inside any of us, but if you knew that something special and unique was there, I mean *really knew*, then it meant that it was real—and that whatever you were dreaming about would actually happen. At least if you worked hard enough and it wasn't too crazy and you were willing to chase that vision to the very end."

"It sounds like some mystical bullshit that I would've said while tripping," I respond. "I dunno if I believe that anymore."

"I don't know if I do either." She tosses the cigarette on the asphalt. "But it was a nice thought."

Back in the interior, the sleazy pseudo-producer who made and sold the Paris Hilton sex tape has appeared with the heir to a hamburger chain. They take the table from DiCaprio, who didn't fall for the charms of the Guess girl. Rod Stewart's daughter is here now with Paris's assistant, Kim Kardashian.

The DJ spots Britney and Paris at their table and queues Elton John's "The Bitch Is Back," which they shout along to like the entire room is watching. It is. At least until a quarter to two, when Lindsay Lohan whorls through the door like a raspy chaos phantom. By now, the Hungarian model has returned to me. She just gave out her number to the actor Lukas Haas.

"I can't remember what he's in, but I know that I've seen him a bunch," she tells me. Then she spots Lohan and whispers, "This is going to be ugly. Paris poured a drink on her last night at Guy's."

The Guess girl tells me about how Lindsay accidentally overdosed at the Chateau a few weeks ago on coke and Vicodin and Ambien and maybe a little nitrous. A friend found her unconscious at 9:00 a.m. and called a doctor, who covered it up, but word still got out, and now everyone won't stop talking about it. Lohan attempts to speak with the burger scion, but he won't entertain the conversation. She's here all alone, scanning the room to see who she should talk to and who to avoid. Lost eyes searching vainly for an escape.

Lohan is the duchess, royalty but a rank below. The true aristocracy will never respect her because she's a striver, forever beneath their bloodless inheritance. Her mother, an ex-Rockette who dreamed of fame but never made it. Her father, a Wall Street trader currently serving a two-and-a-half-year jail bid. According to the tabloids, he wants to become a minister when he's free.

Paris sees Lohan's distress and turns to Rod Stewart's daughter. They point and laugh. Lohan senses the scorn and becomes redder. The bartender screams, "LAST CALL." Lohan heads to the bar to order a drink. A fussy orange man in a suit—who the model tells me is a publicist—whispers something in Paris's ear. She never breaks her haughty expression. Britney bops her head to Prince's "Erotic City."

After Lohan gets a tequila soda, the publicist hurriedly shuffles her to a different corner to sell her on something. The Hungarian model leaves me to talk to Tori Spelling's brother, who tells her that he's filming a reality show with Rod Stewart's son.

Closing time. Security asks people to leave. Liaisons offer after-party options to Paris and Britney. The house raises the lights, causing everyone to squint, and the enchantment to break. Paris and Britney levitate toward the exit. The leathery little man drags Lohan back to Paris, who looks at her like a humbled servant. I can't make out the conversation, but Lohan is talking a lot, and Paris says little. The uninspired nodding of a ceasefire.

For a few breaths, Britney is alone, half-heartedly wandering in my direction. She seems buzzed and distracted. This is the closest that we've ever been. I notice how regular she seems. Gorgeous, sure. But there's something disarming, something still unpolluted by the contrived poses of Hollywood.

She locks eyes with me and smiles. I must have done the same because my feet stutter in that direction. I rack my brain for anything interesting or witty. "Hi" is all I've got. She says hi.

"I was an extra on your first video." The words thump out. "Just one of those guys sitting in the bleachers watching."

"Ohhh, I thought you looked familiar," Britney says.

My mind races toward the other dozen times why that might be the case. I'm pretty drunk now.

"I also wanted to tell you that I'm sorry."

"For what?" She wrinkles her nose, perplexed.

How can I confess everything? It would take too long and I have no business burdening her.

"For what you've dealt with. The paparazzi, the lies in the tabloids, Matt Lauer. You don't deserve it."

"Oh, it's no big deal." She smiles, snapping her head back, putting up her clementine-shaped palm—the people-pleasing way that she was taught when outsiders mention the breaking wheel. She meets my gaze and says, "You're sweet," so demurely that I almost pass out.

Before I respond, Paris links arms with Britney to lead her away. Security clears a path out onto Sunset Boulevard, where one hundred paparazzi gather. I see Tara Reid outside, waiting glumly at the velvet rope. She must have shown up after they hit capacity and been forced to wait. The *Girls Gone Wild* guy gives her a pity kiss on his way out. She doesn't remember me from our night at the Mansion.

Oliver is outside too, trying to get a photo amidst the maelstrom. We briefly make eye contact, but another paparazzo jabs him in the ribs, jockeying for position.

An obsessive fan babbles, "Please, Britney, just one autograph. Please . . . Please!" A female voice unleashes a banshee shriek. The valet is late bringing up Paris's Mercedes. The paparazzi form a flashing ring, asking Paris over and over, "Lindsay Lohan accused you of hitting her last night. Is that true?"

Wrapping her arm around Britney, Paris walks to the Mercedes. The paparazzi creep. Security shove them away. "Guys back up, back up!" Britney frowns, whimpering: "C'mon, guys, let us get in our cars." With fear in her eyes, Britney signs the autograph for the superfan. She tiptoes toward the valet and jumps in the car. The photographers angle themselves for an upskirt shot. Paris snaps at them: "Guys, don't be perverts."

As Paris scurries to the driver's side, the paps ask one last time, "Did you hit Lindsay?"

Spotting Lohan emerging from the club, Paris points: "There she is. You can ask her." The cameras pan to

Lindsay being escorted by the publicist. "Lindsay, tell them the truth!"

"Paris never hit me. She's my friend," Lindsay says robotically. Her head is lowered, and one arm held up in self-defense. "Everyone lies about everything. She's a nice person. Please leave us alone. I've known her since I was fifteen. Please stop making us hate each other."

To the delight of the paparazzi, Lindsay hops into the passenger seat. Britney sits in the middle. Paris beams confidently behind the wheel.

"Oh, this is classic," one paparazzi coos.

Mechanistic flashes. The girls are stationary in the car for only a few seconds, but in the morning, the photos achieve awe, scorn, and eternity. The *New York Post* puts it on the front page with the headline, "Bimbo Summit." Paris favors the kinder appellation: the Holy Trinity. Forever bronzered in immaculate unwrinkled youth, with smoke-glazed irises, beatific smiles, and blinding futures. The McLaren as a V8 Grecian urn, Paris driving off down Sunset, toward the edge of the earth.

They Try to Make Her Go to Rehab: Britney Says NO!! *Terror* in Tarzana!!!!!!

The <u>GREAT</u> Umbrella Assault of 2007

The levee breaks in the back seat of a bullet-black SUV. Winter darkness descends. The last of rush-hour traffic sighs out. Commuters inch home to the two-car garages of Tarzana.

No one knows that they're driving past the world's most famous pop star. Parked on Ventura Boulevard, she weeps softly, incognito, crumpled into the forgiving leather. Her continent-sized bodyguards hover in the front seat, vigilantly ensuring that no paparazzi come too close—or else. The threat trails off like an ellipsis.

Oliver scooped me an hour ago. His psychic intuition for upheaval was unmatched. By now, I've developed a rudimentary extrasensory perception too, but attempt to ignore it. But there are exceptions, and a perverse curiosity draws me toward what's next. You cannot sell half of your soul. So why not agree to ride shotgun in Oliver's Corolla on the way to the Valley? The Escalade was sold to pay off debts, in case you were wondering.

Over the holidays, things always quiet down. I played a lot of pickup basketball and got dragged to an awful local bar where drunk USC postgrads gambled on turtle races. On New Year's Eve, I covered a party on the Paramount back lot hosted by Carmen Electra. *HI!* was tipped that Cameron Diaz might be there—fresh off her breakup with Timberlake—but instead I watched Andy Dick euphorically fist-pump as the Killers played "Mr. Brightside" at midnight. In Vegas, Britney passed out in the club after leading the New Year's Eve countdown at Caesars Palace. Her team said she fell asleep. "A family insider" told the tabloids that it was too much coke, E, weed, and Vicodin.

In the cyanide dawn of 2007, the demons roared back without fear. For the first month, the nation breathlessly followed Britney's drunken nights and impromptu stripteases. But the events of the previous week unlocked a new intensity.

"Vesuvius is finna erupt," Oliver says, peering through binoculars toward Britney's vehicle. "This is what the whole blasted world is waiting on. People pretend they don't, but this is what they really want."

"Man, people don't want to see Britney crack up," I say. "There's a difference between loving drama and wanting to see her suffer."

"Fucking semantics, dawg," he says, sparking a joint. "This past week the rebound boy toy dumped her by text. Her parents and manager pushed her into rehab and she flew the coop, and now she can't even see her babies. They've got her on a fuckton of antidepressants and antianxiety meds. Don't give me the holier-than-thou bullshit like you ain't trying to see what pops off."

These interlocked narratives dominated the news cycles. After a brief fling with Britney, a male model told *News of the World* that Britney was sex-crazed, burnt-out, and desperately sad. A "little girl lost." Her wedding dress was said to still be encased in glass on her bedroom wall. Besides the model, she's romantically tied to Mario Lopez, her producer J. R. Rotem, Arizona Cardinals quarterback Matt Leinart, and Brandon Davis. On top of those rumored affairs, *In Touch* ran a cover about *Britney's GAY SECRET*, claiming that she's into lesbian porn and threesomes.

"You can see right through it," Oliver tells me, blowing smoke rings out the window. "The lezzy shit comes straight from an interview with a failed rap producer who happens to be one of Federline's mates. The worse they make her look, the more anxious she'll be to give him what he wants in the divorce. He ain't going back to delivering pizzas."

Emotions run far deeper than what tabloid suspicions can imagine. Postpartum depression compounds with grief over the January death of her aunt. Her old manager is back steering her career, dredging up primeval feelings of rebellion. He tells Britney that only rehab can right the ship. Her parents agree. So does Federline, who reportedly threatens her with drug tests in his battle for full custody. Anna Nicole Smith just accidentally overdosed at a tribal casino in Hollywood, Florida. Everyone worries Britney will be next.

Britney spends Valentine's Day with her children at the Four Seasons in Miami. In the morning, she jets to Antigua to check into Eric Clapton's Crossroads rehab facility. On arrival, the staff insists that she swap her short shorts for something more appropriate. Group sessions, shared rooms, and regimented schedules are mandatory. It may be located in a Caribbean paradise, but there are still plenty of rules impinging on her freedom. So she bolts after one night.

"The stewardess said she was doing the dash through the airport, late for her flight, and when she finally made it, the door to the plane was locked," Oliver says. "But she begged them to let her home to see her kids like the mum in *Home Alone*. And it's Britney fucking Spears, so what are you gonna do? But first class was booked, so she sat in coach, completely alone, staring into space, zonked, barely able to keep her shit together."

Nothing kicks up unrest like ten hours trapped on an airborne steel cigar with your brain devoured by the gremlins. By the time she lands in LA, the mania heightens. Her children are a sanctuary and reason for being. So she demands that her bodyguards take her to Federline's rental house. But it's his turn for custody, and he won't answer his phone. Now we're here.

Why we're *here* is less clear. We take stock of this distressed stretch of the boulevard: a ribbon of auto body and computer repair shops, small-time optometrists and kosher markets, insurance salesmen and nail salons. A constellation away from Hollywood, where no celebrity would ever intentionally tread.

Her bodyguard exits the vehicle and walks into an inconspicuous shop, set back about fifty feet off the Valley's main boulevard. Two dozen paparazzi and one familiar celebrity reporter burst from their cars like jacks-in-the-box. We're clogging the sidewalk outside of a small hair salon about to close. But before the blinds are pulled down, Esther, the proprietor, is greeted by a knock from a large man who politely informs her that "Ms. Spears is here, and she would like a haircut."

Oliver flashes an *I toldja* expression. Something is about to go awry. Superstars get $1,000 follicular sculptures from master stylists who come to them—not obscure Valley locales a step above Supercuts.

Shielded by her security, Britney scurries in like a frightened deer. A hoodie cowls her puffy eyes. A silver beaded necklace and Star of David poke out over it. The paparazzi pounce to the glass doors, thrusting their lenses against the windows, and the sonata of clicking shutters begins.

Inside the shop, Esther inspects Britney with maternal concern. Amidst the tumult, someone has forgotten to close a side window, so Oliver and I can hear everything. Britney's usually vibrant brown eyes are drained into a glassy onyx. The mirrors hiss. Two days ago, maybe three, she dyed her blonde extensions a chestnut brown, but *ugh, this looks bad, what was I thinking, and why do my extensions feel so itchy and tight?* She feels them clawing into her brain. Why does any of this matter? Why can't she do something drastic? Britney tells Esther, "I want you to buzz my hair off."

Esther refuses. She can't let herself be the one who scalps Britney Spears. Anything else, maybe one of those adorable Audrey Hepburn bobs, could salvage this situation and make her the most famous hairstylist in Los Angeles—provided you don't count any of those snobs in Beverly Hills.

"Honey, are you sure you're not just hormonal? You might wake up tomorrow morning and regret it," Esther counters.

"I WANT IT OFF! ALL OF IT!" Britney replies in a louder monotone.

"I'm not going to do it." The hairdresser throws her hands up.

"Fine, then I will!"

Britney fixates on a cheap rechargeable trimmer. No time to get fancy. This will do. Esther asks the bodyguards for permission. They shrug. "It's her hair."

Britney's eyes are submerged. Then she blinks and the cataracts evaporate. She flicks the razor on, gleefully savoring its cleansing *zzzzzz*.

As Britney stares into the teeth of the clipper, a hush sweeps over the photographers. Their game-winning shot is in midair, but victory is uncertain. For a second Britney contemplates retreat, but this feels right. Arms are raised, razor meets scalp, the extensions are hacked into lifeless scraps. Paparazzi capture this flipbook of despondence, Tourettically shouting, "Take it off, take it all off!"

"Maybe it'll be a nice way to start fresh?" the hairstylist tries to rationalize.

"Yes, yes, that's it," Britney responds, her twang flat-lined into numbness.

After the extensions are lopped off, only four inches of hair remain. Britney keeps going, flashing a fallen angel smile. The stray hairs curl on the floor like writhing snakes. As they hit the dirty tile of this obscure hair salon, I'm seized by an awareness that we have slipped into the other side of a portal with no return. The sins of the recent and distant past have finally caught up to us. We are through the looking glass, wading into a lightless marsh where everything forward exists in living death.

Britney stares into the neon haze of Ventura Boulevard. Her satisfied grin evaporates when she sees the cyclopes outside.

The paparazzi screech. "She's gone mental! What have you done, Brit! Britney, turn your head just a few more inches, show us your new look! We love you, Britney!"

Stepping away from the cesspool, Oliver exhales dramatically and shows me the shot that will be immortalized on magazine covers next week.

"The twenty-first-century *Mona Lisa*," he says.

I ask what we just witnessed, but he shakes his head, lifts his palms, and shrugs. The front of her head is buzzed to a single millimeter. Her crown waits for the final carving. The torment in her eyes coexists with a dazed glint of mystic liberation. Oliver snaps a photo that inspires the headline: *Britney Shears: Bald and Broken*. The chorus says that this is self-mutilation, a cry for help, the rock bottom that everyone can agree upon. For now,

Esther offers to help clean up the mess. Britney remains glued to the mirror, assessing what she has done and the fallout already encroaching.

"My mom is going to be so mad, she's going to kill me." Her eyes well with tears.

She runs her fingers across her scalp like an alien landscape, over and over, as if it could regenerate by force of will.

"It'll grow back, right?" she asks innocently. The stylist smiles and nods and tells her, "Your head is so nicely shaped."

Oliver and a few others scurry off to send the photos. It's like I've been turned to stone. A head hard and dense as granite, ready to cough up a lung. I feel I've been shown an autopsy photo.

The cars honk and hack across the luminous splatter of the Valley. Her bodyguards hand $50 in cash to Esther. Britney stands up, shakily lights a cig, crushes a can of Red Bull, and slowly walks to the door.

The pack follows her to a Sherman Oaks tattoo shack with a sleazy red sign. She gets a pink kiss on her wrist and a cross on her hip, listening to Janis Joplin at piercing volume. When an employee asks what spurred the head shave, Britney blurts, "I don't want anyone touching me. I'm tired of everybody touching me!" The paparazzi will still be there in the early morning when she quickly checks in and out of Cedars-Sinai.

Before that, Esther sweeps up, taking great care to save every strand. In hours, Britney's locks are placed on eBay, along with the empty can of Red Bull and the lighter left behind. The bidding reaches $1 million before the online auction house removes the listing. The authenticity of the hair cannot be verified.

"They're going to have her locked in a rubber room eating Go-Gurt by the end of the night." Oliver ashes out of the Corolla.

It's a week later. I'd agreed to meet Oliver for happy hour at the Red Rock, but two drinks deep, he received a text that Britney was leaving a lawyer's offices a few blocks west on Sunset. Before I can convince him otherwise, we're in a single-file paparazzi conga trailing Britney into the tureen of the San Fernando Valley.

"Who's 'they'?"

"You're still asking this question?" Oliver scoffs. "Label and management ain't gonna let the golden goose fuck off to go eat, pray, love, and sell homemade candles in Bali. Her parents went bloody bankrupt paying for dance classes, acting classes, and New York apartments. She's their retirement plan. None of them have real jobs except the sis, who only got that *Nickelodeon* gig because she's baby Brit. Wake up, mate."

"You can't force someone to rehab. Or make them record."

"No, but they have what she needs. The kids. And if she keeps partying, she ain't gonna see them again."

"A judge would understand the stress of having two kids in quick succession before twenty-five. Then a nasty public divorce. All while being stalked relentlessly. She just needs to get out of this purgatory."

"That has nothing to do with what a judge will say," Oliver retorts, as we cross Ventura, scything into the dull glow of this inert grid. "They'll see the shaved head, the dropped baby, wrong-way car seats, partying with Paris, and say that she's unfit. It don't matter if she is or not. The divorce lawyers will bring up the family alcoholism. Her grandmother that blew her noggin off with a shotgun at the grave of the infant child. Federline will be in an expensive suit that she paid for, pretending to be father of the year. No fucking chance."

The last seven days don't help her case. The morning after shaving her head, Britney popped up in an electric-blue wig at the Mondrian on Sunset. Bystanders described her as "desperate and confused." She tried to get a room, but lacked cash or credit cards. So the manager gave her free tequila cocktails at the pool, at least until she stripped to a bra and panties and started shaving her legs in the bathroom.

This was around the time she switched to a platinum wig and befriended two girls about our age, who were shocked and delighted to fulfill a generational fantasy of becoming best friends with Britney Spears. That Sunday night, her dad took her out for Creole food with the idea of "putting some sense into her." But after dinner, she crashed a private karaoke birthday party above the Roxy. One of my high school teammates danced with her there. He said she seemed "cool but out of it."

The gossip and allegations grew more outlandish. A

"friend" told *Us*, "She's gone crazy. She's on every drug you can name." Another would-be ally said that "she's depressed . . . and everyone has betrayed her. She doesn't know who is good and who is just in her life to make money from her."

There are theories that she shaved her head to seek revenge on her mom, or that it was an attempt to avoid having her hair drug-tested, or that it's a tribute to her late aunt, who went bald from the chemotherapy. All anyone really knows is that on the morning of February 21, she checks into Promises, the preeminent celeb rehab in Malibu.

Within twenty-four hours, she vanishes again. Britney suspects that Lynne and Federline are conspiring against her. Desperate to see her kids, she reserves a bungalow at the Hotel Bel-Air and tries to figure out a way to make the reunion happen. But when word reaches Federline, he threatens to file an emergency court order for full custody if she doesn't reenter Promises. This is why she rushes to see a lawyer on the Strip. It's Mel Gibson's and Lindsay Lohan's attorney, one of Hollywood's most vaunted. The only problem is that the lawyer only does criminal defense and tells Britney that she needs a family law specialist.

None of this matters. Everyone knows where we're going. Britney's distant cousin by marriage, Alli Sims, rides in the passenger seat of the Mercedes. The aspiring blonde singer looks like Britney's stunt double and has just replaced her last assistant, who was fired because management considered her a bad influence.

"I don't know what she expects." Oliver unrolls the window, getting his camera into position, as the procession stops outside of Federline's house. "It's his turn for custody. He ain't giving up the babies. Admittedly, I'll give you that *it is* fucked up that Brit's mum is in the house with him and the kids right now."

"What the fuck?" I scrunch my face. Oliver scrolls to "We Fly High" on the radio. "Of course she thinks they're plotting against her. Why would her mom take his side?"

"Fuck if I know." Oliver takes a break from singing along to the "ballin'" ad-libs. "But listen, mate, does she look well to you? No one knows what the fuck to do. Whether it's drugs or a mental breakdown or both, if they don't get her some kind of help soon, she's gonna find herself in the Twenty-Seven Club."

"She's only twenty-five."

"I'm trying to be optimistic."

Sims gets out of the car and rings the call box at a tall front gate. No one answers, but Britney knows that he's there with her mom and kids. She and her assistant circle the block, slowly being trailed by a train of thirty pap cars. They ring twice more. Finally, on the third attempt, Federline responds. It's Oliver's speech in different words. *No, you can't come in to see the children. This is tough love. If you don't head back to rehab, you won't see them anytime soon.*

A riptide dragging her out into a trench. She could deal with the 24-7 stalkers, the invective and outrageous lies, the creepy old men. She could handle the powerful figures always on the periphery, trying to control her, cynically shape her image, and reap the dividends. But she can't handle this. From here on, it goes black. There are no memories of what happens next.

Digital records and eyewitness accounts are less forgiving than the gainful deceptions of memory. We follow the Mercedes to a nearby Mobil station. Her assistant heads into the convenience store to pay, leaving Britney isolated and vulnerable. Oliver and the paparazzi pop out, a dozen poachers shooting through the windshield, blinding her with bilious yellow bulbs. Britney remains calm, wearing the gray hoodie that has become uniform, fingers pressed to her temple as if to quell a splitting headache.

I hide in Oliver's car, feeling like there's an abscess in my stomach. The windows are down and I can hear them yell, "How are you doing? Are you doing okay? We're concerned about you." Her cousin returns, the Mercedes peels off, the chase resumes.

It lasts a few dozen feet. The car pulls over in the parking lot of a Sherman Oaks Jiffy Lube. The paps form a triangle—where the celebrity turns away from one shooter to accidentally stare directly into another camera's lens. Her cousin Alli hops out and pleads, "Please, guys, don't do this. She's going through a lot right now. Please just leave us alone, please, just for once."

For the last year, X17's eight-man team of Brazilian immigrants, named "the Brazilians," have kept Britney in the crosshairs. They're snowing her: "C'mon, we'll leave soon enough, we promise. Just a few more photos. Just a few more photos."

Oliver barks: "You lames couldn't get a decent photo with all the time in the world. Just buzz off. Leave 'em alone."

Even though no one talks to him, the paparazzo who shoved Oliver outside of the Starbucks last year aggressively steps forward. His name is Adnan Ghalib, a low-level soldier of fortune with a cheap video camera, often risking death to be the top car stalking Britney.

"Why don't *you* pack it in? You're washed-up. No one buys your pics anymore," Ghalib says with a West Midlands accent. He looks like a peacocking System of a Down roadie: a rhinestone skull belt, a newsboy cap, and a scrawny isthmus of a soul patch snaking from lip to chin.

"Get the fuck out of my face, you fourth-rate chav," Oliver spits. "I looked you up. Your whole story is fiction. You didn't get those 'shrapnel scars' fighting against the Russians. You would've been in primary school when they invaded!"

Since joining the pack as a small-time wildcatter, Ghalib has repeatedly told the paparazzi that he acquired his fading facial scars fighting as a mujahideen in Afghanistan—where he was born, before his family moved to England.

"You better back the fuck up unless you want your own scars," Ghalib sneers. He'd also told everyone that hearing 2Pac's "California Love" for the first time inspired his move to the West Coast. "And these are from Kosovo."

Before the confrontation escalates, Britney bounds

out of the car, squeezing a green umbrella so tight it might snap. Nostrils flaring. A bald, clean head given an eerie glare in the chalky street light. Her eyes are dilated and bloodshot. Primordial rage, a half decade of persecution leading up to this moment.

Britney takes long, stabbing steps toward the paparazzi.

"LEAVE ME ALONE!!!!"

No more smiling and nodding. She won't accept the inquisitors anymore. In Abercrombie shorts, she shouts out of her platinum diaphragm:

"FUCK YOU!!!! GO FUCK YOURSELF!!!!!

With the umbrella, she thwacks a photographer in the back. Seeing another X17 paparazzi's empty Ford Explorer, she runs over and stabs the passenger-side door with the pointed end of the parasol. Swinging it like a baseball bat, Britney batters the car until the handle snaps.

Dropping it, she daintily skips back into the car and darts off into the night. No one dares follow. The stunned photographers mill around and examine the damage, murmuring variations on the same theme: the psychotic break is complete, she needs to go back to rehab, these photos are worth a fortune.

The press can only interpret it through a single lens: the victim is the aggressor, Britney's "lunacy" is a mental illness unconnected to daily life. When Chris Martin of Coldplay smashed a pap's windshield and slashed his tires, he was lauded. Slash from Guns N' Roses once got so high that he became convinced that killers with machine guns were after him, and he ran through an Arizona resort naked, using a housekeeper and then a lawn mower as a shield. This behavior will get you enshrined in the Rock & Roll Hall of Fame.

But there is no leeway for Britney Spears, the woman that the Disney conglomerate, then Jive, MTV, *Rolling Stone*, and every willing accomplice mythologized and packaged into the unblemished American ideal. And now Britney is bulldozing their prefabrications, shaving her head and fighting back against her jailers as an unhinged act of defiance. Death to the fake, long live the real—with all of its unhealed head wounds.

Oliver was right. This is the picture the world wants to see, but not the one it wishes to acknowledge. At the scene of the incident, the photographers banter with the gathering crowd. They assess the damage on the Explorer, handling the broken fragments of the umbrella like sacred petroglyphs.

The one who was just attacked turns to Oliver ebulliently, the insults forgiven. He asks him: "How much do you think I can get if I put my car up for sale with the Britney dents in it? Thirty grand? Forty grand? More?"

In a minute or two, a videographer from TMZ pulls up to survey the wreckage. They're currently mired in a cold war with X17, but in this moment, rivalries must be temporarily set aside. As Oliver and I drive away, the TMZ paparazzo begins interviewing the assailed X17 paparazzo, who smiles like a lottery winner, eager for his own turn in the spotlight.

OUT OF CONTROL
& HEADING FOR THE EDGE?

They Try to Make Her Go to Rehab:
Britney Says YES!!

Chicken & Fear!
Photo Shoot Meltdown Madness!

I was there, the seat belt strangling me, when our lives accelerated into a grand prix of blurred colors, fuzzy crowd noise, and Formula One cars buzzing past at high velocity. The audience was tantalized by the prospect of a crash. The winner was a secondary concern to the baleful height of the flames.

Weekly intervals between magazine drops became twenty-four-hour news cycles, which degenerate into an intravenous drip of content. The digital speed inducing a mild schizophrenia. Once-indivisible boundaries between terrestrial and online collapsed. The concept of time flattened to where what happened last week felt like it happened last year and what happened last year might as well have never happened at all. Memory pawned for the instant rush of an absent present. To stand out, everything needed to become a crisis. Nothing was particularly urgent, but everything is happening at once.

What's real and what's false ceased to matter much. We can agree that absolute truth was always unknowable and open for argument, but the mutation became unmistakable. Somewhere in the bardo of 2007, the condition of what was printed and viewed superseded objective fact. Sensationalist narratives sold best. A tabloid *Rashomon* became the images of modernity.

I put my blood money to good use. After a demoralizing year at home, I'd saved up enough to get a studio apartment in Echo Park. My cat was so pleased that she even came out of hiding. The place wasn't lavish, but it was within walking distance of a half dozen decent bars, concert venues, and taco trucks. And it was far enough away from Hollywood to pretend that everything after Western was a lucid dream.

But as Warren Zevon said, my shit was fucked up. The events of the last four years kept looping in my mind, and the footage wasn't soothing. Ever since that first night at the Playboy Mansion, I'd wanted to capture what I'd witnessed, but every attempt felt like cartoonish satire. I was too immersed for real clarity. Every syllable was burdened by shallow pity. Until I watched Britney's torture from up close, the pain and consequences felt like an abstraction.

Late at night, I write about the Vegas trips and Santa Barbara shakedowns, the panopticon monitoring and ethical codes desecrated in pursuit of the Big Story. The cynical mainstream press laundering news through the tabloids, exploiting our appetite for gossip while hiding behind a silhouette of respectability. I was old enough to know the truism that *every writer is always selling someone out*, but at least the celebrity magazines didn't pretend otherwise. They gave people the carnage they demanded, and when that failed they just created it.

I understood Britney as the heliocentric focus. She had been ever since the golden rays zapped me almost a decade earlier on that summer afternoon in Venice. And as you're probably wondering, I realized that I was exploiting her too. I regretted it and still do. But this was the system we were born into, and at some point, my own story became intertwined with hers, and theirs. Telling the whole truth was impossible, but there was the possibility of being sincere.

I was sent to interview the R&B Romeo Ne-Yo about his work on the forthcoming Britney album. No contact with her occurred, only the Jive go-betweens, who wanted something "triumphant but not corny." According to Ne-Yo, Britney was being sautéed for simple mistakes. "Take, for instance, the thing about her almost dropping her baby," he tells me in a golden-arches-shaped tent right before a sponsored concert on Venice Beach. "She was being chased by fifty photographers trying to get a picture of her. They don't tell you *that* side of the story."

At the Comedy Central Emmy party at a nightclub named after a bird of prey, one of the *South Park* guys was there. He'd just won "Best Animated Program." Someone asked if he'd make fun of Britney on the show next year. He replied, "I don't know . . . it's starting to look like Chris Farley territory. If someone's going down that hard, it's less funny. I don't have any compassion, but I don't want to be the last person to make the joke either."

What's really happening? Maybe only a half dozen in Britney's inner orbit have the answer. Their treasons are sold and spun and repackaged with added calumnies and known unknowns. Shortly after the umbrella bashing, Britney reentered Promises under the condition that Federline drop his petition for full custody. Her manager issued a public statement seeking privacy during this time of healing. Jamie Spears told *Fox News*, "She's a very sick little girl, and we're just trying to take care of her."

For the next month, Britney attended Twelve Step classes at a $48,000-a-month rehab. *Us* claimed that Britney was getting into "tons of trouble" for taking shopping breaks and refusing to cop to a substance abuse problem. An "insider" said the doctors were "shocked at what bad shape she's in" and prescribed her new anti-anxiety and antidepressant meds. When she checked out, *Nova* greeted her with a cover about her $130,000 plans for head-to-toe plastic surgery.

Something was different this time. The sweetness was substituted for spiteful wrath. It's said a $10 million memoir is in the works—where Britney will reveal Lynne as a money-hungry stage mom and expose the double-crossings of Timberlake and Federline. Blaming him for forcing her into rehab, Britney fired her manager Larry Rudolph again. Shortly thereafter, Jamie Spears emailed *Page Six* to apologize to Rudolph on behalf of the Spears family.

Through her rehired PR rep, Britney told the gossip mill: "I'm praying for my father. We have never had a good relationship. It's sad that all the men that have been in my life do not know how to accept a real woman's love."

"The comeback" became a collective obsession. Rumors of new music thrill a fanbase that has grown impatient in the four years since *In the Zone*. During this same period, Jive attempted to fill the void (and their coffers) by releasing a greatest hits compilation, a *B in the Mix* dance remix album, and a little-heard soundtrack EP to *Chaotic*. But Britney was supposedly back in the studio. She'd hired a personal trainer and embarked on a rigorous dance regime. Even *Nova* praised her sobriety and discipline. "She looks toned as the Britney of old."

She wasn't. It was obvious when *HI!* sent me to a few secret comeback shows that spring. They were neither a return to form nor a spectacular failure. Something seemed slightly dead in her eyes. The anxiety and fear were enhanced by the long hiatus. She moved a step slower than her dancers; the lip sync was a beat off. But no one minded much. Her shrieking apostles gushed that it was the best show that they'd ever seen. These weren't rubbernecking casuals clucking at her misfortunes; these were the true believers—celebrating her triumphs and suffering from her setbacks, offering unconditional empathy and love without judgment. Her struggles were communal. She's become a heroine for a malfunctioning society. If Britney can come back, hope can never fully be lost.

At Britney's final Southern California show, Lindsay Lohan watches from the VIP balcony alongside the Olsen twins. In a few weeks, Lohan loses control of her Mercedes and runs onto the curb in the early hours of Saturday morning. The Beverly Hills police arrest her after finding coke in the car. She's in rehab again by the end of the month.

Paris Hilton goes to jail too. A judge sentences her to forty-five days at a Lynwood detention center for driving her $190,000 Bentley with a suspended license. Within seventy-two hours, the corrupt county sheriff lets her parents pick her up in the middle of the night and whisk her back to Bel Air. Shortly thereafter, her *Simple Life* castmate, Nicole Richie, serves eighty-two minutes of a four-day sentence for cruising the wrong way on the 134 Freeway in Burbank off a blunt and some Vicodin.

Still, it's the summer of Britney. She's rid of her meddling parents and ex-husband. She dyes her hair antihero black. She has no management. Just a publicist, rotating assistants and bodyguards, several semiferal designer dogs, and us. Even joyrides to nowhere dominate the news.

A short list of the allegations from that season: Britney is drinking again and stripped to her bra in a club. She cut a deal with X17 and walked out in the middle of a photo shoot for her Elizabeth Arden perfume line. She got into a "horrifying slapping contest" with her mom and was fucking the security guard who rescued baby Sean Preston from falling to the pavement last year—at least until she discovered that he leads a double life selling sex toys over the internet. She applied for a waitress job at the club of the moment, Les Deux, where one night a mob of crazed stans ripped out a heckler's hair extensions for the crime of calling Britney a "whore who should go home to her babies."

Everyone vies for an exclusive interview, but *HI!* wins. My editors are ecstatic. This is their chance to replace *People* as Britney's preferred mouthpiece and elevate themselves to the A-list. It's their the biggest story since launching in America two years ago. Which is why I'm surprised and flattered when Alice Van Bronx tells me that she wants my help.

The idea was that I'd come up with questions, which I'd give to Alice to add to her own list. She'd be the chief interlocutor, but I'd get to ask a few at the end. Everything felt like it had been building to this. I didn't have any delusions about some revelatory confessional, where we'd develop an instant mind meld over art, music, and generational laments. But I was excited to talk to her, temporarily free from the layers that divide the divine from mortals.

I was spared from the more invasive questions. Alice would ask about Britney's irate trip to the set of her sister's television show, where she handed her mom a mysterious letter. She'd investigate the claim that the umbrella attack was the result of taking an acting role too seriously. She'd get to the bottom of the report where Britney supposedly claimed to be able to fly an airplane, and attempted to eject the pilots and stewards from the cockpit at thirty-five thousand feet.

I took it more seriously than anything previously assigned. I read fan sites, excavated old *Rolling Stone* covers, and watched clips on YouTube. There were questions about working with the Neptunes and LCD Soundsystem in the past, and Keri Hilson and T-Pain in the present, and queries about her initial inspirations, the new album, and her role in the songwriting process.

For preparation, I analyzed a letter that Britney published on her website in late spring. She described herself as a "bad kid running round with ADD" who hit rock bottom in rehab. It wasn't alcohol or depression, she wrote, but being overwhelmed, sad, and lost in the wake of her divorce. She feels that she's never good enough and misses her lost childhood. The time when happiness was as easy as dancing, singing, and watching movies every night with her family. Parenthood had dredged up buried memories and insecurities.

The diary entry sought understanding from a world far more interested in consumption. She just wanted "people to look at me differently . . . When you are a real woman and say what you feel . . . people just say you are a 'bitch.'" She acknowledged the surrealness of being twenty-five with your mistakes simulcast on *Good Morning America* and CNN. It's imbued with some self-awareness too: "There is your side, my side, and the truth."

Did I believe all of it? Not exactly. But that's not the

point. Since she was a teen she'd been taught to lie as a matter of survival and advancement. The truth was something to be stage-managed. The glossy persona eventually became inextricable from the actual person. *Swear to be a virgin, always exude sunshine cheeriness, present as wholesome as the milk from grandpappy's dairy farm.* Anything can feel honest when nothing seems real.

I wanted to understand what isolated her from her more conventional peers. What aroused our sublimated fantasies and allowed her to turn overlooked rhythms into colossal anthems? What numinous quality let her move the needle in ways that million-dollar marketing teams could never conceive? It was more than startling beauty, being surrounded by the right people, and selecting the right songs. What made Britney, BRITNEY?

These questions congeal in my mind as I drive up to a Hollywood Hills mansion on a Thursday morning in the middle of July. It's a Spanish Revival estate in the nosebleed altitudes that looks like it was originally built for a silent film star who failed to successfully transition to the talkies. About twenty-five of us are here. Top wardrobe, hair, and makeup artists. Video and photography crews. A half dozen writers, editors, assistants, and runners to handle last-minute whims. No expense is spared. If it all goes smoothly, it'll mean millions in newsstand sales, and if it doesn't, it could mean more.

It's ninety degrees by 10:00 a.m. but the house is frigid. Magazine photo shoots are always stressful—a banal orchestra of hired hands and talent trying to get what they need and get out. The idea is that she'll take the pictures first and then talk to us. But even under the most ideal circumstances, someone is always late or forgot something on the other side of the city, or the star storms off the premises when the cable channels are all wrong on their dressing room TV.

It's a soulless day rental with the gloomy ambience of a place uninhabited for decades. An expensive mess of overstuffed rococo couches, French windows, and Roman vases. High heels click down empty hallways, and weathered men rig hot studio lights. The junior *HI!* staffers try to guess how much Britney is getting paid to be here. "She's pocketing a cool $250K for this." "Nah, $500K, at least. She wouldn't get out of bed for less— even if you threw in all the Red Bull and Cheetos in the world."

With artists, you expect unpredictability. But this is abstract expressionism at its most experimental. Around 10:30 a.m., Alice Van Bronx answers her phone and immediately starts frowning. She rolls her eyes and puts one frustrated hand on her hip like a vice principal. When she hangs up, she's cursing under her breath.

"It's going to be catastrophic. I can sense these things," she tells me, an air of resignation already in her voice. "Britney *insisted* upon bringing her own clothes, as if Mr. Blackwell hadn't named her 'worst dressed.' Twice! But now, her assistant—who even knows which one this is—is begging for us to dress her."

I ask what we're going to do.

"Don't be stupid." She laughs like she's told a joke. "We've planned for every last contingency. We have exquisite gowns and dresses ready—if she's willing to come to her senses. You heard what happened Tuesday, right?"

I nod my head. A few days earlier, Britney took her toddlers to the beach and *shocked onlookers* by stripping to her underwear and plunging into the water. It was eccentric by Malibu standards, but conservative for the south of France. Nonetheless, the gossip world played it up like she'd posed for *Penthouse*.

By noon, the panic becomes contagious. No one necessarily expected her to show up on time, but *HI!*'s calls to her assistant are going straight to voicemail. By 12:30, I overhear Alice on the phone to New York attempting to figure out next week's cover in case Britney doesn't show. It's not lost on anyone that Britney recently blew off four straight *Allure* cover shoots.

By a quarter to one, Alice is convinced that the magazine should proceed with backup plans for another Tom Cruise and Katie Holmes cover. But then, outside, a screeching car and slamming doors. A paparazzi cortege bays in the distance. Britney and her entourage burst through the heavy Renaissance doors. The *HI!* staff exhale with relief.

Britney's almost an hour late, but Alice, the head photographer, and the crew are fawning. *Can we get you water? Coffee? An ambrosia smoothie carried up Coldwater Canyon by a passel of white-winged doves?* Britney wants none of their offerings. She's a rain cloud of nervous gestures, rambling speech, and distracted eyes. Her latest look-alike assistant handles all communication with *HI!*'s team. Three of her friends wander through the house inspecting the furnishings and searching for snacks. Her bodyguard keeps a close watch. Britney keeps a close watch on her new Yorkie puppy, London.

The stylist, a fashionable brunette woman in her thirties, gently guides Britney and the assistant over to a rack of clothes hanging in the middle of the living room.

"Ugh, this is, like, for gross old people," Britney scoffs, rolling her eyes and flipping through the wardrobe that the stylist agonized over for weeks. "Do you have anything, like, short? Or, like, tight? Or, like, sexy?"

"This" refers to a $5,600 Versace gown, a $6,000 pink silk design from Zac Posen, and a Vera Wang dress that costs more than my rent.

Alice turns to the photographer, out of earshot from Britney.

"She's out of her gourd." Alice sighs. "Poor thing. Which drugs do you think she's on right now? Coke? Adderall?"

"Is she drunk? She seems drunk," says the photographer, a trim graying man in a pin-striped suit.

"It's too early," Alice responds. "Who even knows anymore? She could just be on the Anna Nicole smorgasbord."

Britney looks like she hasn't seen the backs of her eyelids in forty-eight hours. The last thing she should do is a photo shoot and interview. I hear her friends complaining about how after this, they have to go film the video for her new single.

Hastily selecting an outfit, Britney banishes everyone to a different floor, save for hair and makeup. After twenty minutes, they glumly report back that Britney has exiled them. She and her friends are handling the styling now. This is when I realize that the interview will probably never happen, and even if it does, it won't be a multi-dimensional exploration of being Britney Spears. It's just as well. This is all contaminated anyway.

Another hour passes and we're summoned into the foyer. For five minutes, Britney and the photographer exchange ideas, which means that she's mostly snapping gum and saying, "Yeah," counting the seconds until dismissal. Then Britney barks to one of the shoot assistants, "I'm starving. We need lunch! Where is lunch?"

On command, the assistant sprints toward catering to prepare to serve the fried-chicken-and-vegetables feast. Alice paces anxiously, terrified that any error will be used as an excuse for Britney to leave. And until the food is brought to her, Britney will not proceed. To make the point clear, she and her assistant vanish into a different wing of the property.

I'm tired of playing *Snake* on my phone, so I wander into the backyard, one of those Southern California miracles of flaming birds-of-paradise, pink roses, and late-blooming jacarandas. But as I arrive in the garden, security captures and ejects several paparazzi for scaling the walls.

Time for lunch. After a few bites, life returns to her eyes. "Thank god," Alice whispers to me. "She probably hadn't eaten in days." We're clustered a couple yards away—close enough so that she can't escape after eating, but not so much that it's weird.

For a minute or two, things seem almost normal. Maybe this will work out after all. But then after cleaning the plate, Britney wipes her greasy hands all over her $6,000 gown, and Alice Van Bronx gasps like she's seen Greta Garbo's ghost.

Mumbling a half apology, Britney shrugs and summons me like she has something important to confess. My heart performs aerodynamic tricks. But the glory is immediately dashed. She thinks that I'm one of the assistants. Her pupils look like popped balloons. She hands me her empty plate filled with bones and fat to throw away.

No time to ruminate because the Yorkie is yipping in circles. Someone has been giving it chicken, and now it's shitting all over the hem of a Versace dress. The stylist unleashes a death rattle. The assistant—who looks like the long-lost middle sibling between Britney and Jamie Lynn—frantically tries to clean up the mess with a tissue. A distraught Alice Van Bronx looks like she's just lost a decade off her life. I'm trying not to let anyone see me laughing.

Britney heads into the bathroom to change into the Vera Wang dress, the last sartorial option. After thirty minutes, she and her assistant reemerge for test photos. But Britney barely makes eye contact with the camera. She could not give a fuck and demands that someone get her Janet Jackson *Rhythm Nation* CD from the car. It's the most sense that anyone's made all day.

We're ready to go again. No, wait, Britney say that she has to pee, and her assistant needs to come. And look, I don't want to snitch or cast aspersions, but I spent a year hitting LA clubs nightly, and there's not much doubt what they're doing. Britney comes back sniffing; her eyes are like Edison bulbs.

"Please, Britney, can we just get back to the shoot?" the photographer whines.

She's making cutesy baby talk to the Yorkie now. When their moment is over, she bolts up and does a few lackluster poses in front of the camera, looking like a wax museum statue.

I don't know what to make of it, but neither does anyone else. "It's better than nothing." Alice Van Bronx nudges me. But after about two minutes, Britney halts the proceedings.

"I'm done. You've got enough," she tells the photographer, rushing over to cradle the Yorkie in her arms.

"But we haven't even started!"

Ignoring him, Britney orders her assistant to fetch the CD. Alice begs her to reconsider. The bodyguard politely intercedes: "Ms. Spears says she's finished. Please respect that." The photographer and photo editor join the chorus in a salvage attempt. But Britney traipses toward the exit, still wearing the dress, heels, and jewelry borrowed from the magazine.

We follow her to the hand-carved cedar door, watching as she skitters out into the searing heat. The paparazzi are shouting outside, snapping at every step into her Mercedes. The cars drive down the mountain, leaving *HI!*'s dreams of defeating *People* in the exhaust.

Back inside the mansion, indignation reigns. *How dare she do this to us? All this time and money squandered!*

The unmitigated nerve! But well before everyone has packed up to leave, Alice says that she has already begun to see the silver lining. Only *HI!* will have the exclusive on "Britney's Meltdown." Millions will pay to hear about this "heartbreaking day." This "emotional cry for help" that will leave readers "shocked and sad!"

She's not wrong either. The magazine's publicist seeds the "explosive news" about the photo shoot, which elicits hundreds of blog posts and nightly news hits before the issue even drops. And when it does, the editor in chief writes a scathing attack on Britney and the people surrounding her. They're all "spoiled, disrespectful children pretending that nothing is wrong."

14

Gimme More!
D.O.A. at the VMAs!!

FEAR and LIP-SYNCING
in Las Vegas

How to Impersonate a Security Guard:
AN INSIDER'S GUIDE!

'm surprised that more people don't try it. The uniform is almost always identical. All you really need is a black suit, slacks, and leather dress shoes. If you want to ensure extra costume fidelity, I'd recommend bringing a fake earpiece too. Just in case. The only thing that actually requires foresight is finding an engraving shop to make you a personalized metal name tag to pin onto the fabric. But that's just a Yelp search away. At that point, even the authentic security guards can't tell you apart.

"Pretty damn convincing," I mumble to myself, straightening my tie in the mirror of my room at the Palms in

Vegas. Oliver performed the due diligence. We even sourced the official vendors used by the hotel. His resourcefulness remains unmatched.

Of course, the plot hinges on having an inside man. Do you remember Gutierrez, the bellhop-turned–limo driver who drove Britney to get married on New Year's Eve 2004? Oliver did. What's more, he knew that he'd been switched to security detail at the Pearl Theater, the site of the 2007 MTV VMAs. For the right price, he'll sneak us backstage, right outside of Britney's dressing room.

I stride through the garish wallpapered hallway. The hotel guests nod with deference, acknowledging my implied authority. "This is fucking ridiculous," I extend my soliloquy as I enter the elevator. But I agreed to it, so there's only me to blame.

The original itinerary involved hitting the VMA pre-parties at the clubs, covering the red carpet, and conducting interviews in the press room. But yesterday, Oliver finalized a deal with *HI!*. If I joined him on this ethically imperiled scheme, the magazine would give him a windfall.

"Do me a solid, mate. *Please*," Oliver begged.

Earlier this summer, *HI!* declined to renew their exclusive agreement with him. With greater frequency, they're relying on the cheap hired guns of the digital wave, and sometimes even citizen paparazzi, newly empowered by camera phones. Word has spread around LA that a competent pic of the right celebrity can mean a payday.

For all of my failings, I'm loyal. "Besides, it'll make for a good story, another chapter," I rationalize to myself.

When I meet Gutierrez in the hotel lobby, we're perfectly matched. My anxieties about getting ejected fall away.

"Oh, shit, *you* again?" He smiles widely. I nod and exchange pounds with him. "Smart kid like you, I'd have figured you'd have gotten out the game by now."

Gutierrez leads me through a door marked PALMS EMPLOYEES ONLY.

"Bro, shit's getting gnarly," he explains, as we walk past Akon. "Britney's tweaking. She's locked in her dressing room and won't let anyone come in. And she showed up, like, super late to the rehearsal yesterday with a frozen margarita and fries. I dunno, I remember her from like four years ago, and now, this shit just feels like the pod people snatched her, y'know?"

Live from the intestines of Sin City, September 9, 2007. Flocks of celebrities and their entourages slip across the faux-marble floors. They're joined by battalions of ear-pieced producers, wired-up assistants, label executives, MTV minions, barking managers, eager valets, clammy talent agents, unctuous bookers, Moonman waxers, sprinting gofers, and death-stare security guards.

Outside of Britney's dressing room, Gutierrez approaches her bodyguards to tell them that we're two of his best soldiers. Ideal candidates to help protect Britney. Then he nods and gives us a goofy wink, which we ignore. We bob our heads at her minders like we're made men. Someone shouts: "TWO HOURS UNTIL SHOWTIME!"

A slick MTV producer in a blazer approaches. He lingers a few feet from the dressing room, talking on his cell, trying to convey anger without attracting too much attention.

"You think I don't know that she was partying with Puff until four in the morning?!" he rages. "Yeah, yeah, she better be ready . . . Yeah, it better be her flu game. Look, you need to get someone here from Jive immediately if you ever want your artists to perform here again. Because my bosses are going apeshit!!"

Technically, Britney only partied with Puffy until 2:30 a.m. They hung out all weekend. Last night, they went from 50 Cent's album release party at the Hard Rock, to the Samsung party at the Venetian, to Cassie's twenty-first birthday at the Mirage. When everyone was getting ready to leave the club, Diddy told Britney to go home and rest up for her performance. But she kept raging in a hotel suite until almost 5:00, only slumping back to the Palms in the migraine dawn. At least that's the rumor flying around the backstage area.

What a scene. Oliver and I watch Lil Wayne strutting imperially alongside Birdman, Tyga, and a dozen models in skimpy dresses, tendrils of blunt smoke trailing in their wake. In a pink mermaid gown, Rihanna searches for her boyfriend and coperformer, Chris Brown. Upstairs, cameras roll from four "Fantasy Suites" hosted by Kanye, the

Foo Fighters, Fall Out Boy, and Justin Timberlake and Timbaland.

No one is more anticipated than Britney. With her comeback album *Blackout* finally dropping in the fall, the label convinced her to play the game. And they all agreed that the VMAs were the rightful arena for her return—where she hasn't performed since that Madonna kiss choked the world's oxygen supply four years ago. Only at this axis mundi of pop culture can she reclaim her throne.

MTV wasn't leaving anything up to chance. Stipulations were placed on her participation. For it to happen, Britney needed to rehearse for five weeks and have professional representation. So she signed with The Firm, the industry's most powerful management company, and spent ludicrous amounts of time practicing one song for an awards show that she's ruled since she got her driver's license. A week ago, the suits watched a competent trial run in a Los Angeles dance studio. Everyone was pleased.

Everyone is no longer pleased. The unraveling is underway, their worst fears realized. A blonde who looks like Reese Witherspoon raps on the dressing room door, begging Britney to open up. Oliver whispers that it's her new paid-for assistant/best friend hired by management to replace Alli Sims, her old assistant/best friend. But shortly before Britney's Gulfstream jet departed from Van Nuys to Vegas, she refused to get on the plane unless Alli came too.

After a few minutes, the door cracks open. Sims's eyes slide out.

"Britney doesn't want anyone near her!"

"But we wanted to check in on her and see how she was feeling!"

"She's *feeling* like she doesn't want to talk to anyone!"

The door slams shut. Knocks go nowhere. The bodyguards escort Britney's crestfallen new assistant out of the path. Within minutes, the Jive cabal attempts to enter. But they're boxed out too, and after lingering for a while they decide to go for backup.

"You think I should go in and talk to Brit?" Oliver whispers to me. It takes a few seconds to realize that it's not a bit.

"That's probably the worst idea you've ever had."

"She needs motivation right now, and I'm a fucking walking TED Talk."

"You'll blow up the spot." I cover my mouth with my hand. Johnny Drama and Turtle walk past us, slapping each other on the back.

"Not if I'm the hero."

"Just chill."

He sulks but abides. You can see the huckster's gleam in Oliver's eyes, the wild look of someone who never considers anything but doubling down, but who should have learned by now that the house always wins.

"90 MINUTES UNTIL SHOWTIME."

The tequila shots start. A conversation between Britney and her assistant bleeds through the dressing room walls.

"Maybe some shots will help loosen me up!" The familiar Bible Belt twang.

"It'll at least get rid of the hangover."

"Cheers, bitches!"

This isn't always a terrible idea. Vladimir Nabokov once said that before job interviews, "you must have one martini, but not a drop more." Ron Artest took Hennessy shots at halftime and won NBA Defensive Player of the Year. And nothing could be more on-brand for the promotion of an album called *Blackout*. But downing Patrón before a balletically complex dance routine beamed live to seven million viewers can go only one way.

When you start drinking an hour and a half before the performance, you have to keep going to stave off the crash. It also doesn't help your nerves when your canonical ex is tapping on the door. Yes, Timberlake himself is here to see Britney. He knocks with a corny rhythm that you can tell that he used to do when they were dating.

For the most awkward minute of our lives, we pose in the hallway. Oliver and me and Timberlake and four bodyguards. All of us completely silent: the professional defense experts and the pop star in a suit who looks like he's trying to sell you the world's sexiest adjustable-rate mortgage.

Of course, she *has* to open the door. If she doesn't, it's admitting defeat. He's America's teacher's pet, frictionless as aluminosilicate, nominated for VMAs in all but one category that he's eligible for. No matter what she does, she only catches demerits and censures. The consensus is that if she doesn't pull off tonight's performance, her career might be over.

I won't lie and tell you that I heard whatever Timberlake told Britney. Some mysteries are better unsolved. All I know is that after he leaves, I catch her eyes rolling back like he offered her a hemlock dick in a box.

"What do you think that turkey said?" Oliver asks me.

"Probably some played out Bible quote or a cliché like 'break a leg.'"

"I bet he was trying to get inside her head. Y'know, a little last-minute psych-out to remind her that he's top dog."

"Maybe he's reminding her about their first VMAs, when she brought out *NSYNC for 'Tearin' Up My Heart' and they looked like twenty-five-year-olds trying to pick up high school girls in a Mitsubishi Eclipse."

"What do you fellas think?" Oliver asks Britney's bodyguards. They refuse to acknowledge him. I flash him a *what the fuck is wrong with you?* glance. LC and Audrina from *The Hills* skip past.

Bryan Spears enters to stanch the bleeding. He's Britney's sometime manager, elder sibling, and the only adult member of the family still in her good graces. He offers a hug.

"I don't want to do it anymore. Tell them that I'm not going to do it. Tell them, *tell them*."

"Brit, you're going to be fine." Big bro tries to calm down baby sister. "You've done this a million times. Remember, you're Britney fucking Spears!"

"Not anymore. I can't do this. I'm scared," she says,

her voice cracking. "Everyone is going to stare and laugh and I can't. I just can't."

"You have to." His voice lifts an octave. "The show can't go on without you. It's in your contract."

"Fuck my contract."

"Alli, turn down the lights. Why are the lights so *bright* in here?"

"They seem normal, Brit," a female voice counters.

"They're blinding me. My head hurts. Everything is blurry. Turn them down!"

Through the transom, the lights noticeably dim.

"Have a shot with me, Bry."

"Go Tigers!"

The patter of whispered conversation. The door re-opens. Bryan Spears raises his eyebrows and pats the chief bodyguard on the chest: "She's better now, I think." A Gym Class Hero scampers past us.

"ONE HOUR AND FIFTEEN MINUTES UNTIL SHOWTIME!"

Time to get her hair done. Golden extensions to channel Old Testament Britney. Management conscripted the in-demand Ken Pavés, who was booked to tousle JLo tonight until she backed out. Pavés sweeps inside, carrying his Rapunzel tresses in a jewel box. After a few minutes of calm, the commotion returns.

"I don't like him! I want his assistant!" Britney shouts.

Outside, Oliver makes a gun-to-head gesture and presses the trigger.

"I work with Ken, Britney! We're a team!"

"Then both of you need to leave! I'll do it myself!

You're really annoying me. Get out of my dressing room! *GET OUT!*"

Muffled chatter. Alli enlists a bodyguard to eject the stunned A-list stylist. A Jive vice president tries to apologize, but Pavés wants none of it. "I've never been so insulted in my life." He sulks off with the tissue-wrapped locks.

Representatives of The Firm and Jive pound on the door, demanding to be let in with a gravity that not even Britney can dismiss. Her manager, her assistant, and several label vice presidents burst in. Britney tells them that she didn't like Pavés's attitude.

"YOU NEED HIM! HE HAS YOUR HAIR!"

For the next ten minutes, more VIPs dart in and out, attempting brinkmanship between stubborn star and outraged stylist.

"Where the fuck is Ken?! He's not picking up his phone!"

An apoplectic Jive executive screams at a shook Britney representative. I recognize him as the A&R who signed Britney, the one I spoke to at Venice High a lifetime ago. He's a little balder. He's removed the earring to reflect that he's a boss now. The sport coat upgraded from Nordstrom to Neiman's, but it's definitely the same estimated prophet.

"He's in his room and refuses to talk to anyone," the underling from Britney's management company meekly responds. "He's beside himself. Believe me, we're trying!"

"Well, try the fuck harder!"

"I believe his exact words were 'tell that self-righteous cu—'"

"Okay, I get it. Keep trying!"

Our eyes connect.

"Do I know you?" the A&R asks, trying to place my face.

"I think so," I say. "I was one of the extras on the '. . . Baby One More Time' shoot. You told me that she was going to be the biggest pop star in the world."

"Sounds like something I would've said." He gives a salesman's smile. "I mean, shit, was I right?"

He's staring at the locked dressing room door.

"What's going on in there?" I ask.

"Fuck if I know." He sighs. "She's got the yips. We figured this might happen, but she looked fine in rehearsals, and her manager . . ."

His voice trails off.

"What happened?"

He looks around to see if anyone's paying attention, but her bodyguards are inside the room, and no one else in the hallway is listening.

"I'm not Sigmund Freud." He shrugs. "We thought it was drugs, so we put her in the best rehabs in the world. But she says it's not drugs, so we got her the best therapists in the world, but they say they can't do anything and maybe she's just rebelling. So we got her a new manager and a new assistant and a new puppy and the best bodyguards to keep the paparazzi away, but she loves the attention at the same time she hates the attention. And all anyone just wants her to do is get well and sing songs that people love, but no one knows how to make that happen."

"So why don't you just let her be. She's almost twenty-six."

"Ha!" he snorts. "I love Britney—we all do. But she doesn't know how to open up her own mail, let alone pay a credit card bill. Every four weeks, she'd have a bench warrant out for her arrest for unpaid parking tickets or worse. You probably think that we're just trying to exploit her, but I promise you, if we disappear, the real vultures will get to her."

"Well, does the new album sound good at least?"

"That's the thing," he says. "It's one of the best pop albums I've ever heard."

"ONE HOUR TILL SHOWTIME!"

Pavés is never coming back. Unbothered by his absence, Britney knocks down another tequila shot as the departing executive runs his hands over his scalp. She commands Alli to turn the lights down further. I hear a glass bulb shatter. Walking past us, T-Pain stops, stares, reads the grave expressions of the producers, and keeps gliding. One of them tells his assistant to send a Mayday flare to all hairstylists within a five-square-mile radius.

Nelly Furtado's hired gun appears to save the day, but there's not much to work with. The hair extensions belong to Pavés, and that's where they'll remain. Alli Sims and a Palms employee scour the hotel's hair salon and bring back generic blonde extensions for the stylist to clip onto Britney's bob. It won't win an Outstanding Achievement in Hairstyling Emmy, but anything will suffice.

"THIRTY MINUTES UNTIL SHOWTIME!"

Clear the dressing room. Britney needs privacy to change into her custom corset, made by Dita Von Teese's stylist—the one that she had specifically requested. Her hair and makeup are decent enough. All she has to do is put on the tasteful but sexy one-piece, hit the right cues, and the crisis will be averted. But panic escalates. She locks the door again. Label executives, managers, and show producers keep battering without success.

WILL SHE COME OUT? WHY CAN'T YOU GET HER TO COME OUT? DOES SHE KNOW HOW IM-PORTANT THIS IS? WE'VE BEEN PROMOTING HER PERFORMANCE FOR A MONTH! MILLIONS OF PEO-PLE ARE WAITING ON THIS! MAKE HER COME OUT! BREAK DOWN THE DOOR IF YOU HAVE TO!

"TEN MINUTES UNTIL SHOWTIME!"

They're sweating, shaking, convulsing, screaming. No one has ever seen anything like this, at least not before an event of such global import. With seven minutes to go, the door snaps open. Britney stands before us, hands on hips, eyes flambéed, anxiously seeking approval. She is not wearing the corset.

"What the *fuck*?" someone shouts.

No one will ever really know what spurred Britney to ditch the artfully sewn and meticulously fitted outfit. The only theory that makes sense is that this was what she'd done since the ". . . Baby One More Time" video— when she ordered the wardrobe team to Kmart to buy the discount-store blouse and skirt now on display in the Rock & Roll Hall of Fame. But that was nearly a decade ago. Instincts are immutable, but times change. For all its charms, tequila doesn't aid sound decision-making. Even the most powerful spells only last for so long.

Britney sparkles in a black bra, a jewel-encrusted bikini bottom, and fishnets. Nothing else. No one knows where she got it from, and nobody knows where her mind is. Yes, the physical form of Britney Jean Spears appears before us, but her spirit has departed.

Maybe Britney's thinking about what's happening back in LA, where her mother, father, and other guests are gathered at Federline's house to celebrate the first and second birthdays of their sons, which fell three days apart, astrologically intertwined with VMAs week. Maybe it's an existential crisis. Maybe the lyrics to "Once in a Lifetime" are running through her mind. *You may find yourself . . . opening the VMAs.*

Glimpsing the shock in the executive's eyes, Alli Sims smiles and tells the room: "Britney really wants to go for it!"

"You need to change into the original outfit, Britney," her manager insists.

"I'm wearing this," Britney responds flatly, staring at the ground, then at the recessed LED lights in the ceiling. Anywhere but at the people yelling at her.

"ONE MINUTE TILL SHOWTIME!"

A column of backup dancers rumbles past: whooping, cheering, eager for their chance.

"It's too late, it's too fucking late. We've got to get her onstage," one of the MTV producers yells at Britney's manager. He shrugs his shoulders and turns his palms up. Escorts surround Britney, grabbing her elbows and steering her toward the bright lights.

All she has to do is utter the magic words: "It's Britney, bitch." No need to even mouth them into the wireless mic. Just lip-sync those four syllables with a diva's swagger, follow the dance steps, and let "Gimme More" work its strip-club-on-Sirius gris-gris. If Britney can do that, victory is assured.

I watch from the monitors backstage. The first shot reveals the scavenger-hunt hair extensions. A man-eating timbre cascades from the speakers. "If you're looking for trouble . . . look right in my face." A winking allusion to Elvis's 1968 comeback special.

The cameras freeze on Britney. She shimmies her shoulders, whips her hair, and whirls around to the whistling audience. But she can't fake it. A half smile becomes a confused frown. Her blue colored contacts block the natural warmth of her cocoa eyes. She's lost in the high beams.

A dramatic pause.

She misses the beat. The icy robotic prerecorded voice purrs, "It's Britney, bitch," but her lips don't keep up. The cameras pan away.

Underneath a neon arch and black-and-red Tetris blocks, six leather dominatrices prowl and kick, arching their spines, thrusting their hips, and writhing in tribute. But Britney goes blank. Her muscle memory abandons her. Her body stiffens. She's a time signature off, stumbling and lethargic.

Britney glances back at the dancers to try to catch up, abandoning the lip sync, unable to remember any of the words, forfeiting all illusion. She sees her reflection on the jumbo theater screens, and we see the horror in her eyes. The panicked nightmare that we've all had at some point in our life. When it's time for the test but your memory completely malfunctions.

The pantomime obscures the song's brilliance. It's our first time hearing the pole-dance funk of "Gimme More." The beat comes from Timbaland's in-demand protégé, Danja, and the lyrics from the moment's preeminent songwriter, Keri Hilson, but Britney's recorded vocals lend it a full frontal decadence. She sounds like Donna Summer for the damned. The soundtrack to a cocaine orgy at a dystopian disco. But no one will listen closely until later.

At the moment, the cameras do few favors. Britney is remarkably fit. But when you're dancing in your underwear under unyielding light, the high-definition lenses can capture you at warped angles. The sense of watching a disaster unfold is amplified by the audience responses. 50 Cent is flummoxed. You can practically see Diddy regret not ending last night's party a little earlier. Rihanna laughs.

In evanescent bursts, you can see hints of the past brilliance, but they don't last. Britney wobbles to the lower level of the stage like she has a broken stiletto. It's two hundred agonizing seconds of feeling like you're swimming underwater in slow motion being chased by piranhas. I wanted to scream at the producers to let her try it again. She'll get it right next time! But there are no do-overs. We're live. The lights flicker; the audience applauds tepidly. Britney disappears.

Sarah Silverman alights into her opening monologue. It's a comic bonfire. Even the normally stoic bodyguards wince while we watch on the monitors.

"Britney Spears, everyone . . . she is twenty-five years old and she's already accomplished everything she's gonna accomplish in her life . . . It's weird to think that just a few years ago on this very show, she was this, like, sweet innocent little girl in slutty clothes writhing around with a python . . . But have you seen Britney's kids? Oh my god. They are the most adorable mistakes you will ever see . . . They're as cute as the hairless vagina they came out of."

Britney's dressing room becomes a crucible. Her managers and label representatives stream in to offer false praise. *No, really, you were great, really. The outfit looked amazing, for sure, everyone was saying it. Ten out of ten.* Exiting, they mumble cloak-and-dagger invective to one another. "What the fuck was that shit? How could we let that happen? She'll never live this down."

Britney demands that a producer show her the replay. Her team—mostly older white men in suits and slacks and silver rings and receding hairlines and dress shirts buttoned either a button too high or too low—try to convince her otherwise. But her rage shuts them down. Confronting the calamity on the monitor, she bursts into tears.

"OH MY GOD, I LOOKED LIKE A FAT PIG!!! I LOOKED LIKE A FAT PIG!"

One by one, everyone leaves to let her change. Oliver turns to me.

"Okay, now it's my turn."

"Bro, she just humiliated herself in front of the entire world. The last thing she wants is false comfort from a random."

"Are you daft? The perfect time to talk to her is when she's at her lowest."

I grab his arm to stop him from doing it, but he slaps it away. I'm not exactly sure what possessed him. There was something about Britney that made everyone in her vicinity want to take advantage, even under the auspice of good intentions. She was susceptible to manipulative and greedy men who thought that they could make her do what they wanted, so long as they whispered the right password. And somewhere in this slow erosion, Oliver lost both his grasp on reality and his water-into-wine touch.

Oliver steps toward the dressing room, eliciting a warning from one of her bodyguards: "Where do you think you're going!?"

"Step aside, mate," Oliver says rudely. "I just want to have a few words with Brit. I only need a second."

"Miss Spears is indisposed right now, *mate*," says the

bodyguard, who outweighs Oliver by at least a hundred pounds. "Why don't you do your job and let me do mine."

Oliver brushes past him and pounds on Britney's dressing room door. "Brit open up, open up, it's Oliver, remember me?"

The lineman-sized bodyguard grabs Oliver, lifts him like a Slinky, and pins him against the wall.

"LISTEN, MOTHERFUCKER! I SAID SHE DOESN'T WANT TO SEE YOU!"

I try to remove Oliver from the giant's grasp, but his partner blocks my path. People are starting to notice the skirmish. Oliver screams for the bodyguard to take his "filthy mitts off him." Thankfully, Gutierrez appears and quickly negotiates his release. He aggressively clenches Oliver's shoulder and leads him out the exit doors. I'm left alone, feeling vile and disgusted, wondering how it all went so wrong.

The dressing room door flies open. Alli wraps a robe around Britney. The tears have become cataracts. With a guttural whimper, Britney slips on a hoodie and beelines toward a nearby emergency fire exit, heading out onto the casino floor, which has been cleared as a security precaution. The assistant and a security guard follow.

After a few minutes, I leave in search of Oliver. Truthfully, I don't want anything to do with him, but I figure that I should make at least a cursory attempt to see that he's okay. He's nowhere in sight, and I'm too angry to text. All I want to do is rip off this itchy con-man suit and throw it atop one of the *Deal or No Deal* slot machines.

Instead, I'm staggered by the sight of Britney on the second floor of a shuttered chain restaurant in the Palms, slumped against a granite wall. She's splintered, miserable, trying to make phone calls and sobbing louder when each one goes unanswered. I've never seen anyone look more alone.

The next morning, the *New York Post* puts her on the cover with the headline *LARD & CLEAR*. *The New York Times* says she was "awful." *Entertainment Weekly* calls it "the worst public performance of her career." Jokes about her weight are ubiquitous for weeks. But this is later.

Right now, the VMAs aren't even halfway over, and I attempt to honor the journalistic ambitions that originally brought me out to Vegas. From the press room, I watch the rest of the show, medicating myself with free liquor as Timberlake takes home the most awards of the night (four), including "Best Male Artist of the Year."

While the winners and presenters are paraded backstage before the media, it's clear that Britney overshadows everything. No one escapes without being asked for comment. Most take the bait. The lead singer of Green Day compares it to watching a public execution. Akon says it "definitely could've been a lot better." Dave Grohl sneers, "I don't give two fucking shits. She doesn't even sing live." Her idol, Janet Jackson, offers sympathy: "My heart goes out to her. We shouldn't pass judgment. We have no idea what she is going through."

Kanye has thoughts too. He's pissed off after losing all five awards that he's up for, even though he defined the night and the dying age at large with his performance of yet-unreleased songs from *Graduation*. In a tuxedo and white stunner shades, he raps "Good Life" with the holy-rolling fervor of someone who is certain that the bottle will never go empty—with its lyric about impressing his mom by being on TV. In two months she'll be dead from plastic surgery complications.

When the press asks him about tonight, about Britney, Kanye shakes his head: "They exploited Britney in helping to end her career," he says with disbelief. ". . . I felt so bad for her. I said, 'Man, it's a dirty game. This game will chew you up and spit you out.'"

15

JUDGMENT DAY:
Britney Battles for Her Babies!

Cold as Fire!
Blackout Is a Hot Mess Classic!

Is Svengali Sam *SUCKING OUT* Brit's Soul??

It's the last week of October, and Los Angeles is burning. I know that old line about the city on fire being the deepest image of itself, but I promise you, that's a poetic misrepresentation. Fire isn't our reflection, but our shadow. It's the unwanted reminder of ecological and eschatological consequences ignored until the issue is forced.

It's one of those skies that will leave you believing in

apocalypse. A psychedelic hallucination of burnt cinnamon and marmalade. Toxic ash in the air. A barbecued-woodlands odor sticks to your clothes even when you're inside. I've never seen wildfire burn with such mutant intensity. The climate feels juiced.

People greet each other by talking about the weather: *It's just like in a movie.* All the Santa Ana clichés are true. Aggressive freeway cutoffs send pacificists into spasming road rage. In the sweating flatlands, underneath nervously swinging palms, vendettas reemerge and pistols are wiped down. Divorce lawyers populate recent call lists. The mansions in the Santa Monica Mountains are aflame, and the wind won't stop blowing.

Britney's life forms a Bermuda triangle between her suite at the Peninsula in Beverly Hills, the criminal justice obelisks downtown, and her coastal compound. But Malibu is currently under evacuation order. Neither *Billboard* chart history nor S&P fortune can protect its residents from the inferno. For the paparazzi, the flames are a momentary distraction. The fainthearted shooters retreat to safety, which means less competition for the most dedicated. But eventually, the traveling circus simply relocates east.

Her court docket is a Bavarian nightmare, a labyrinth of short-lived fiats and lurking bureaucrats constantly taking notes, writing reports, observing. A Superior Court commissioner forces her to take coparenting classes and forbids alcohol or drugs within twelve hours of being with the kids.

After Britney misses a drug test and fails to produce

a California drivers' license, Federline receives temporary full custody. She has ten days to "get her act together" or the order will become permanent. Her principal defender is a teenage YouTuber whose "Leave Britney Alone" video goes viral. It's a straightforward and tearful plea for the media to stop dehumanizing her, but the clip is roundly mocked.

The judge sets a showdown for October 26, the same day that Lynne Spears announces that she's writing a tell-all memoir. AccessHollywood.com is broadcasting a live feed from the courthouse where Oliver and I are headed.

"You hear Brit got banned from the Chateau last week?" Oliver says, driving through Echo Park, underneath the wormwood sky.

"I didn't even know that was possible."

"Always a first. She rubbed mashed potatoes on her face in the restaurant and people started complaining. It got bloody wacky."

I haven't seen Oliver since Vegas. A few hours after the incident, he called me and profusely apologized. He didn't know what had gotten into him. It was inane and shortsighted and he was just trying to make moves. For all the ill-advised maneuvers, I couldn't stay angry at him for long.

In the Corolla, Oliver settles on Soulja Boy's "Crank That," currently in its sixth week atop the charts. Of course, he's doing the dance, lit joint in hand.

"I never took you for a hipster." He laughs as we pass a clump of bespectacled and bearded twentysomethings who look like they have Decemberists tattoos. I tell him to fuck off. For all the pretentiousness on the eastern side of Sunset, it feels like a reprieve after a half decade in Hollywood.

"You thought shit was bad before?" Oliver says. "This is the hide-all-the sharp-objects, prepare-the-butterfly-net phase."

Shortly after the VMAs, Britney's management dropped her. They claimed that "current circumstances are preventing us from doing our job." On the same day, Britney's lawyer recused herself and told the press, "There's a time for fresh blood."

Oliver fills me in on what hearsay I've missed.

"So, right, mate, check it. She's been talking in a British accent, and the Marilyn Monroe obsession is getting mental. Dr. Phil said that she's got 'toxic brain' and should be involuntarily committed. *In Touch* said that J. R. Rotem slipped one past the goalie too, but I don't believe that shite. And our old homies at *Nova* are saying they saw a Myspace page where Britney posted a sonogram of the fetus."

"Didn't someone print that she's trying to adopt six-year-old Chinese twins?"

"Precisely," he snorts. "Who the fuck even knows!"

I grab a handful of tabloids scattered in the back seat. In the latest *Nova*, the cover yawps that Britney's "Hit ROCK BOTTOM. She's lost her kids and risking her life on a binge and purge!!!! SHE'S OBSESSED WITH PARTYING AND HER PUPPY!" She's supposedly using amphetamines and laxatives to shed weight, and they include a photo of her carrying Provigil, a trucker drug that will turn you into a babbling zombie. Without irony, they tear into the junk-food diet that's left Britney with a "triple chin, big belly, and excess fat all over."

"Her fam came back from crocodile country a few weeks ago to help out, but they couldn't get a bead on her for almost a day."

I ask what happened.

"Well, her mum and her sister went to Malibu, but Brit wouldn't pick up the phone because she was actually up on Mulholland, convinced that someone had broken into the mansion," he continues. "But when she calls 911, the cops come and tell her she's just being paranoid. So she decides to go to the 'Bu but has to ask the paps how to get there because she don't remember. And then she discovers she's got a flat, which one of the X17 wankers fixed. By that time, her mum had tracked her down and they reunited in BH."

The songs turn into commercials. Sunset becomes Cesar Chavez. Oliver twists the radio dial and lands on "Gimme More," currently #3 in the country, her biggest single since ". . . Baby One More Time." All prognostications that the VMAs would torpedo her career were completely wrong.

"You hear the album yet?"

I nod and ask him what he thinks of it.

"I gotta give it to our girl." He takes a huge hit of the joint. The music starts. "This shit goes hard."

Blackout was undeniable from the first notes. A pop masterpiece recorded during biblical duress. A crystal strobe light exploding inside a black hole. It embodied

the hedonistic sleaze of the late Bush years, but anticipated our joyless mechanistic future. Only one ballad.
Almost nothing but literal and figurative bangers. The
all-night binges, 3:00 a.m. tequila shots, flashing cameras, impromptu stripteases, animalistic sex, five-star
hotels, impulsive weddings, designer spending sprees,
tabloid scandals, and court drama have all led to this. It's
the definitive Britney Spears album, a lost weekend of
one-more-gram indulgence to push away the despair and
loneliness waiting when the high wears off.

Let's be clear, listening to it in broad daylight in an
economical Japanese sedan on the way to her custody
battle is not the ideal first listen. But some things tran-
scend. I glance down at *Nova* on my lap, promising
"shocking truths" from "Brit's crazy house"—a Mulholland Drive villa with a fantasy room on the second floor.
It reportedly has ceiling mirrors, blackout curtains, and
a king-sized bed with fur handcuffs. The pink walls are
covered in provocative photos of Britney. Light comes
from bordello red bulbs. The closet is stocked with Catholic schoolgirl, French maid, and Cinderella outfits. In
the drawers, sex toys vibrate next to blindfolds, whips,
and a spanking paddle. *Blackout* sounds explicitly made
for this room.

Critics considered the album an enigma. Even the
ones who deemed it a classic wondered how it was created
amidst a whirlwind of mental instability, relationship carnage, and Cartagena excess. But if you believe the myth of
the tortured artist, this is the exact arithmetic for creating
something indelible. No one asks David Bowie how he

wrote the Berlin Trilogy on nothing but red peppers, milk, and astronomical quantities of cocaine.

If you attribute its vision to the talent assembled by the Jive megalith, all of Britney's collaborators still regularly praised her ingenious pop instincts. Keri Hilson raved about Britney's intense focus while doing vocals in her home studio at eight months pregnant. Danja compared her to Michael Jackson. T-Pain said that he thought she was going to be sitting on the couch eating Doritos: "But she came in, shook my hand, gave me a hug, went right in the booth, and put it down." Her chief A&R said that Britney's "magic turns these songs into what they are." For all the chaos, this was the first time that she earned an executive producer credit on an album.

It was recorded over the last two years in Los Angeles, New York, Vegas, and Miami. Beats mostly came from Danja and Bloodshy & Avant, the Swedish producers behind "Toxic." *Blackout*'s final song, "Why Should I Be Sad," is one of the last gems from the era of peak Neptunes, a seafoam funk kiss-off to Federline.

If the current charts are run by ringtone rap, Toys "R" Us pop, and whatever Akon auto-tunes, *Blackout* taps into what's next: the space-shattering dubstep rumbling in the London underground, the chromatic rush of Berlin techno, MDMA-fried electro-clash. It's bereft of the reworked samples and retro pastiche starting to become the norm. At times, it sounds like Kraftwerk at a candy rave. At others, it sounds like Giorgio Moroder scoring an Ibiza *Girls Gone Wild*. There is a push and pull between automaton perfection and messy human soul that recalls *OK Computer* if the computer's homepage was Pornhub.

Blackout glows with a glossy hypermodernity that sounds like the digital age becoming a disruptive reality. This isn't the 3D glasses and shiny space suits of utopian dreams, but the bleak chill of a postindustrialized algorithmic mind virus. Lost futures only imagined as a collection of pixels. You can practically see her face projected on a million screens, small and large, prefiguring a millennium where, whether you know it or not, you are always consenting to be filmed.

The tabloids are a recursive theme. "Piece of Me" foregrounds the paparazzi, lawsuits, and fixation about her image. The American dream since she was seventeen wants vengeance. She's shameless, mocking industry panic, aware that no matter what she does, they'll still put pictures of her "derriere in the magazine." The ravenous desire for sex, attention, and confrontation melds with the music. Themes of fire and ice mirror an artist prone to emotional polarity.

Her vocals are frequently splintered into staccato bytes, chopped and chirped, and auto-tuned to a fembot moan. In the Dionysian rites of ancient Greece, there was something called "sparagmos," where, at the peak of worship, ecstatic devotees tore victims limb from limb in a form of deranged sacrifice. This is that, but at a bottle service club with a velvet rope outside.

Everything from the Catholic schoolgirl uniform on was an elaborate tease. This was the final uncensored form. An autoerotic disassociated femme fatale who wants love but will settle for raw, no-safe-word sex, leaving stains and inhibitions under the black light.

Blackout silenced many of the doubters who considered her a washed-up vestige of the Clearasil pop past, a sock puppet for the suits, too reckless and scattered to deliver anything great again. But no matter how good the songs were, some cynicism remained. In an otherwise favorable review, a *New York Times* critic sniped that "she has done almost nothing, in the recording studio or outside it, to convince fans that *Blackout* is really hers, or really her."

But for Britney's army, *Blackout* was proof that she was, is, and always would be "the one." As for Timberlake, they used most of the same producers and she'd made something more futuristic, sexy, and destined for a lasting influence. Her onetime rival Christina Aguilera's "Dirrty" phase seemed tame and contrived in comparison. This is the pinnacle of boundless American extravagance and appetite. Gravity was bound to exert its cruel dominion sooner or later.

The scene outside the downtown courthouse is pandemonium. A dozen sheriff's deputies direct traffic and clear a path for Britney's white Mercedes coupe, but the paparazzi outnumber them ten-to-one. In front of the colorless six-story cube where they shot *Perry Mason*, Oliver and I are surrounded by nattering reporters and a failed comic wearing a dream castle on his head.

Britney steers through the horde, gently denting two paparazzi when they get too close. By now, you know how it goes. But it's also somehow worse. There must be a hundred of them, and as Mobb Deep said, you can run, but you can't hide forever. After the cops finally carve out a path, Britney escapes into an underground parking lot, leaving the locusts clicking outside.

It's easier to understand the physical laws of nature than the man-made code of justice. In every other aspect of life, Britney bulldozed her way. The power of her celebrity, beauty, money, charisma, and talent allowed her to circumvent regular constraints. But you can't negotiate a judicial edict. And there's no shock as severe as when the system exerts its immovable force in your direction. For someone usually able to snap her fingers and realize impossible visions, losing her children is an axis-shattering blow.

It's been constant legal hell ever since the divorce papers were filed. In late July, the split was finalized with a fifty-fifty custody arrangement, but Federline's attorney is an aggressive reader of the tabloids. Just one week after things were settled, Federline filed for primary custody of the children. In mid-August, he hired a process server to stake out a house party in the hills and serve Alli Sims with a subpoena when she stumbled out with Britney at 2:30 a.m.

To enhance the indignity, Federline's attorney claims that Britney should pay his legal fees because she's earning $737,868 a month and K-Fed is out of cash. His $20,000 in monthly spousal support is set to end this month too. The judge agrees, ordering Britney to pay $120,000 to Federline's lawyers as they attempt to destroy her.

An absent-minded functionary gave *HI!* two press passes for the proceedings, which meant that Oliver joined me in the packed courtroom. They're all here. The big weekly magazines, the AP, Reuters, the *Los Angeles Times*, CNN. Pens in hand, notebooks on laps, spectacles misting with excitement.

When Britney walks in, the room sucks in its stomach. She's wearing a short Native American–inspired turquoise-and-black dress, cowboy boots, and Dior shades. A cream Versace bag. Her hair is natural brown. She looks elegant but nervous. With her head down, she coquettishly bounces to a reserved seat up front. Federline is already here, trying to project grown-up authority in his Lexus salesman suit. He's got about $20,000 of diamonds gleaming in his ears, but he isn't taking them out, no matter how much the lawyer tells him that it's a smart idea.

"Who's the little general?" I ask Oliver, nodding at a tanned, soul-patched, wet gnome in a black Dodgers cap. He's sitting inches from Britney, tugging at her dress, whispering into her ear, commanding the operation.

"You don't know Lutfi?"

"Who the hell is Lutfi?"

"One of the lizard people."

"What the fuck does that mean?

"You know the people that show up at the rave at dawn when everyone is too smacked to see straight and

know who's who and what's what? He's the lizard that
tells them what to do and where to go. The one who always has the answer, who knows the guy that knows the
guy. I hear the feds are looking at his ties with the
Saudis."

Lutfi's appearance is unremarkable. He could be any
number of monochrome supplicants begging to slip past
the velvet rope after a long day toiling at a T-Mobile in
Van Nuys. What set him apart was his stare. Beneath ta-
rantula brows lay eyes that looked like they could cure a
czarist princeling of hemophilia.

Oliver offers a quick background sketch. Lutfi claimed
to be the thirty-three-year-old progeny of wealthy Leba-
nese immigrants who owned a couple gas stations in the
Valley. No one knew the exact story behind Britney's Ras-
putin because it came out slightly different in each retelling. He said he went to USC, but they had no record of his
enrollment, either under Sam or his birth name, Osama.
He purported to be a producer, but his sole movie was a
1997 straight-to-VHS Antonio Sabato Jr. vehicle. His only
clear means of income was "consulting" for his parents'
gas enterprise.

Unbeknownst to Britney, Lutfi had racked up three
restraining orders in the last three years. The first was
from a neighbor who claimed that in the autumn of '04,
Lutfi tried to kick down his front door while yelling ho-
mophobic slurs. A year later, a Santa Monica business-
woman claimed that Lutfi unleashed an "overwhelming
nightmare" of obscene emails, late-night voicemails,

hang-ups, and faxes after she wouldn't cancel an escrow check.

The final petition came from a twentysomething ex-roommate trying to protect a secret past in homoerotic porn modeling. After meeting on Myspace, Lutfi allegedly lured him in with celebrity connections and promises to rescue him so long as he pledged total honesty. But Lutfi flipped after the victim regained his self-confidence and reestablished ties with his conservative Mormon family. An $18,000 loan went unpaid. Then Lutfi supposedly left creepy voicemails telling his ex–best friend that he hoped his "sister would be raped to death," his mother would have her "flesh and bones devoured by Satan," and he'd commit suicide by sleeping pills ("lots of them"). Afterward, Lutfi emailed naked pictures of the plaintiff to his family, friends, and employer.

For most of '07, Lutfi tried to penetrate Britney's inner circle. First, he posed as a private investigator hired by Federline who possessed career-killing kompromat about Britney. He'd hand the dossier over to Britney's assistant only if she was willing to take a meeting. But at a Santa Monica Starbucks, his claims were outed as total bullshit.

Plan B was to befriend Britney's mom. Late one night, Lutfi anonymously cold-called Lynne Spears and claimed that drugs had been planted at Britney's Malibu house as part of a Federline scheme to make Britney look like an unfit mother. But after an extensive search, no contraband was found. Shortly thereafter, Lutfi approached Lynne with a plan to hawk jewelry on a home shopping network. It went nowhere. The "high-quality cubic zirconia" was actually cheap costume jewelry.

Lutfi remained undeterred. As the crack-up summer sweltered, the aspiring mogul managed to meet Alli Sims at a club, who introduced him to Britney, who became intoxicated by his promises and attention. Roughly a thousand Sam Lutfis roam Hollywood on any given night, with production companies whose web pages are always "under construction." But these amateur Machiavellis possess the gift of knowing what to promise. They can make outlandish claims sound convincing and usually believe their own lies. Lutfi has all the answers: all Britney has to do is let him take the wheel. After the VMAs, after all the professionals abandon her, he receives his chance. Now he's her unofficial manager, confidant, public mouthpiece, and consigliere.

The judge calls the court to order. A pudgy gray old man with a juddering chin and the *my way is the highway* mentality of a cop-turned-prosecutor-turned–berobed kaiser. It'd be hard to find anyone less sympathetic to Britney. You can see the derision in his watery silverfish eyes. No multimillionaire, hoo-ha-flashing, leading-America's-daughters-to-sin pop star will come under his bailiwick and think that they don't have to play by the rules.

What no one ever tells you about the legal process is that most of what's admitted is up to the judge's discretion. Of course, there are penal codes, but nearly everything is open to specious arguments. There's no jury in family law cases. Until the appeals stage, it's just one fallible human's opinion. And the judge is letting everything fly in favor of Federline.

"Your Honor, if it may please the court, I would like to call attention to a deposition from a Mr. Ray Barretto, a professional security officer in the employ of Miss Spears from late March to the middle of May this year."

"You may proceed," the judge tells Federline's attorney, a ratty man in an expensive suit, who looks a lot like one of Mr. Burns's high-priced lawyers.

"Objection, Your Honor," Britney's attorney speaks up. Oliver whispers that this distinguished bald gentleman in his late seventies was once Cary Grant's lawyer. "The court has already been apprised of Mr. Barretto's deposition and we see no reason to rehash testimony about events from six months ago—when we are here to establish my client's ability to be a responsible guardian today."

"Overruled," the judge says. "Since you're the third attorney to represent your client in the past three months, perhaps you are unaware of her recurring pattern of insubordination and irresponsibility before this court. She has habitually refused to follow orders, missed drug tests, appeared late or not appeared at all, and neglected to inform both the court and Mr. Federline of out-of-state trips with the kids—in violation of the terms of their agreement. What's more, she has used too many excuses that the court finds dubious—including, but not limited to, constantly losing her phone and changing her number to be unreachable. Actions that make her unable to meet responsibilities that this court deems necessary to regain custody."

"Thank you, Your Honor," Federline's attorney says smugly. "We repeat this information not out of a desire for redundancy, but to establish a pattern that illustrates why my client deserves full custody to ensure the safety and well-being of the children."

Lutfi tugs at Britney's attorney to give him information. The lawyer looks irritated.

"If you recall, Your Honor, Mr. Barretto gave testimony pertaining to an event that he witnessed on May 2nd of this year," Federline's attorney continues. "It involved a suspected overdose in Ms. Spears's hotel room at the Mondrian hotel in West Hollywood, where Mr. Barretto arrived after several distress calls from Ms. Spears seeking help. In his testimony, he described finding Ms. Spears crying and shaking, surrounded by empty liquor bottles, white powder, and a glass pipe. In his words, 'We thought she was dying. Her skin was all waxy. It was bad.'"

"Fat Tony found her with Howie Day! And in six hours she played the show in Anaheim!" Oliver whispers to me.

Fat Tony was actually the bodyguard's nickname. Howie Day was a one-hit wonder who Britney met at rehab. You probably heard "Collide" in a CVS once. In retrospect, the Anaheim show was more impressive than I remembered.

"This was but one of several incidents that left Mr.

Barretto convinced that Ms. Spears was putting her children at risk," Federline's lawyer continues in his reedy voice. "He witnessed her driving around with Styrofoam cups of Jack Daniel's and Coca-Cola, as well as snorting a 'powdery substance' in a nightclub."

"Objection, Your Honor," Britney's lawyer interrupts again. "Mr. Barretto's testimony should be considered highly uncredible and stricken from the record, considering that he sold his story to a tabloid for the reported sum of a hundred and eighty thousand dollars."

"Overruled," the judge replies. "That has no bearing on his testimony."

The reporters frantically jot everything down. The overdose, the judge's contempt for Britney, the Howie Day cameo—they can't believe what A1 fodder it is.

"In addition, there was a pattern of eccentric behavior and suicidal ideation that left Mr. Barretto of the belief that Ms. Spears was undergoing severe mental distress."

"Objection! Mr. Barretto is not a trained medical doctor."

"Sustained. Focus on his observations, not his conclusions."

"Mr. Barretto reported that Ms. Spears told him not to stare at her or sweat in her presence. Other members of her staff instructed him to, quote, 'act coy' during her frequent bouts of nudity. Mr. Barretto said that she spent so little time with her babies that Ms. Spears didn't even know when they were hungry. He also says that he was once asked to babysit while she went tanning."

"Is that all counselor?" the judge says impatiently.

"One more thing, Your Honor. Mr. Barretto told the court that Ms. Spears was forbidden to swim alone with her children. When he asked another security officer if that was because they were worried that she would drown them, the officer shrugged his shoulders and replied, 'I don't know.'"

"Objection! Hearsay!"

"Sustained."

"We would like to point out before the court that Ms. Spears has passed her last ten drug tests," Britney's attorney counters.

"She's also missed eight of the last fourteen tests that have been ordered," the judge thunders.

"Your Honor, my client is a pop star with a single at the top of the charts," Britney's lawyer says.

"Counsel, I don't care if your client is the Queen of Sheba," the judge interrupts him. "This court has already found her to be a habitual, frequent, and continuous user of alcohol and controlled substances."

"She's promoting an album, Your Honor! Her life-style presents extenuating circumstances that do not allow her to be up and ready to take twice-weekly tests at one hour's notice—especially not before nine in the morning! It's unconstitutional!"

"Unconstitutional." The judge laughs. "Listen, counsel—and I assume you too are listening, Ms. Spears—if you want to disobey my rulings, then you are more than welcome to do so. But under no circumstances will I put your children at risk."

Britney looks shattered but tries to keep her composure. You can see Lutfi's neck veins bulge as he tries to stifle the rage. Oliver jabs me in the ribs and nods.

"Your Honor, if the court will allow it, we are prepared to present more recent exhibits of the unsafe environment for the children," Federline's attorney continues. "Earlier this month, her bodyguards were seen fighting off two aggressive paparazzi who had bumped into Jayden Spears. We would also like to present the court with a recent copy of *HI!* magazine, in which Ms. Spears is described as 'acting bizarre' and amidst an 'emotional cry for help.'"

"Objection." Britney's attorney raises his arm. "Reports from tabloid magazines should not be held on the journalistic level of, say, *The New York Times* or other publications with more rigorous standards."

"Overruled. Counsel, you may continue." He turns to Federline's lawyer.

"We are prepared to depose the editor in chief of *HI!* as well as present additional affidavits from two more former bodyguards and a nanny—who claim that Ms. Spears has given the babies soda and coffee, put whitening strips on their teeth, and forced them to sit in soiled diapers for hours."

"That will be enough for now, counselor," the judge responds. "Is the report from the monitor ready?"

A clerk hands several pages to the judge. We wait while he scans it. For the last several months, a court-appointed parental monitor has shadowed Britney during the intervals in which she's been allowed to see her children. The findings are due today.

"Your Honor, we would like the court to focus on the part of the report where Ms. Spears is said to be 'unfocused' and 'operating in her own world,'" Federline's attorney says. "The mood at home is, quote, 'chaotic to almost somber.' And her parenting style is described as 'not abusive in the *traditional sense*.'"

Britney's best option is to throw herself at the judge's mercy. She'd need to publicly cop to past wrongdoings, find God again, become a *changed* woman. And show a little charm while doing so. The judge wants her to submit. He requires it. This was a former police detective who had probably long divided the world into good guys and bad hombres. If you did drugs, especially if you were a rich and worshiped young woman, you fell into the wrong category. He saw himself as the neutral arbiter tasked with the awesome power of the state to ensure that there would be consequences for those subject to his control. And for Britney, he symbolized every oppressive reactionary she had become conditioned to loathe.

The lawyers volley back and forth a little longer. The monitor's report is picked apart. It contains mostly uncontroversial observations about her parenting style, which, to be fair, would not necessarily be reprinted in child-rearing manuals. Britney's lawyer keeps returning to her clean drug tests and the ineffable love that she feels for her sons. They need to be able to see their mother—it's for all of their benefit.

In the end, the old man is hard, but not heartless. The judge grants Britney two daytime visits and one overnight a week. But she and the children must be supervised at all times—with no exceptions. As he delivers the news, tears stream down Britney's cheeks. Lutfi securely wraps his arm around her. Federline never breaks his poker face.

Outside, Grand Avenue is a hungry blob. The smoke from the fires has turned the sun the color of a rotting orange. An overmatched Superior Court press coordinator attempts to corral what feels like a fifth of the active media on the West Coast. The roving TV eyes and disorienting camera flashes and the babble of the same question being asked a thousand different ways. Federline's lawyer appears to love the attention.

Britney and Lutfi walk out from the glass doors of the lobby. For a few seconds, they stand confused beneath carved statues dedicated to the Mosaic Covenant, the Magna Carta, and the Declaration of Independence. They're accompanied by several deputies, who look like they're trying to help them figure out where they parked.

A few dozen members of the scrum swarm Britney. The cops create a buffer, but one *Us Weekly* reporter practically flings herself over the perimeter, her voice piercing through the din: "How are you feeling about the decision, Britney?"

The question severs any last hint of self-restraint. Leaning in, Britney hisses from somewhere broken: "Eat it, lick it, snort it, fuck it." Then she's escorted back into the building, down the elevator shaft, back to the cocoon of her car.

Oliver tries to convince me to get a drink at the Short Stop. But I don't feel like rehashing the details of this downward spiral. I don't care about the biographies of bottom-feeding scammers. I don't want to hear about how another one of today's brightest stars will be the next to stagger down Via Dolorosa. I no longer want to have to lie about what I do or wrestle with the insomnia that arrives when you aren't sure if you believe in the soul, but you know that if it exists, yours is a ruin of guilt and soft corruption.

It doesn't help that my birthday is tomorrow at midnight. I'm supposed to go to a bar this weekend with a few high school friends, but nothing feels worth celebrating. I head home and crumple into a time warp, listening to records that I used to love, smoking a joint while staring at the ceiling. My cat periodically screeches at me whenever I'm not paying her enough attention.

Around 8:00 p.m., I realize I haven't eaten and slide west to the Apple Pan on Pico, in search of a hickory burger, fries, and a pecan pie to go. But it's too packed, and I've already blazed another joint on the way here, which left me so high that I'm somehow not even hungry anymore. I hop back in the car and instinctively drive in the direction of the water.

A left on Bundy, which becomes Centinela, then an automatic right on Venice Boulevard, where an atavistic urge compels me to pull over in front of my old high school. Forgive my sentimentality, but I turn twenty-six tomorrow, a forgettable blip that you might as well not even commemorate. I wasn't quite twenty-seven, the rattlesnake year that killed all the rock legends whose bootleg T-shirts they sell by the pier. But I was now older than

Biggie and 'Pac were when they died. All I had to show in this quarter century was a few novel rejection slips, tabloid ephemera, and a *Page Six* humiliation that would shadow me until my own long kiss good night.

The campus is technically closed, but it's an LA public high school, which means that you can basically wander in whenever. I'm engulfed by ever-dimming memories of three-week crushes and ditching computer class to get McDonald's and watch *The Matrix* on the Promenade, the locker by the stairwell with the 18-24-36 combination, the puffy, tasteless cafeteria pizza, the geometry class where I usually had to sit in the hallway because I preferred to play *Drug Wars* on my TI-83.

Basketballs bounce and sneakers squeak in the gym. The lights are on. The season starts in a couple weeks, and one of the entrances is unlocked. No one notices me in the rafters. The coach is new. None of the players would know that I was once them in a bygone universe. A sense of intense familiarity washes over me, and then a dislocating sadness. I remember the afternoon watching Britney here, sitting in these same bleachers, envisioning a cloudless future where unearned laurels, fantastic wealth, and beautiful lovers all seemed assured—for me, for us. I swear it was written on the scoreboard.

The coach notices me and politely tells me that's a private practice, which sends me back out into the end of the night. The smoke from the nearby Malibu fires has turned the moon the color of blood. The steering wheel is pointed straight toward the beach. I park a few blocks from the boardwalk and take a basketball out of my trunk. In one hand, I light a spliff; in the other, I dribble past the shuttered souvenir vendors and corn-dog kiosks.

It's so late that the mixtape hawkers have all gone home, the turbaned roller-skating man with the electric guitar is nowhere to be found, and no one is trying to sell me a henna tattoo. It's just the spectral thunderclap of the waves and a hot whistling wind attempting to shove me backward like an uninvited guest.

I have the courts to myself. No streetlights, but the fires cast an atomic pink tint, which coupled with the light pollution offers just enough glow. My mind quickly retreats into the Zen nothingness of the thousands of hours of my childhood spent shooting until my hands were black and my shirt was damp and everything smelled like the metallic tang of asphalt, chain-link nets, and synthetic basketball leather.

I hoist jumpers until I'm certain the calendar has flipped over to the next day—as if this ritual is some placebo act of penance, a nepenthe for guilt and depression and loneliness. If I sink ten free throws in a row or sweat enough of the toxins out, I may be able to restore the equilibrium that I have never found since the afternoon when I walked out of the artificial lights of the gym into the frying glare of the imprisoning sunshine.

The wind keeps blowing harder, knocking my shots down. The palm trees look like swaying witch doctors. I keep thinking that if I time it right and angle it correctly, I can defeat the meddling of the gusts. All I need to do is shoot straighter, jump higher, adjust to the shifting vectors.

I start sprinting to the ball after every missed shot, until I realize that I can hardly breathe anymore. The acid gases and carbon monoxide are poisoning me. I sit down on the concrete, dizzy and nauseous, putting my head between my knees. The ocean waves crash on the edge of the continent, and I start to notice tears streaming down my cheeks. I can't be sure if it's from the residue of everything burning around me or the illusions that I have allowed myself to believe.

16
Spears vs. Spears:
IT'S WAR!

SLEEPING WITH THE ENEMY:
Britney's Paparazzi Love Affair

THE *NIGHTMARE*
on Mulholland Drive

The days are wandering but circular, the nights cold and wired. Sometimes, the pursuit is plodding. At others, it's a rosary-clutching death-plunge. The fifty-photographer plague trails Britney from the Topanga mall to the Barstow Taco Bell. Never before had there been so much documentation about so little. A reality show about nothing, and the ratings are spectacular.

For someone whose adult life was beset by transactional relationships, it's understandable that Britney mistook the attention for affection. The paparazzi cultivated this destructive addiction. They counterbalanced the negative with constant validation. Conditional love at a steep cost.

When Britney's sixteen-year-old sister, Jamie Lynn, gets pregnant, Britney learns about it from the paparazzi. Each day, they offer directions, buy her McDonald's, and tell her that she's fantastic when she's in tears. They shadow her to Starbucks, the hospital, and runs to Larry Flynt's Hustler store, where she changes into BARELY LE-GAL booty shorts in the middle of the aisle.

Lutfi exerts martial control, playing organizations off each other, and calling in tips about their daily itinerary. He even negotiates a deal with X17 to auction off signed copies of the new album for charity.

Despite fan adulation and appearances on Best of the Year lists, *Blackout* is considered a disappointment. The would-be comeback sells 290,000 copies in its debut week, her first to miss the top spot, and half of what *In the Zone* moved in 2003. Illegal downloading has decimated the music business. It's now Myspace and 99-cent iTunes singles. A new generation of teen pop stars have become more commercially dominant: Miley Cyrus, Taylor Swift, the cast of *High School Musical*.

Steroidal gangsta rap and *American Idol* pop have receded in favor of something more underground, less controllable. Terrestrial radio and MTV lose their gatekeeping monopoly to online tastemakers. Indie rock, French blog house, and Day-Glo rappers in skinny jeans are in vogue. The internet's second wave fractures the monocultural world that produced Britney.

An aura of decline becomes unmistakable. There is the widespread sense that this samsara will end, but no one knows when or what will come next. By the middle of November, Paris, Nicole, and Lindsay have all cycled in and out of jail, experiences that tint the campy hedonism of the near past toward a numb anhedonia.

The paparazzi money begins drying up too. With thousands of blogs and websites posting the same photos daily, often without permission, the picture values continue to crater. The gossip rags brawl for scraps. The tabloids still sell, but newsstand circulation begins its decline. Perez Hilton and TMZ are trouncing print with online breaking news. And with camera phones becoming ubiquitous, celebrities reconsider the perils of club excess.

It's in this cuticle of the year when something tears inside me again. My patience for treading in this stagnant canal was always limited. I start applying for other jobs and use the holidays as an excuse to lie to Alice Van Bronx about being on an extended vacation in Big Sur. *No phone service—what a pity.*

There are a few exceptions where I accept assignments. In early December, a slippery Dane named Claus throws a swag party disguised as a twenty-sixth birthday celebration for Britney, at something called the Scandinavian Style Mansion in Bel Air. Claus drives a blue Porsche and claims to be one of her new best friends. He aims for old Hollywood glamour, but the mood is neomodern managed decline. In this packed but empty room, few actually know the birthday girl, and everyone feels like they're on some vague audition. In a gifting area where the press are corralled, Paris Hilton poses for photos, sips champagne, and accepts all material tributes. In exchange for her appearance, Britney collects $45,000 worth of fur coats and diamond rings. Then she blows out the candles on a dinky chocolate cake.

Once or twice that winter, Alice Van Bronx pressures me into riding around with Oliver on the Britney trail of tears. A few nights before Christmas, somewhere in East Hollywood, Britney pumps her brakes to photograph a graffiti mural.

"LOOK AT THAT! THAT'S ART!" she screams to the philistines stopping traffic on Santa Monica Boulevard to take pictures of her taking a picture.

Britney curses out the convoy, slams her camera against the hood of a paparazzo's car, and yells to be let back to her Mini Cooper. But before leaving, she realizes that she's lost her memory card, and enlists them to help her find it. At some point, amidst the commotion of this chilly winter night, Adnan Ghalib—the paparazzo engaged in a low-level cold war with Oliver—slips Britney his business card.

When Britney makes her next stop to buy snacks at a gas station, she hops into Ghalib's silver Mercedes. As he drives off with the prize, the cameramen ask her, "How does it feel to be in a paparazzo's car?" Britney smiles faintly. By her next ampm spree, she bops out with a huge grin, toting Ghalib's video camera like a kidnapped heiress with a semiautomatic.

Maybe it was natural to fall for someone who knew her daily habits, routines, and desires. Or maybe it was a good old-fashioned case of Stockholm syndrome. Either way, the night ends with Britney dreamily waltzing through the lobby of the Peninsula hotel in Beverly Hills, holding hands with her latest infatuation, vanishing from sight until late the next afternoon.

"It should be me!" Oliver grumbles inside the Red Rock. "A-Fed is such a bloody charlatan. Can't shoot a photo. Works for a failing fourth-rate company. An ego-maniac fake pimp who looks like he's trying to sell you a bootleg Ed Hardy phone case outside the Cinnabon! And he's married!"

"Aren't *you* married?" I light up one of his Benson & Hedges.

"That's fucking immaterial," Oliver says, taking a tremendous drag, lazily fixating on the newly shuttered Tower Records across the street. "Didja see his blabbering bullshit on *20/20*?"

Within hours of spending the night with Britney, Ghalib appeared on ABC to tell the world that Britney was "unpredictable" and "lucrative." He claimed to have sold a forty-second clip of her stealing a cigarette lighter for $40,000. When asked if her life would improve if the paparazzi left her alone, he admitted, "I'd be lying if I said no." But because even villains believe that they're antiheroes at worst, Ghalib explained that his presence was vital: "If we're not there, who's going to pump her gas? The photographers who work her twenty-four hours a day are the only ones who treat her with respect. We're her friends now."

Ghalib's marriage ended up being a minor nuisance. After the news broke, his second wife, a part-time model, filed for divorce—irate that her husband of five years was taking his work home. Britney's new beau didn't mind much. He leveraged his burgeoning relationship to broker photo exclusives with his company, Finalpixx. The also-rans become titans, which made him Lutfi's nemesis. Worried about losing power, Lutfi began leaking rumors that he was the only thing keeping Britney sober. Without him, *who knows what might happen*?

"So what's the deal?" I ask. "You got a parlay in Las Vegas when she'll be institutionalized? When she'll marry Adnan? When she'll join the cargo cult in New Guinea?"

"Dawg, for once, I ain't got the faintest fucking idea. It could be manic depression, it could be the world's worst case of ADD. She's been taking so many Addies that she calls 'em her vitamins."

The anguish metastasizes. The judge forbade her from seeing her children over Christmas. She reportedly spends the holiday in Malibu, alone with Ghalib, collapsed and weeping at the foot of a massive tree wrapped in ribbons, angels, and stars. Lonely gifts lay underneath, waiting for the toddlers the state of California deemed her too unwell to mother. Ghalib told a paparazzi friend that she was the unhappiest person he'd ever seen.

By New Year's, LA County investigators have begun looking into "multiple child abuse and neglect" allegations, asking the judge to unseal the case file for inspection. Britney's third set of lawyers file a motion to withdraw. In court documents, they claim that a "breakdown in communications" makes "further representation impossible." The lawyers are said to believe that Britney's actions are "sinking the case."

Britney is spotted with Ghalib at a resort hotel in Palm Springs. Wearing a black wig and black sunglasses, she checks in around 2:00 a.m. and leaves five hours later. She speeds back to Beverly Hills that afternoon, getting clocked at triple digits. Abruptly, she veers toward Malibu, then hooks an illegal U and returns to 90210.

The anxiety isn't pure neurosis. Federline's lawyers are about to make their final plea for full custody. Nearly everyone in her old orbit has given their sworn testimony. The judge requires that Britney be interrogated about her substance intake and psychological well-being. Two deposition dates have already been blown off. After the last cancellation, he threatens to take away her kids forever. No more deferments are possible.

Her last chance is scheduled for today at 9:45 a.m. Alongside dozens of news cameras and paparazzi, Oliver and I wait outside of Century City's twin towers. Britney arrives an hour late, petrified in a hot pink dress, accompanied by Lutfi. The deposition only lasts fourteen minutes. Federline's attorneys seem aggrieved about Britney's tardiness and curt answers, but describe her to the press as "cooperative."

With his crowbar charm, Oliver cajoles me into joining him for happy hour. After all, it's only January 3, and half of LA doesn't start the year until half-way through the month.

"Someone's gonna step in to take control," Oliver says. "Nature abhors a vacuum."

"Lutfi doesn't let her buy a pack of cigs without a permission slip," I respond. "When he's gone, your boy Affliction Adnan runs the show. She barely talks to her mom and dad. The old managers got axed six months ago."

"I dunno, mate." Oliver sighs, running his fingers through his hair—the once-thick rotini curls now look like tattered ribbons. His wardrobe has adapted to the times: shredded jeans, an unbuttoned chartreuse Henley shirt, and a scarf. "The American fucking dream can't be running around with a shady manager named Osama and an Afghan pap who says that he fought on the same side as bin Laden."

"We funded that side."

"It ain't the point." He exhales smoke doughnuts. "If she makes ten milli a year for herself, how much do you think she makes for other people? You think they're gonna let her send the kiddies to a madrassa in Malibu?"

"'They'? You about to explain what's *really* on the dollar bill?"

"Dawg, with all due respect, you predicted K-Fed and Brit were going to live happily ever after. Your predictions are shit. The courts are involved. The county is investigating. You can fire a lawyer, but it don't make the problems go away."

"She's practically the only one from Hyde who hasn't

gone to jail. The drug tests were negative. No felonies. It's her American right to make bad decisions."

"Exactly. It's America, and she's a priceless asset depreciating rapidly," Oliver continues, as the passing cars bray in Sunset traffic. "Her family wants to save her, but she don't want to be saved. Jive needs what's left of her carcass to avoid getting swallowed whole by BMG. And Federline wants those kids full-time because that's seventeen years of child support. You know how many durags that buys?"

A MIDI rendition of "Duffle Bag Boy" blares from Oliver's pocket. He rolls his eyes and silences it without looking.

"This nimrod!" he says venomously. "I told him that I'd paid him what he was owed, but he keeps trying to extort me for a bigger cut of some photos that he didn't even really take."

I bob my head. The phone keeps ringing. Finally, Oliver takes the BlackBerry out of his pocket and reads a text. His eyebrows threaten to escape his forehead. "Oh, shit, it's going down at Brit's house!!! Let's bounce!"

Britney's barely slept in days. The Adderall that she needs to function kills her appetite. Her lungs are aflame from all the cigarettes. She shouldn't be driving, but she needs control. The car is a sanctuary. She can play her music and scream as loud as she wants or have total silence. Sometimes, the silence is worse.

Fuck Kevin for trying to steal the kids, and fuck his lawyer for the nosy questions that he has no right to ask. Her parents might as well be dead to her. She's supported them since she was sixteen, but they somehow keep siding with her ex. As for her old management, who tried to lock her in rehab, they can kiss her ass too.

Who hasn't sold her out yet? Maybe Jamie Lynn and Fe, wherever she is. Her first boyfriend, Reg—back from when she was fifteen and praying to Jesus that someone would save her from Kentwood—keeps telling the tabloids that, actually, he was the one who took her virginity. Way before Justin Timberlake, who is still everywhere. How strange that the paparazzi *never* seem to fuck with him.

Adnan went to Santa Barbara to visit his sister. He should be here now. Then she remembers that the kids are waiting at her house. Fuck that court monitor for never giving them a second alone. Sam was gone for a few days over Christmas. His mother had cancer or something, but he's back. The paparazzi follow her on the short ride from Century City, but she doesn't feel like games today. Sunset to Beverly to Coldwater to Mulholland, back to her babies.

This is the only afternoon that the old-ass judge lets her have the boys. Right now, they're playing with their new Christmas toys. Britney wants to join them, but there are pins in her skull, and she needs to puke. Nothing's coming out, though. Fighting the chills, she thrashes in bed, trying to remember what happened this morning in court. In the shadows of her mind, Kevin's shriveled-up lawyer plots and waits for a slipup to destroy her.

No point in trying to rest anymore. She can't sit still, but her head keeps hammering away. Her mouth is alkaloid bitter and dry. A couple pills might help. The doctors say it's good for her. Even eight-year-olds take Adderall, and *everyone* is on Prozac. Sam keeps track of everything, but he's on his cell, talking business, he says. But he never makes a deal. When was the last time she had a cigarette?

Britney's pulse is fast and irregular. Her lungs feel full of bleach. Water would help, but another Red Bull will *work*. She cracks open the one on her nightstand. Maybe Adnan will know how to fix it. But he doesn't pick up. Nine rings and nothing? He must be with his ex! Someone needs to come stroke her hair and say that it will be okay. The babies are here, thank god. If she asks Kevin nicely, maybe he'll let them spend the night. The judge doesn't have to know.

Nothing ever goes right anymore. Kevin refuses, of course. When they first met, he would always tell her that she was his goddess, and now, she's *nothing*? What a phony, pretending to be a serious grown-up when all he ever did was smoke weed, hang with his dumbass friends, and make that rap album everyone hated. She keeps crying every few minutes. It feels like red ants are crawling across her skin.

"Is something wrong?" the court monitor says. With scalding water, Britney washes her hands and arms in the sink. Her flesh is bright pink.

"Where are my babies?!" Britney says, panicked.

"In the living room," the monitor says. Concern

grows in her voice. "Kevin's bodyguard is on his way to pick them up, *remember*?"

"Kevin said the boys can stay here!"

"I would need to hear verbal confirmation, and besides—"

"I just spoke to him!" Britney interrupts aggressively.

"Ms. Spears, Judge Gordon makes the rules," the monitor says primly. "You cannot be legally left alone without my supervision, and I leave at 7:00. No exceptions."

"You don't make the rules," Britney spits, then starts grinding her teeth. Running into the next room, she stares into a full-length mirror; the frame is decorated with gold angels.

"My eyes look so big. I look so short. I'm so freaking hot, ugh." She removes her sweater to reveal a skimpy tank top. She swivels around, staring at her back in the mirror.

"My tattoo's still there, right?" Britney points at the nape of her neck. She addresses the nanny, a pretty twenty-something blonde girl who looks like she dresses up as Britney Spears at children's birthday parties. The nanny nods and gives an unconvincing smile.

"It says MEM HEI SHIN, Seventy-Two Names of God! Kabbalah. Nothing is what it seems, and I need to be pure."

She stares in the mirror again, her eyes spinning like shellac discs. She concentrates on the veiny purple bags. "I need new moisturizer and face wash!"

She spins again to the nanny. "Have you ever seen me do a handstand?"

Federline's bodyguard rings the intercom. He's here to take Sean Preston and Jayden back to Tarzana. The monitor keeps asking Britney what's going on. But Britney sends her nanny to distract the bodyguard. This ought to buy her a little more time.

"I need to go home," the monitor keeps whining. With a bit more force, the bodyguard demands that she let the boys come home with him. *PLEASE!*

Here comes little Sam telling her to calm down. Calm down. That's easy for him to say when he doesn't know what it's like to have the only thing you love ripped away.

"HE'S GOING TO TAKE MY BABIES!! I'LL NEVER SEE THEM AGAIN! HE'S GOING TO TAKE MY BABIES!"

Everyone offers reassurance. If she lets the babies go, it will be fine. She'll get to see them next week. Maybe sooner. If she doesn't, things will only get worse. Her ex, his lawyer, the judge, her parents, the press—they'd all like that. Everyone will say that they're better off. She was a terrible mother anyway. But you can't be a terrible mother if you need your babies this much. *NO ONE* on earth has the right to take them.

They tell Britney to go into the TV room. There's a rule change: she can keep the kids for one more night. Some ground rules need to be established, that's all. But it's a trick. As she steps away, the bodyguard snatches Sean Preston, taking the two-year-old to the Escalade with the court monitor's help. Now the tears really won't stop and her makeup is smearing and her brain is infected.

If they want war, she'll show them. Locking the court monitor outside, Britney grabs sixteen-month-old Jayden, and barricades herself in the bathroom. No one, not Sam, not the bodyguard, not even the police are going to take her children from her.

"KEVIN CAN HAVE SEAN, BUT I WANT JAYDEN WITH ME!!!"

In the Escalade, the bodyguard calls Federline, who calls his lawyer. Shivering in the cold canyon darkness, the court monitor dials 911, asking for police assistance. "Something has gone terribly wrong. Two young children are at serious risk!"

In Los Angeles, helicopters are symbols of celebration and tragedy. They can be whirling tools of police surveillance or iron albatrosses illuminating the latest celebrity saga. Sometimes both. Right now, six soar above Britney's compound, beaming their searchlights onto the neighborhood estates. Four are local news, and one belongs to the LAPD. The final chopper is anyone's guess.

Oliver and I arrive at Britney's gated community shortly after 8:00 p.m. The security detail is overwhelmed, and we slip past the guardhouse in the wake of several wailing police cruisers. At the imposing black fence in front of the mansion, bodyguards keep us at bay while waving the cops inside. We know a custodial dispute is brewing, but the exact circumstances remain mysterious.

The tabloid reporters and paparazzi cluster around the perimeter of the 7,800-square-foot faux-Italian villa. I see Neil David, my sphinxlike former colleague from *Nova*. He looks giddy as a guillotine. We ask what's going on.

"I thought you'd forsaken us for the literary dreams you always spoke so lustily about," David snickers. I may have drunkenly told him at a *Nova* Christmas party that I was working on a book. "It's an absolute farce. Brit is a walking telenovela."

"You doing your typical bullshit, David, or you have any real dirt for once?" Oliver barks impatiently.

"First of all, it's Da-veed," he says, smoothening his rumpled white J.Crew dress shirt. "And yes, I've actually heard from a valid source that Sam and Adnan got into a vicious fight in front of the kids. And now the cops are attempting to resolve this mayhem."

"No, no, no," says one of the Brazilians who stalks Britney for X17. He overheard our conversation. "She tried to commit suicide and swallowed too many pills!"

"Are you sure?" another X17 Brazilian interjects. "Sam *just* texted the bossman to tell him that one of the kids accidentally swallowed something and they had to call 911."

All or none of these things could be fully true, completely false, or somewhere in between. The police take statements from the bodyguard and court monitor and devise a plan. First, they'll knock. You don't just batter-ram Britney Spears's door. But Lutfi won't let them enter without a search warrant. The cops can get one if necessary, but for now, the manager tries to convince her to leave the bathroom of her own volition. Everyone starts worrying that if they scare her too much . . . well, let's not consider that.

Around 9:30 p.m., Federline's lawyer arrives and hands the police the court documents that allow them to enter without a warrant. Cops keep popping up, more out of curiosity than official duty. Outside, the crowd expands from paparazzi and gossip reporters to the Associated Press and nightly news. Next to me, a correspondent offers a somber monologue for the viewers at home:

"We're here tonight at Britney Spears's house for what appears to be the latest in a long line of tragic incidents that have many questioning the star's psychological well-being. According to law enforcement officials, around 7:00 p.m., a previously scheduled routine custody transfer between Britney Spears and her ex-husband, the backup dancer Kevin Federline, turned into what some are calling 'a hostage situation.'

"Our sources are telling us that it appears that the '. . . Baby One More Time' singer has barricaded herself in a downstairs bathroom with one of her children, and refuses to hand him over. So far, we have been told that no one has been injured, but we are actively monitoring the scene and will continue updating you as the crisis unfolds. Back to you, Christine."

Sickly silver shafts of camera light flood the property like a hellish Hollywood premiere. The helicopter din forces us to shout. No one says much. I wander around the perimeter, contemptuous and disgusted at myself and my contemporaries—all of us so ruthlessly effective at isolating human emotions from profit margins. But for all the abuse, even the most hardened paparazzi would never wish harm upon Britney. Good intentions or not, this was bound to happen: a standoff where worst-case hypotheticals became viable outcomes.

The policemen keep their red, white, and blue flashers on to jangle our nerves. Blazing lights and agitated wind, paparazzi scuttling around, rich neighbors walking their dogs and stopping to gawk at the chaos. It's a vortex. By 10:00 p.m., there are ten police vehicles, two ambulances, and a fire truck.

An exact record of what happened inside Britney's house will never be known. It was only later that I pieced together a loose chronology from sources closer to the reactor core. And even if they attempted to tell the truth, trauma and time distort memory.

This is just what I was told:

Inside the house, Lutfi loses all composure. He's tried flattering lies and despotic commands, gentle nudging and pragmatic reasoning. Finally, he starts sobbing. Maybe if he calls Britney's mom, she'll know what to do. Except she's thousands of miles away in Kentwood, watching the TV news in horror. Jamie and Bryan Spears are nearby, though. After Lutfi hangs up, Lynne begs her ex-husband and son to check on Britney. But they roll their eyes and tell her that that slimy Lutfi dipshit is blowing things out of proportion, per usual. She'll be fine, just wait and see.

Britney is not fine. Unable to stop crying, locked inside the bathroom, she cradles her baby tighter. Outside the door, a half dozen cops admire the double-height foyer and crystal chandeliers. They inspect the vaulted ceilings, the home theater, the master suite, the built-in bookshelves, and the saltwater pool outside the French windows. A few even try to coax her out of the bathroom. "Please, Ms. Spears . . . It's going to be all right. We only want to make sure that you and your baby are safe. We promise."

She's heard this before. A cop's guarantee is as worthless as a label executive or agent. Then Federline's lawyer speaks in his salty peanut whine: "Britney, please come out. Kevin *wants* you to have custody of the kids too. This isn't the last time you'll see them, I assure you!" Hearing the voice of her bully, Britney shrieks like Niobe: "GET HIM THE FUCK OUT OF MY HOUSE!!!"

The baby cries. The cops huddle. *Is she suicidal or not?* Lutfi tells them she hasn't slept in days. He swears that she's not on drugs beyond what's been legally prescribed, but her screaming convinces them that she's on something. The baby bellows louder, ratcheting up the tension. Then it stops. Everything goes silent. *Is she okay? Is he okay? Did she hurt herself? Did she hurt him?*

This is no hostage situation. It's a young woman chased by monsters until she falls backward into a vat of boiling acid. The cops shout; the steel vultures hover above. Her remaining options are surrender or say goodbye. She yelps that she can't live without her kids. The baby cries again. She'd give anything to make him stop, to give him happiness, to hold him for another minute.

"THIS IS YOUR LAST WARNING! IF YOU DON'T COME OUT IN THE NEXT THIRTY SECONDS, WE WILL BREAK THE DOOR DOWN. I REPEAT, OPEN THE DOOR IMMEDIATELY!"

"OKAY, OKAY," she coughs meekly, sobbing. The resistance dissolves into dehydrated fear. "You can come in."

With a roundhouse kick, the cops burst through. The baby screeches. Britney writhes in the bathtub in darkness, half-naked in a bra and panties. Sweating, shaking, crumpled, fetal. The unharmed Jayden is ripped from her arms and passed to Federline's bodyguard.

The police surround Britney. Half of them are our age. They've grown up with her, lusted after the cheerleader fantasy, panted at the python-draped postadolescent, then watched as she partied all night with Paris Hilton, shaved her head, and beat that paparazzi car with the umbrella. Now they gaze with pity at the pop star in a heap, tearing at her dirty, tangled hair, her face blotched and smeared, eyes like black pinholes, shattered. They are used to scenes like these by now, their jobs regularly forcing them into situations of last-resort distress, but they have never seen anything like this.

Only two options are offered: leave in the back of a cop car or an ambulance. Britney is in no condition to

decide, so Lutfi picks the latter. There are no decent
choices. You either look crazy or criminal. With lo mein
legs, she tries to stand but buckles and begs Lutfi for her
vitamins. A police officer offers a sweater, but she snaps:
"DON'T COVER ME UP. I'M FUCKING HOT!"

The gates admit the ambulances. The barred congregation, including Oliver and me, rush in. Solemn medics
wheel out a gurney underneath the eaves of slanted roofs,
palms adorned with fairy lights, and a garden of roses
and bougainvillea in permanent bloom. The wide balco-
nies above us are still draped in Christmas wreaths.
When the paramedics emerge from the house, Britney is
strapped in at the wrists and ankles, writhing but re-
strained, surrounded by officers of the state.

Ask anyone close enough to have heard her above the
cry of emergency vehicles and scudding helicopters: they
all remember the same thing. A high-pitched and doomed
laughter, a cursed transmission from the slaughterhouse
of the soul. There are the tears, the pale infected grief of a
mother forcibly surrendering everything that matters to
her. A CNN reporter next to us mutters that it's a total
psychotic breakdown.

Britney's eyes are cryogenic, frozen with confusion.
As a half dozen firemen and medics cart her into the
ambulance, the assembled cameras capture the nightmare of imploded dreams and carcinogenic fallout. The
sirens grow so loud that you can't hear a word, but it
doesn't matter much; no one knows what to say.

◆

We chase the ambulance, a ghoulish parade of red wagons and police and press and paparazzi flying down the hill to Cedars-Sinai. But even this elite hospital isn't prepared for the bombardment. The cops attempt to handle crowd control, but the entire Western world has now gotten wind of the story.

Federline shows up to collect his children. Jayden is scanned for injuries. He's scared but fine. Lutfi appears with the court monitor, and tries to negotiate entrance to the eighth floor, the one reserved for celebrities. Security rebuffs him. *Family only.*

Jamie Spears stomps in at 1:00 a.m. in a purple LSU hat. Britney hasn't seen her father's scowl in at least eight months, but Federline summoned him on the way over. He's the only one at her side while the doctors run a battery of psychiatric and drug tests. No illegal substances are detected in her bloodstream. The hospital places her under a 5150 involuntary hold, pending an evaluation of whether she poses a threat to herself or others.

When it becomes clear that Britney will spend the next few days enduring psychological and physical examinations, we dip. It's past two, but Oliver insists that he needs to head to his office to start editing the photos. He'll call me a cab from there. It's on the Strip in a postmodern cube next to the Cabo Cantina.

In the elevator, Oliver feels prophetic.

"That's what they were hoping for," he opines. "A shit show starring the police, CNN, and photos of her looking like the end of *A Clockwork Orange.* Now her dad's back in the picture. Her mum will return too. The walls are closing in."

"Does this shit ever bother you?"

"What?"

I give him a dirty look. He knows.

"What, mate? Do I want to see Brit on suicide watch? Fuck no. But dope sells itself. Customers always find a dealer. You'd rather TMZ push it?"

"Let 'em." I shake my head. "You're a smart guy. There's a thousand other ways to survive."

Before he can explain why I'm wrong, Oliver notices the office lock is broken. Flinging the door open, he looks inside and gasps. The place has been ransacked. Splintered glass everywhere. Framed action shots from his biggest scores are ripped from the walls: prints of Ben Affleck and JLo in Georgia, Britney in various states of distress, all of the decade's large game tracked and tagged.

"MY COMPUTERS, MY HARD DRIVES, MY CAMERAS. WHAT THE FUCK, WHAT THE FUCK!!! WHAT THE FUCK!!! THEY'RE ALL GONE!!!"

He sifts for remnants, but it's all stolen: desktop computers, laptops, backup hard drives, and a half dozen of the most expensive high-speed cameras on the market. The thief waited for the precise moment to strike, knowing that Oliver would be out all night waiting for Britney.

"I knew I never should have hired him. I paid him all that he was owed, I swear!" Oliver looks at me with fury and sadness. I murmur, "I'm sorry, bro," and stare at the photos on the floor, his life's work in jumbled disarray.

Oliver runs his fingers through what's left of his hair, attempting to figure out what to do, where to go from here, and how to get revenge.

His eyes eventually land on a partially destroyed photo of Britney and Federline, fresh in lust from that first day on the beach nearly four years ago. The frame is mangled, a huge gash through Federline's head. Picking it up off the floor, Oliver stares vacantly—as if this is the closest he'll come to a regret. Shaking his head, he hurls it out the window, the glass shattering on the sidewalk. You can hear the deafening crash down the block, all the way to the early morning stragglers leaving the Body Shop.

In that first month of 2008, the dream where I'm flying through the desert returns. The pattern remains almost identical. First, I realize my powers of levitation, then I soar over the badlands until I reach the same place of refuge. The little one-bedroom house surrounded by a spectacular bloom of wildflowers—the only sign of life amidst the vast oblivion.

I walk in through the unlocked front door. I see the TV and the rollaway bed laid out for me. I climb under the covers and click on the remote. Unlike in the past, there is no black-and-white image on the screen. There is nothing whatsoever. Before I can even try to fix what's broken, I wake up in a sweat, feeling like I've been saved from something that I shouldn't see.

My other visions are much more direct. Over and over, I see Britney manacled and carried out on the stretcher. Something seems transfigured at a mitochondrial level. Her eyes are always scared, tranquilized, gouged. Other nightmares include car chases and crashes—where I stagger from the wreck with singed flesh and a sense of gruesome complicity.

I start distancing myself from Alice Van Bronx, returning her calls late to ensure that she can't send me out to report on any sudden tragedies. On my free evenings, I keep writing about what I've witnessed, but the evidence I've collected lets me imagine only one ending.

Britney checks herself out of the hospital after thirty-six hours. Her father attempts to force her into a long-term mental facility—even soliciting Dr. Phil to help the cause—but Britney flees to the desert with her paparazzo boyfriend instead. The getaway lasts a day before she returns to Beverly Hills and Lutfi. In her absence, he obtained Barbara Walters's number to let *The View* know that Britney was doing better and all her mental issues were treatable.

The Associated Press bureau chief tells his staff that "now and for the foreseeable future, virtually everything involving Britney is a big deal." They even write her obituary, just in case.

Britney's lowest moment haunts every supermarket checkout line: On the *Nova* cover, she's called *INSANE!*. They offer a look *Inside Britney's Tragic Free Fall into Madness.*

THE STANDOFF: Holds Jayden HOSTAGE in tub, BITES BODYGUARD

THE AMBULANCE: Hysteria and RESTRAINTS

THE HOSPITAL: *Trashes room, rips out IV*

THE GETAWAY: On the loose with a <u>MARRIED</u> man!

<u>NEW</u> DETAILS ON THAT NIGHT

Jayden's terror, Kevin's DESPERATE CALL to Lynne, inside the LOCKED BATHROOM

DANGEROUS LOVE with a MARRIED paparazzo

Aunt: "SHE NEEDS TO BE ON SUICIDE WATCH."

I didn't think it was possible, but the number of photographers, videographers, and reporters doubles again. Things become twice as weird. One night, Britney gets a flat tire on the way back from a drugstore run. Rather than call AAA, she abandons her car in the middle of the street and hitches a ride home with the paparazzi. In a pink wig, she goes to Mexico with Ghalib, whose photo agency exclusively captures them sipping Frappuccinos while traipsing through the souvenir shops of Baja.

Britney is spotted wearing her wedding dress to go lease Ghalib a Mercedes. On several different nights, she leads 100-mph chases through the Valley. There are 2:00 a.m. Kitson shopping sprees and manic trips to the mall—where a young girl meekly asks for a photo for her little sister, but Britney snaps, "I don't know who you think I am, bitch, but I'm not that person."

Most evenings are spent at the Four Seasons in Beverly Hills. The lobby becomes a black market of celebrity profiteers, aspiring entouragists, gossip hounds, sheisty lawyers, and other spiritual ambulance chasers. Suge Knight is constantly there, puffing Cohibas in his corner. No one thinks that he has anything to do with the Britney saga, but no one will bet against it either.

On January 22, the NYPD discover Heath Ledger dead from an accidental overdose. When the paparazzi ask for comment, Britney ruminates in a British accent: "He's still here. Oh, yes. No one ever really dies." Reports from the psychiatrist's office are so-so. Britney apparently doesn't want to be there and isn't taking it seriously. But to get her kids back, she agrees to take the prescribed meds.

By now, the courts have stripped Britney of child visitation rights for at least another month. The LAPD isn't filing charges, but "an investigation is ongoing." A war breaks out among Lutfi, Ghalib, and Britney's parents for her body and business. After a year of near-total estrangement, Jamie and Lynne attempt to claw back into her life. They're said to be devastated and terrified of Lutfi's diabolical control—as well as the paparazzo love affair that keeps getting more torrid. Every day, rumors abound about Britney getting married or pregnant. Her cousin Alli Sims calls Ghalib "a snake with bad intentions." To the family, creatures of the Bible Belt, Hollywood is Gomorrah. And no escalation is too drastic if it allows them to stabilize their daughter.

Even Oliver has had enough. After his office was plundered, his wife convinced him that it was time to return to England. His former financial backers won't accept his calls. The bigger agencies won outright, and he would rather commit ritual suicide than take orders from "the cheese-eating surrender monkey"—his preferred nickname for François Navarre, the Frenchman running X17.

On the second-to-last night of January, Oliver throws a Viking funeral for himself at the Red Rock. Sometimes, it's only years later when you realize the moment that marks the end of an era; sometimes, it's so on the nose as to be awkward. Of course, Oliver isn't one to weep about the golden days. In an upstairs private room, twenty depressive tabloid journalists trickle in and out, complaining about the industry in a drafty, half-empty pub.

Mostly, everyone talks Britney. Beneath a fraying GUINNESS IS GOOD FOR YOU ad, Alice Van Bronx and Oliver dissect the latest crisis that unfolded late Monday night off Mulholland.

"Sleazy Sam *hates* Adnan and told Britney that she cares more about her boyfriend than getting her kids back," Van Bronx explains, sipping a martini in her blazer. "He called her a 'whore,' an 'unfit mother,' every name in the book. She tells *him* he's a 'piece of shit.' Next thing you know she's bawling, grabbing the Yorkie, and slamming the door. The paparazzi found her outside, smoking cigarettes, squeezing the life out of that poor dog."

"It's a coup, mate," Oliver continues. "The paps want Lutfi's neck. If he's moving his lips, he's lying. Brit's mum says that he's sprinkling pills in the food to control her. None of us wants to see anything drastic. Death is bad for business."

"You didn't even tell him when things got really interesting," Van Bronx says, caressing her Donna Karan handbag. "Britney got a Brazilian to take her to purchase a chalupa. Then one of the paparazzi called Jamie, who has been paying top dollar to let him know when things go *really* haywire. He's all lawyered up. They're calling it an 'intervention.' LAPD is even advising them on the best way to get Britney committed."

Oliver gives me a smug eyebrow raise.

"So Jamie hops in his pickup and calls up Lou Taylor, the mastermind." Oliver grabs the baton.

"Wait, who's Lou Taylor?" I interject.

"You ain't seen Lou Taylor on the *Today* show slagging off Dr. Phil for double-crossing Brit's fam?" Oliver squints at me. Clearly, I have not. "Lou Taylor is Jamie Lynn's business manager from Nashville. She's been waiting in the wings to grab big sis for years. And Papa Spears is broke as a joke. Lou Taylor lent him forty grand, but the catch is, she needs to be a part of the new team. And now her job is to find a legal way for Jamie Spears to become Britney Spears."

"All they need is the right judge who will let Jamie tell Britney what to eat, what prescriptions to take, and what the salary should be for his *inconvenience*," Alice explains.

"Exact-a-fucking-mundo," Oliver continues. "So on Monday night, Lou Taylor calls Lynne and the whole Spears familia flocks to Brit's house like the bloody *Beverly Hillbillies*."

"Jamie Spears doesn't exactly *blend*," Van Bronx says snidely. "When the photographers saw him, they swarmed. But no one saw Lynne hiding in her friend's car. Sam gave Lynne permission to come in, but as soon as the gates opened, Jamie rode his F-150 in after her like a monster truck rally!"

"Lutfi's about to shit his trousers. Jamie Spears barging into the house like, 'Who the fuck are you?! Get out of here, shithead, I'm taking over!!'" Oliver affects a bad hick accent. "Big papa starts chasing Yosemite Sam around the wet bar, threatening him like, 'You better not be hurting my little girl! Where is my Brit Brit?!'"

"Of course, Lutfi knows *exactly* where Britney is," Van Bronx says, pausing to tell a junior staffer to order her another dirty martini. "Lutfi's not stupid. He knew the Clampetts were going to stage an intervention. I'm sure he told X17 to take Britney away so they couldn't get to her. He even got the security guard to escort Jamie off the premises."

"How much of this do you believe?" I ask.

"I'm sure they're all massaging the truth," Van Bronx says. "But Lynne isn't creative enough to dream up that Sam steals Britney's phone chargers, cuts the landline wires, and hides her dog so he can be a hero."

"I can't stand the bloke, but you have to admire the dedication." Oliver shrugs his shoulders. "This is his fucking meal ticket, and he doesn't care if he's considered the enemy. If she marries Ghalib, if her parents get the reins, Lutfi will be canned pronto."

"So what happened?"

"Brit finally shows up, but now she's with Adnan. So Lutfi kicks *him* out too, which makes Brit go apeshit," Oliver continues. "Then Sam starts texting Adnan: 'Delete Britney's number! You'll kill her! The only way you can help is by disappearing!'"

"What's Britney doing while this is happening?" I ask.

"Completely off her noggin," Oliver says. "Cleaning the house nonstop. Changing outfits over and over. When she got bored, she put the doggies in fancy sweaters. They've got her on two heavy antipsychotics, plus Addies and nighttime knockout pills. Lutfi controls her like a marionette. Downers to rest, uppers to wake. He's living there rent-free, and he's the point man with the lawyers, the press, the business manager, the security blokes at the gate. No wonder she's a fucking mess."

"What do you think she should do?"

"What she should do and what she *can* do are very different questions." Van Bronx takes a lusty gulp of the martini. "Let's face it, the girl is tragically bipolar. It's probably genetic. Of course, stress plays some role. She needs professional help, ideally from someone who isn't there to take fifteen percent or lock her in the castle. She despises her father and hates her mother for letting him run over everyone."

"It ought to be a movie, but it seems too daft," Oliver quips. "Lynne ends up calling the police that night. Brit is a bloody wreck. Sam tries to get everyone to take tequila shots to *relax*, but they settle on red wine even though everyone knows that Brit can't mix her meds with booze. It set something off, because after midnight, she *needs* lipstick from Rite Aid. And that started a whole bloody pap chase."

"Oh, it was a glorious mess," Van Bronx adds. "We may sell a million copies next week. Lutfi told Lynne that only *he* can give Britney her medicine. If not, she'll kill herself. And if they fire him, he'll piss on her grave!"

"So how did it end?" My curiosity once again outweighs the disgust.

"Eventually, the Addies and wine wore off, and they tried to get some Zs," Oliver says. "But the next morning, Papa Spears came to pick up his ex-wife and told Lutfi he was gonna beat his fucking ass. Lutfi claims that he got socked in the stomach and he was so scared that he locked himself in the game room."

"You dream of copy like this." Van Bronx sighs happily.

"Where does it stand now?"

"Her parents are about to file the paperwork to take over any day. They just need to topple Lutfi," Van Bronx explains. "Britney took her brand-new Mercedes out today for a spin. But on the way home, she had a panic attack looking for a shortcut. She got dizzy and almost ran the car off the cliff. The paparazzi had to help her turn it around."

"She ain't slept in four days," Oliver tells me. "The paps followed her at 5:00 a.m. today to the Rite Aid in high heels and the pink wig to buy Windex and sunglasses. Then her and Sam stopped at a gas station for a Red Bull. At 6:00, they went to the Beverly Hills Hotel for who the fuck knows what. Then on the way home, she cussed him out in the British accent and made him pull over so she could drive."

"However will you live without these thrills?" Van Bronx jabs Oliver.

"I'll manage. It's only a matter of time before someone gets killed, and fuck if it's going to be me. I got a daughter now."

"I never expected you to go soft," Van Bronx snorts.

"Maybe you should have extended my contract." He looks around the room, sees no one to stop him, and lights a cigarette. "But it don't matter. There won't be an industry in a few years. You don't hire photographers anymore. You hire stalkers with video cameras, jumping in celebrity's faces."

"Can't beat the price."

"Right." He takes a drag and exhales exhaustedly. "We've cannibalized ourselves. Rats in a fucking barrel, and I'm not trying to be one of the last fighting to survive. Eventually, it'll just be random nobodies taking pictures of celebs on the street, or the stars will just stage fake scenarios to post on their own. Cut the middleman right out."

"And here I thought you had told me that your dream was to be the world's most famous paparazzo," Alice taunts.

"I was," he says. "But fuck that, fame is like seawater: the more you drink, the thirstier you get."

"What about you?" Van Bronx wields her salamander stare on me. "You're not going to abandon me to become a wedding photographer, are you?"

"Maybe we'll become a package duo. He'll shoot the ceremonies; I'll DJ the after-party."

"You joke, but I see a bright future for you. You're only getting started. Stick with it and you could be a bureau chief."

"I don't think that's the career that I have in mind."

"No one reads anything longer than a text anymore," she scoffs. "Do something that'll pay your bills. You'll never go broke betting on Britney."

Van Bronx's phone rings, and she excuses herself to take the call. It's just Oliver and me.

"You gonna swing by K-Fed's house one more time before you dip to see if he'll sign you? You're not even thirty. There's still time to launch your rap career."

"I need a break from this shit," he wheezes. "My visa is expiring. I'm tired of fighting the bodyguards, the other paps, the editors at the magazines nickel-and-diming for every photo. I'm burnt, mate."

I'm unsure how to respond. He catches himself in this moment of reflection and reverses it.

"But you know what, we had some good times." He flashes a conniving smile. "I accomplished what I set out to do. I came to LA with a camera bag and a suitcase, and I'm leaving with a legacy."

Alice Van Bronx returns, on edge.

"Something is going down again at Britney's," she tells me. "We need you there immediately!"

"Can't someone else do it?"

"Sure, but I'm asking you. I think tonight is the night."

"Give me a second to think about it?"

"I'm getting another martini. Let me know when I return."

When she steps away, Oliver paternally throws his arm around me.

"Just go, dawg."

"Fuck that. I'm done. I know I've been saying that forever, but this is really it."

"You need to be there."

"I'm sure a dozen helicopters and one hundred paparazzi are already circling the house. No one *needs* me."

"Someone needs to write what *really* went down."

"You, of all people, know how stupid that sounds."

"Sure, but at least you might come close."

◆

The familiar climb up the mountain. The neon glare of Sunset submitting to the calming womb of Coldwater Canyon, ascending to the dizzying tightrope of Mulholland, past Eden Drive and Hidden Valley Road and all the other idyllically named streets, a poison paradise for celebrities to periodically vanish into.

Mulholland slices through the mountain center like a meridian. From one curve, you can see the opalescent pinpoints of city lights, glowing well past midnight in artificial hues of green, yellow, and red. At another angle, there are the wild ravines and seasonal arroyos still prowled by coyotes, scorpions, and even mountain lions that occasionally wander into someone's backyard and prey upon whatever household pet they can find.

At Britney's, the siege is already underway. Police helicopters tear across the pink-gray sky. Platoons of motorcycle cops aggressively rev their engines. They're joined by another dozen uniformed patrol officers, standing outside their Crown Victorias with flashing lights warning the paparazzi gargoyled outside. From here, three emergency vehicles have their doors wide-open like waiting jaws.

It's clear that this is the result of an elaborate plan. The roads are blocked off; the airspace is cleared. Whatever happens in there will not be the result of free will. Britney will soon be extradited to the hospital of their choosing. Who is doing the choosing remains unclear. I approach an X17 shooter, a middle-aged former federal police officer from Brazil, to ask what's going on.

"An hour ago, Sam told us that he heard that they were sending Britney to the mental hospital. And not just overnight this time."

"What did she do?"

"Her psychiatrist came by a few hours ago to check on her. I guess Britney hasn't been sleeping," the paparazzo says. "She refused to take her meds or stop driving. They're saying that the doctor had her committed."

"Brit's mom showed up an hour ago," he continues, double-checking his camera battery. "Right before you arrived, twenty cops pounded on the door and entered. Everyone is saying that Sam is trying to convince her to leave without a fight. You remember what happened last time."

It's one of those cold LA winter nights that always throw off the transplants who move here, animated by the delusion that the sun never actually sets. Someone overhears the cops referring to Britney by her code name: "The Package." A rumor circulates that it's an allusion to suicide. The photographers chatter about what a photo of Britney in a body bag might be worth. A pap in a blink-182 baseball cap laments about how he'll be out of work if Britney dies.

For all the morbidity, or maybe owing to it, the mood is carnivalesque. Everyone waits for the prize. I understand that if I stick around this malignant sphere, there will be no hope of rehabilitation. There will be nothing left to save.

Only later do reports seep out about what happened inside. This too is mere approximation, the self-interested explanations spun by those who spend their lives deflecting themselves from blame.

The story goes: Lutfi called Lynne Spears, hysterical and frantic, informing her that the decision had finally been made. No more mood swings and manic depression, early morning shopping runs and shouting matches. The mother blames the manager for the hospitalization. He claims that Britney's psychiatrist called the LAPD's Systemwide Mental Assessment Response Team (SMART) to ask for another 5150 because Britney had been "driving recklessly, not taking her medication as directed, and not sleeping properly." It has finally been determined that she is a threat to herself.

Lynne Spears will claim that she tried to save Britney from returning to the mental institution, but that her fate was already sealed. When the cops arrive, they shove Lynne out of the way, insisting that if she tries to stop them, she'll leave in handcuffs. She backs down and calls her ex-husband. It's time for him to call the lawyers and let them know that now is the time to strike. This may be the moment that they have been waiting for. Their prayers have been answered.

Sam Lutfi will claim that he was merely following the psychiatrist's wishes. Before she is taken away, he says that Britney asks if he believes that there's really something wrong with her.

"I do think there's something wrong, and I'm your

friend and I love you," Lutfi tells her. "This is what you have to do to get your babies back." Britney responds that she will go peacefully then.

The officers prepare the stretcher and lift Britney onto it without resistance, shackling her in at the wrists and ankles. She doesn't cry or yell or laugh this time.

As policemen carry Britney out of the house, her face is stoic and emotionless. The charge in her eyes is extinguished. A mask of someone numbly accepting her sentence.

The paparazzi scale roofs and leap onto their cars, but no one gets a clear shot for once. Everything is blurry and out of focus. The police are prepared this time and shield her.

Shoveled into the ambulance, the sirens screech, the motorcycle engines growl, the helicopters stampede to the south, kicking up a ferocious wind. Alice Van Bronx texts me: *SHE'S GOING TO UCLA MEDICAL CENTER. FOLLOW HER!* Shoving my phone in my pocket, I dart back to my car, surrounded by paparazzi unleashing primal whoops. The chase begins one more time.

Descending the same way, past the arcadian roads sealed off by the police, all the way back down to Sunset, slicing into the emerald vacancy of Beverly Hills and the aloof mansions of Bel Air, toward UCLA Medical Center, where Britney will spend the next six days.

During this time, a court will grant her father dictatorial control over her financial decisions and physical well-being. She becomes a twenty-six-year-old woman legally incapacitated and bound by law to Jamie's de-

mands. The judge insists that her decision is only temporary, but refuses to let Britney hire a lawyer to intervene
on her behalf. Her parents successfully obtain a restraining order barring Lutfi from coming within 250 yards of
their daughter.

Before this can happen, there is the funereal, wailing,
flashing seventy-five-car parade in the grim predawn.
The ambulances lead the cops, who lead Lutfi and her
mother and Ghalib, who in turn lead the paparazzi.
When it comes time to hook left through the university
campus, following Britney to the sliding doors of the
hospital, my phone rings. Alice Van Bronx. I silence it.

There are no more excuses or interpretations left. All
the secrets have been exposed, dissected, and filed in a
fluorescent morgue. The shimmering dream was destroyed first by intent, then by design. She resisted the
gilded confinement and set fire to the plastic fantasy, but
there were spies and cameras at every corner. And everyone was ready to cash in.

We wanted more and more, until she had no energy
left to resist and no place left to hide. The victim of a sinister inertia, a corrupting force that, once unleashed,
could never be unlearned. After all, the sacrifices and
destruction of the gods were our original form of entertainment. But now we have learned to become slyer and
more evasive about calling it religion.

There is no shame in believing the fables for a little
while. They can give our lives shape, meaning, and direction. But anyone navigating by the lurid glow of this
artificial North Star will eventually find themselves

irredeemable and off course. I can't tell you that I knew where to go from here, but I understood that whatever I did would require a complete recalibration.

I needed to put what was left of my faith in whatever resembled the truth. The past was past, the present was perdition, but the future offered a slim promise of reclamation—a chance to try to create something yet unseen, to discover the pockets of pirated frequencies that still existed. To join those survivors resisting the greater conspiracy to keep growing and expanding until we're somehow all the private property of the publicly owned machines.

But for the moment, I am still on the road. A fleet of paparazzi in all-black SUVs screams through a red light into Westwood Village. Maybe this time they will finally get the photo that makes them rich. My phone keeps ringing, the texts keep coming, but I ignore them all.

I'm long gone now, leaving the race in the rearview, accelerating through the synchronized green signals and blind curves of Sunset. Heading west until the land runs out of breath and the bewildering lights vanish into the black water, forking toward whichever direction allows me to forget the bright lies and block out the sirens.